Praise for

FISH OUT OF AGUA

"Poignant, funny and authentic. Michele Carlo writes about a lost New York with a cinematic eye, a keen ear, and a huge heart."

—**Janice Erlbaum**, author of
Girlbomb and *Have You Found Her*

"If you've sadly suspected that the last decades have somehow left us with a New York far too polished and antiseptic clean, way too fashionably heeled, sexually savvy, snarky and glib, then you have every reason to celebrate Michele Carlo's writing for reassuring us that this is clearly not the case.

The humor, heart—and every alternately sweet and razor-sharp note of her writing—reach far past the edges of this island. Her houses, her boroughs, and every crack in every sidewalk weave a strangely beautiful and universal map of that thing doomed and damned, charmed and graced: the human condition."

—**Dan Kennedy**, author of *Rock On* and *Loser Goes First*

"Michele Carlo is a force to be reckoned with. I have worked with her at the Moth for six years, and she has a unique talent for bringing to life, onstage and in her writing, the many wonderful characters from her life. Her stories are extremely original, and yet she tells them in a way that makes them completely relatable to anyone. I am a fan, and if you read her work, you soon will be too."

—**Catherine Burns**, artistic director of the Moth

"I have known and worked with Michele Carlo since 1995, and each and every time I have seen her perform she has delivered funny, warm, insightful and touching stories. Her take on life as a Latina is the most original I have ever seen. She is an important voice who makes a huge impact."

—**Linda Nieves Powell,** author of *Free Style*
and director of Latino-Flavored Productions

"Michele Carlo's writing captures the electricity and insanity of a moment in time that always seems equally capable of either blossoming into utopia or spiraling into apocalypse. It has a sweetness and danger that never feels forced and a crackling sense of humor with its own brand of seriousness."

—**Patrick William Gallagher,** editor, *Animal Farm,* former
managing editor of *Mr. Beller's Neighborhood*

FISH OUT OF AGUA

*My Life on Neither Side of
the (Subway) Tracks*

Michele Carlo

CITADEL PRESS
Kensington Publishing
www.kensingtonbooks.com

CITADEL PRESS BOOKS are published by

Kensington Publishing Corp.
119 West 40th Street
New York, NY 10018

Earlier versions of some of the chapters in this memoir were previously published as follows:

"My Fundillo" in *Chicken Soup For The Latino Soul* (2005); "After Dark" and "Kill Whitey Day" in *Mr. Beller's Neighborhood Lost & Found: Stories from New York, Vol. 2* (2009); "Night of The Black Chrysanthemum" as a webcomic by *SMITH Magazine* (2009).

All Kensington titles, imprints, and distributed lines are available at special quantity discounts for bulk purchases for sales promotions, premiums, fund-raising, educational, or institutional use. Special book excerpts or customized printing can also be created to fit specific needs. For details, write or phone the office of the Kensington special sales manager: Kensington Publishing Corp., 119 West 40th Street, New York, NY 10018, attn: Special Sales Department; phone 1-800-221-2647.

First printing: August 2010

10 9 8 7 6 5 4 3 2 1

Printed in the United States of America

Library of Congress Control Number: 2010924997

ISBN-13: 978-0-8065-3146-5
ISBN-10: 0-8065-3146-0

For all who knew I could do this.
And for those who thought I couldn't.
Both know who they are.
But most of all . . . for Lucy and Rudy.

Certain identifying names, characteristics,
dates and places have been changed to protect anonymity.
Some characters and events are composites;
some timelines have been expanded or compressed; some dialogue
has been reconstructed.

CONTENTS

Contents

FISH OUT OF AGUA

INTRODUCTION

SPANISH ON SUNDAY (part 1)

I was ten years old when my mother told me my great-grandmother was dead. My immediate reaction was relief. There would be no more riding the subway, the bus, and another bus to that island where all the buildings looked like prisons and no more visiting the hospital there that smelled of chicken soup, Clorox, and puke—where even the trees and pigeons looked as if they had been exiled there to die too.

On the day of the funeral, my family gathered at my *abuela*'s apartment in Washingon Heights to mourn: six sprawling rooms with French doors, crumbling moldings, and a long dark hallway with framed prints of John F. Kennedy, Martin Luther King, and a blond, blue-eyed, long-haired Jesus.

As always when all the family were together, the kitchen table had been moved into the living room and held enough food to feed an entire neighborhood. Pots of *arroz con gandules*, trays of *pasteles* and *alcapurrias, perñil*, a roast turkey, *tostones, maduros*, and my favorite, *salujos*, spilled over its edges, but for once I wasn't hungry. The grownups took their plates to the dining room to eat while my brother and cousins, all younger than I, went to the back room to play. I didn't feel like playing either, so I wandered off alone.

I stopped at the beginning of the hallway and looked at John F. Kennedy, Martin Luther King, and Jesus. Why did almost every house I had ever been brought to have these pictures? I knew Kennedy was supposed to save the country, and "they" killed him. I knew King was supposed to save the black people, and he was killed. I knew Jesus was supposed to have saved mankind and they, of course, killed him, too. Jesus stared back at me. He looked like a hippie. My family told me to stay away from hippies. They were dirty and they were on drugs. Drugs were what made people not come home anymore and made whoever was left behind cry. I tried to knock Jesus off the wall, but he was way beyond my reach.

The sound of my *abuela*'s slippered footsteps interrupted my communion with El Señor (literally: "The Man;" figuratively: Our Father, a.k.a. God). She readjusted the Jesus photo I never touched, took my hand, and led me a little farther down the hall, into the bedroom where once I had lived with her. The bedroom smelled of powder, Jergen's hand lotion, and Tigress perfume: just like any ordinary churchgoing grandma type of a woman.

On top of the chenille bedspread was an ancient-looking cardboard photo album. My *abuela* sat down, opened it, removed one of the photos on the page, and handed it to me. It wasn't in black and white or color; it was an artifact in shades of sepia brown, with lines of glue dried along its edges.

A little girl, with short, tight braids that looked like they hurt, stood next to a seated older woman with posture as straight as her chair's back. Standing behind the two was a younger woman with a flower in her long, wavy hair. She was the only one smiling. My *abuela* looked at me as if I should know these people. They looked vaguely familiar, but I wasn't sure, so I said nothing. My *abuela* waited another second and said, "This is your mother," pointing to the child with the braids. "This is me," pointing at the woman smiling. "And this"—pointing to the woman in the chair—"is my mother, your great-grandmother."

The woman in the chair was not the shriveled thing I had known only from a hospital. A thing with foggy eyes from cataracts and glaucoma and clenched bony fingers that gripped you with otherworldly strength. The only trace that she had once been human was her mane of straight, waist-length, silver blue hair. I used to watch my *abuela* brush it for her.

I took the photo from my *abuela* for a closer look. Despite the sepia coloring, you could tell her hair had been jet black. Her hands were not claws, but were long and smooth. Her unblemished skin was the color of a cinnamon stick. Her eyes had a clear, knowing gaze, and she had the highest, sharpest cheekbones I had ever seen. She looked like a princess—or a priestess. She was beautiful.

I put down the picture, walked over to *abuela*'s dressing table, and knelt on the bench to look in the mirror. My pale, yellow-tinged round freckled face and halo of frizzy red curls made me cry. *"Abuelita*, I said, "why don't I look like you . . . like great-grandma?"

"Como?" she said, shaking her head, because I always spoke English too fast for her to follow.

"Por . . . que," I began, *"Por que . . ."* The tears stopped and frustration set in. I was angry with myself for not knowing her words and angry with her for not knowing mine. *"Por que . . . yo no* look like the *familia?"*

"Oh, *pero,* you do," *abuela* said. "You have look like *mi . . . como se dice en ingles . . .* mother of . . . mother of your mother's *padre. Ella tiene pelo rojo tambien y . . ."* She was speaking entirely in Spanish now, but it didn't matter because I couldn't understand her—and I didn't believe her anyway.

A couple of weeks later, my mother, grandmother, *titis* (aunties), brother, cousins, and I went to the Puerto Rican Day Parade together. We had never gone before. Or at least I didn't remember ever going to the mid-June, all-day celebration of all things *Boricua,* Puerto Rican, where the *gente* march, the *musica* plays, and the *banderas* wave.

Cordoned off along the sidewalks stood tens of tens of thousands of varying shades of beige and brown pride crammed *cabeza* to *cabeza,* head to head, *hombro* to *hombro,* shoulder to shoulder, and *nalgas* to *nalgas,* swaying hips to swaying hips, letting New York City know, *"Wepa, Boricua! Eso es nuestro dia."* (We are Puerto Rican and this is our day!) Everyone, that is, except for me.

I'd become separated from everyone in my family and meandered down crowded Fifth Avenue looking for the nice policeman my mother told me to find if I ever got lost. The fact that all the policemen were chasing and grabbing at a group of paraders who were shouting, *"Arriba, pa bajo, los puercos va a carajo!"* (Up, down, all around, pigs go to hell!) puzzled me. Why were these people yelling about pigs? That was stupid. They were all going to be in trouble. I wasn't. I decided I was going to stand right where I was until the nice policeman came to me.

When he finally came, I told him I was lost and followed him to a bandstand filled with men in white suits, *guyanaberas*, and straw hats and women in tight pretty dresses and high heels. They were all very nice to me. They bought me a hot dog and a Sun Dew and told me not to worry. They said my family would come, and "Please, sit down." I obeyed. I was tired from all that walking and waiting.

While I ate and drank with my best manners—because I remembered what my mother always said, "People are watching you all the time."—a loudspeaker screeched on. I heard names: "Herman Badillo, Geraldo Rivera, Pablo Guzman . . ." Who were these people? I saw a Good Humor truck and wanted ice cream. Maybe I could get one of those pretty ladies to buy me a Strawberry Shortcake.

Before I had a chance to ask, the voice from the loudspeaker blared again, "Will the family who brought the little redheaded white girl to the parade please come to the Bandshell to pick her up?" Did I hear that right? Wait a minute, I was at the Bandshell. I looked around to see where that poor, unfortunate child who didn't belong here was, but only saw grownups in suits and dresses looking everywhere but at me. Then it hit me. I was that lost girl.

As I sat there holding my half-eaten hot dog and Sun Dew, I cried for the first time since my *abuela* showed me the photograph of my great-grandmother. I was not a priestess like my great-grandmother, a little girl in braids like my mother, or a woman in a pretty dress like the women at the parade. I had no idea where my family was, or who I was. I was a fish out of *agua*.

1

A TALE OF TWO ABUELAS

The first thing you need to know is that the *abuela*, or grandmother, is an integral part of every Latino child's life. *Abuelas* provide moral guidance by dragging you to their place of worship, be it *Catolico*, *Luterano, Pentecostal*, or *the Way of the Saints*. There, they test you by giving you the envelope to put into the collection plate, and when you try to slip their $5.37 into your pocket, *tenga cuidado!*

They are also valuable sources of medical knowledge and can discern between *una monga*, a feverish condition that isn't really a fever, *cuerpo cortao*, a general disability that isn't really debilitating, and *dolor de los cocotazos*, the headache caused by the rap of knuckles against your skull when you are caught placing the oral thermometer under a radiator in order to skip school and watch reruns of *Bewitched*.

Abuelas are also dispensers of justice, usually in the form of *la chancleta*, the slipper. Whatever their provenance, all *abuelas* possess this unique weapon as well as the inherent, expert knowledge of its deployment. Whoever invented the laser pointed weapon must've grown up in a Latin household because when an *abuela* throws a *chancleta* it morphs into a heat-seeking device with unparalleled pinpoint accuracy that will find you anywhere. It doesn't matter if you're under a bed, behind a door, or behind your younger sibling, the slipper will hit *you* square on the forehead, *ping!*

But *abuelas* don't just pass judgment. They also provide absolution. After all, they've lived longer than anyone else on their watch and have heard, seen, and, done (or at least wanted to) it all before. If you need someone to predict the future, *nadie*, but no one, can do it like an *abuela*.

My Grandma Marisol or Mari, was my mother's mother. She came from Corozal, Puerto Rico, a town near the center of the island, named for *"la palma de corozo,"* a type of palm tree. Today it is a modern city, but in the late 1930s it was just another mountain village caught in the Great Depression. A single mother with a small child and invalid mother had two choices: remarriage and emigration or staying put and starving. Grandma Mari chose to remarry and come to the mainland where she hoped she would find the man who deserted her, my mother's father. She arrived in New York City in December 1938 and in her fifty-seven years in Nueva York, she had three more children, never mastered English, and never reunited with her first love.

My Grandma Isabel, or Izzy, was my father's mother. She was also from Puerto Rico, from Cabo Rojo, a resort city on the island's southwest coast. The name means Red Tip or Red Cape. On an island where every coastal town claims to have the most beautiful beach, this one *really* does. It's called El Buye. Like Grandma Mari, Grandma Izzy also came to New York City as a newlywed. I have a photograph of her with my grandfather Ezekiel, circa 1928, in which you can tell she's just a teenager by the look on her round moon face. Her expression is free of frustration, resignation, and grief—the failed businesses, unfaithful husband, and five sons all still ahead of her.

Both of my *abuelas* were there for me the day I was born. According to my mother, it was the hottest day of the year when she unexpectedly went into labor. She was only eight months pregnant and wasn't prepared for it. When she started to feel pains, my father was driving a forklift at a construction site somewhere in Queens; my mother's half sisters, Carmen, Ofelia, and Dulce, all still teenagers, were out with their friends; and her one best friend, Daisy, was on her honeymoon. She called her mother, but she wasn't home either. Her stepfather, Papa Julio, worked nights and was annoyed by the early afternoon phone call, but agreed to leave his wife, Grandma Mari, a note. As usual, my mother was on her own.

My mother grabbed her already packed little suitcase and jumped into a taxi. "Columbia-Presbyterian/Sloane Hospital, 168th Street and Broadway, please." She leaned back against the seat and rolled down the window. Lucy had been warned about the horrors of childbirth, but she took pride in her ability to withstand pain.

By the time she arrived at the hospital, the pains subsided. The resident who examined her said, "Your water hasn't broken, the contractions have stopped and you're not due till the end of the month? False alarm. Go home, take two aspirins and take a nap." Back then people listened to doctors, and my mother left to do just that.

Except in the taxi home, her water broke and the contractions resumed. Violently. She told the driver to turn around and go back, quick! "Hold it in," he said. "No babies in my cab!"

When she got to the hospital again, she was immediately rushed into an operating room; her little suitcase was left behind.

"Breech!"

"Caesarian!"

"Stat!"

Lucy felt a mask over her face, heard the tang of what she guessed to be a scalpel, and thought, "After all I have been through, I do not want to feel this." She inhaled the anesthesia as deeply as she could.

As my mother went under, Grandma Mari burst into the hospital waiting room. Upon finding the note left by her husband, she ran the twelve blocks from her apartment, with asthma and in high heels, to get to her daughter. There is never a *guagua*, bus, or *un taxi* when you need one (or when she needed one). She sensed something had gone wrong with either my mother, but no one would tell her exactly what. She knew exactly what she had to do.

As people streamed in and out of the waiting room, they beheld Grandma Mari, with her salt-and-pepper hair streaming out of two real tortoiseshell combs and her beaded straw summer handbag at her feet, leading a charismatic prayer. Many of the visitors joined in, although in support of what exactly, they weren't sure. It was a multigenerational, multiethnic congregation of minds, hearts and *Espiritu Santo*, the Holy Spirit.

A couple of hours into the prayer session, breathless from an hour-long bus ride from The Bronx, burst in Grandma Izzy. She was also in heels. Her bouffant was damp and collapsed, and her green patent leather pocketbook hung open. Bracelets jangled up and down her arms, and a crumpled pack of Belairs was in her hand. Her keen hazel eyes scanned Grandma Mari and the prayer group as she asked, *"Por favor,* does anyone have a light?"

The last thing Grandma Izzy expected to find at the hospital was a mini *iglesia* revival. The phone call she received from Grandma Mari only said, "Lucy is having the baby. Come now." Grandma Izzy wasn't particularly religious and wasn't what you would call a joiner, but she did have *cojones*: nerve. She also had a good command of the English language and the inability to take "maybe" for an answer.

While Grandma Mari continued to pray, Grandma Izzy, who realized that *something* had gone very very wrong, canvassed the hospital floor until at last she found a doctor who told her that my mother would live, but I might not. By this time my father had arrived (going straight to the ICU and my soundly sleeping mother) along with the balance of both families (minus the nightshift-working Papa Julio).

I was cut free in that late afternoon, cold and blue, with no guarantee of surviving. I had turned in the womb multiple times, and became stuck, butt first and strangled by my own umbilical cord. It was a talent I would repeat in many variations, many times later in my life. To my family's relief though, the doctors resuscitated me and placed me in an oxygen pressure incubator—the rare and latest technology for treating infant asphyxia.

I'm not sure if they stayed at the hospital that night, but the next morning both of my grandmothers stood in front of a glass window that separated them from my incubator. The doctors warned them that even though I'd lived, I was without oxygen for almost four minutes and there was a 50 percent chance that I'd be "mentally compromised," blind, or both. My grandmothers were prepared for this as much as anyone can be.

But they weren't prepared for a thrashing, squalling, *carrot-topped* bundle. As they stared at me through the glass pane, their conversation probably went like this:

GRANDMA MARI: *"El Señor* will decide if she lives."

GRANDMA IZZY: "No, she will decide."

GRANDMA MARI: "She will need us to protect her and guide her."

GRANDMA IZZY: "She will learn the only one you can depend on is yourself. *Por favor,* Mari, do you have a light?"

GRANDMA MARI: *"Mija, no puedes fumar aqui.* Let's go get *un café."*

Thirty-six hours after the two longest taxi rides of her life, my mother woke up with her jet-black hair slowly turning white and a healthy baby girl to bring home. Even Grandma Izzy had to admit it was *un milagro,* a miracle—one that both of my grandmothers would always take full credit for.

From Grandma Mari, I'd learn to find hope in things both unexpected and unseen. From Grandma Izzy, I'd learn that when you want something, you must try for it as hard as you can, pretty much any way you can, and when you think that you can't possibly go any farther, take just one more step because that's when the door will open.

2

THE ILLUMINATION OF ST. LUCY

The day after my mother arrived in New York City, she woke up to find the world had turned *blanco*. White things had taken over the sky, swirling over the ground, the running boards of cars, and the limbs of what she thought were dead trees (she had only known the Caribbean's eternal summer). Barefoot, with her short braids sticking out behind her, she ran out of the apartment into the magic street, and bolted, just as quickly, back inside.

"It burns. It burns! I want to go home."

"You are home," her mother said.

Running innocently into unfamiliar and hurtful things was the story of my mother's entire childhood. What I know, what I've been told is this: Grandma Marisol's first husband, my mother's father, was a man named Beltran. He was a musician who went back and forth between Corozal, the rural town where my mother and Grandma Mari lived, to New York City. "I'll come back for you," he said. "I'll bring you and the baby to Nueva York. We'll have a new life. A good life." He kept his word, at first. He did come back a few times. But when my mother was two years old, he left Corozal and didn't return.

When my grandmother eventually realized she had been abandoned, she moved her daughter, *Luz,* whose name means "the light," and her mother, Mami Marisol, from their *finca*—the little farm where my mother drank fresh goat's milk every morning and my great-grandmother swung chickens by their necks before slicing their heads off—to the city of Old San Juan. There, my Grandma Mari met a man named Julio who wanted to marry her and move to Nueva York. It was the 1930s, the Great Depression. Jobs and food were scarce.

Julio said to my grandmother, "You have to leave the child and your mother behind."

"I will not," my grandmother countered. "You want me, you take all of us."

My grandmother had a plan. Once in Nueva York she would track down Beltran, who, last she heard, was living in El Barrio, Spanish Harlem, the place where everyone from the island went to live—where they were going to live. It would only be a matter of time until she found her lost love. And when they reunited and Beltran saw his then five-year-old daughter's ivory complexion, Roman nose, and tightly spiraled jet black hair, the exact reflection of his, he would, without any doubt, immediately fall in love with both of them all over again and they would all live together in bliss. At least, that was the way she imagined it. I do not know if Grandma Mari ever bothered to actually get divorced from the long-gone Beltran or not, but back then, who checked? No one cared about the details of yet another deserted mother, child, and *vieja*, elderly woman.

In December of 1938, after a week on a boat (a large, clean, and nice one, according to my mother), Grandma Mari, Papa Julio (as he insisted on being called), Mami Marisol, and my mother arrived at their new railroad apartment on East 103rd Street between Park and Madison Avenues in El Barrio, New York City. In most ways they were a family, though Papa Julio would never replace the father my mother had never really known. On the contrary, as my mother's half sisters were born: quiet, heavy Carmen; sharp, willful Ofelia; and the affectionate, inquisitive Dulce, my mother was seldom allowed to play in the Conservatory Garden in Central Park anymore, her refuge where she climbed trees and read books about faraway places; she had to help Mami take care of them. She would now often find the kitchen cabinets locked to her because she ate too much, taking food away from Papa Julio's *real* daughters.

And worst of all, she'd endure the unspeakable shame, the *vergüenza*, the thing that happened here and there in the night that my mother could tell no one. The thing her Mami should have known and should have stopped from happening. Did her Mami not see? Or did she not care? Why didn't Mami leave that monster and take her and *abuela* away? But, by now, Mami was plagued with health issues: asthma, migraines, *mal de estomago*, and distracted, . . . by her own mother's withering health, . . . and by her other three daughters. Maybe, and it made my mother cry to think of this, maybe Mami didn't *want* to know. The *vergüenza* would eventually stop, but my mother never ever forgot she was not Papa Julio's daughter.

In 1951, when my mother (her Spanish name long replaced by the Americanized "Lucy") turned eighteen, the age where a girl today is planning her prom outfit and matching her pedicure to the upholstery in the limo, she had been working for three full years. In ninth grade, when she turned fifteen, she was told she would have to leave school to work, when what she had dreamed of doing after graduation was becoming an interpreter at the brand-new United Nations offices and traveling the world. She managed a compromise by entering Julia Richman High School's co-op program, where she worked one week and went to school the next. It took longer to graduate that way, but Papa Julio got what he wanted, her income, and my mother got what she wanted, a high school diploma.

On a Saturday evening in early December, Lucy and her best friend, Daisy, went to the holiday bazaar at St. Lucy's Church. It was the Catholic Church and school around the corner on East 104th Street that almost the entire neighborhood attended but not my mother or her half-sisters. My grandmother had grown to prefer the immediacy and intensity of storefront *iglesia* worship to the restrained hierarchy of the Catholicism in which she was raised.

My mother was naturally shy and cautious and didn't have a lot of friends. But Daisy Varela, who lived in the building next door and had been my mother's one close friend since grade school, had no trouble meeting people and dragging my mother out with her. The two were opposites in every way. Daisy was tall, flat, and outgoing; my mother short, curvy, and reserved. Their friendship worked because my mother kept Daisy from getting into "too much" trouble, and Daisy had the unique talent of being able to make my mother laugh.

Daisy's motive for going to the bazaar was to look for boys; my mother's, to be out of the apartment. The bazaar took place in the school's gymnasium, decorated chock-full of post-World War II overabundance including loads of pine-bough garlands with icicles and red velvet bows; a life-size panorama of a Christmas crèche (with actual livestock); and the main attraction, an entire aisle devoted to holiday food, drink, and lesser gambling games like "Under and Over." Daisy and Lucy ignored the tables selling treats like *pasteles* and *coquito* (*virgen*, of course, since this was a church), and pushed their way toward the end of the row where Daisy had spotted a group of cute boys.

On their way, they passed two priests selling raffle tickets for five cents each, twenty for one dollar, with prizes of bottled wine, boxed chocolates, various trinkets—and a grand prize that stopped them dead in their tracks. Daisy and Lucy stared in awe at the item sitting on the floor.

It was a massive, carved, dark wood piece of furniture holding a Philco black-and-white TV with a built-in AM radio and Hi-Fi record player, which made even Daisy momentarily forget about boys. It was the pinnacle of entertainment technology, whose offerings, presence, and status could transform the poorest railroad flat into a middle-class temple of conspicuous consumption. No one in the neighborhood could afford to buy it. Hardly anyone in El Barrio could afford *any* TV. As far as Lucy and Daisy knew, there wasn't a single one on East 103rd Street at all—yet.

"Let's get it," Daisy said. "Let's try! If I win you can come over all the time and if you win I'll come over all the time. We can invite boys!"

My mother told me her first reaction was to say no. It was her initial response to everything. Say no and you can never be disappointed. But as she stood in front of the block of wood, glass, and tubes, her mind turned to one thought: This is something Papa Julio could never afford.

"Yes," she said. "Let's." Daisy bought two tickets. Lucy had her weekly co-op pay of $32.50 in her pocketbook and traded an entire dollar for the chance to win.

An hour later my mother's number was called. Daisy leapt at her screaming, "We won! Lucy, we won!" My mother, who was just as jubilant as Daisy but as usual held her feelings inside, extricated herself from her friend's embrace, smoothed her hair, and brought her winning ticket to the priests. The TV was delivered that night.

Two days later the priests from the bazaar, one young, one old, knocked on my mother's apartment door. Both were tall, bespectacled Irishmen straight out of *The Bells of St. Mary's*, and both wore their best vow-of-poverty faces. When my mother answered, they said they'd come because she, the petite, baby-faced girl who presented them with the winning ticket, was obviously underage and therefore disqualified from the raffle. They hadn't wanted to make a scene at the bazaar where everyone seemed so genuinely happy for her, so they decided to allow her to keep the TV over the weekend before taking it back.

My mother said, "I'm not underage. I won." The priests moved to Plan B.

They then told my mother there had been a terrible mistake. The TV had been meant for the church all along; it should never have been raffled at all. "Don't you want to donate it to St. Lucy's so that the poor and indigent can enjoy it, instead of just your family?"

"No," my mother said. "I won it. We're poor. It's mine."

The priests looked down at my mother, who, after a brief adolescent growth spurt, had remained just a shade over five feet tall.

"But you're just a child. Children aren't allowed to gamble; it's a sin. Let us speak with your mother."

When my four-feet-eleven-inch grandmother came to the door and saw the collars, she crossed herself and said, "*Ay bendito, que paso?"* as my mother translated why the priests were standing there. Now my *abuela* was religious, but she was not a fool. Maybe gambling was a sin, but having Milton Berle and Ricky Ricardo in your own living room was A Gift from El Señor. My *abuela* straightened her back, thrust out her chin, and enunciated slowly, "My daughter have eighteen years. *Televición* ours. Thank God. Thank Lucy," before gently closing the door in their faces.

There was nothing the priests could do. My mother had won the television fair and square. She was eighteen, of legal age, and since the family didn't belong to St. Lucy's Church, they couldn't even use shame as a weapon. St. Lucy's had lost to a higher-powered Lucy.

The black-and-white Philco console was the first TV in my mother's building. Every Sunday night, family, friends, and friends of friends would gather before it to experience *Tio Miltee* in *una falda*, a skirt; *Lucy y Ricky*; and other audiovisual delights. Daisy came often, as promised, but sadly, never brought any boys. Lucy had won the TV, but it was still Papa Julio's house.

The TV did nothing to change anything between my mother and Papa Julio, but it did open her mind to a crazy idea: maybe, just maybe, it was okay to say yes once in a while.

3

TURKEYS

(Or, The Brief, Wondrous Life Of Señor Pavo)

"Don't name it," my Grandma Izzy ordered. "It's not a pet. It's for *eat*."

But of course, it had already been named as soon as my father and his three brothers woke up and saw the long-necked bug-eyed squawking bird with a rope around its neck tied to the kitchen steam pole. Of course they named it, *"Señor Pavo! Señor Pavo!"* Mr. Turkey! Mr. Turkey!

It was March 1944. After three years of World War II and food rationing, there was hardly a scrap of meat to be had in all of New York City, never mind in El Barrio. But on one still-frozen morning, in a second-floor railroad apartment on East 106th Street between Park and Madison Avenues, there did appear a live and intact young turkey.

My Grandpa Ezekiel was a blackout warden, one of the guardians who walked the city streets every night after lights out. For someone who'd been classified as 4F, unfit for the military (due to asthma, flat feet *and* a punctured eardrum), it was an honorable way to serve one's country. He'd check building after building to make sure not a sliver of light escaped the mandatory black curtains each apartment had to draw after sunset. Armed with only a flashlight, he'd inspect every doorway and vestibule to make sure no stray Japs or Nazis had parachuted in to spy on, or even worse, blow up El Barrio.

There was another advantage to being a blackout warden, one that I'm sure was foremost in my grandfather's mind when he applied for the job. As that March night slowly edged toward gray dawn, either in some nameless back alley or perhaps even smack in the middle of Madison Avenue, a live turkey pullet somehow "fell off the back of a truck" and into my grandfather's waiting arms.

Grandma Izzy was ecstatic, or what would pass for ecstatic for her. She had come to Nueva York with my grandfather in 1928, which made them the equivalent of Mayflower Puerto Ricans (the great island diaspora would not begin until *after* the war was over). And like many pioneers, they found the natives were not particularly welcoming. For the past sixteen years, she had endured not only poverty, prejudice, and multiple pregnancies but the bombardment of constantly being told to go back to her country by fellow emigrants, (and/or their descendants) who were too ignorant to realize that Puerto Rico actually *belonged* to the United States, so if anything, *she* had more right to be here than they did.

Now after three years of eating little else than rice and beans, which, to put it bluntly, even she was damned tired of, there was a Real American Thanksgiving tied up in her kitchen. Grandma Izzy was truly grateful, not only for the promise of meat, but also for the chance to show up the *a quién qué tu crées* (who do you think you are), *blanquitos* (white people) who lived on the ground floor below.

Who *did* they think they were, those Blanquitos? That, of course, wasn't their name. That knowledge has, alas, been lost to the ages, but according to my father, these "Blanquitos" were the last Irish family left on the block. As would soon occur in countless other New York City neighborhoods, a changing of the guard had begun. As Latin families moved in, the *Ingladesas, Judeos,* and *Italianos* moved out—seeking safety in Washington Heights, the South Bronx, or, at the very least, six blocks east on Pleasant Avenue—as close to the East River as you could get and still be in Manhattan.

By all accounts, the Blanquitos were no worse than any other family in the Barrio. Mrs. Blanquito was clean, soft-spoken, and amazingly cheerful, considering she had nine (yes, nine) children, who were actually better behaved than some of the other neighborhood tribes. Her boys wouldn't play with my father and his brothers, but didn't fight with them either, which in a neighborhood like Spanish Harlem in 1944 was something of a miracle. Her husband, the gangly, affable Mr. Blanquito, who suffered from sporadic bouts of employment that interrupted his steady job of drinking and disappearing—only to reappear days later propped against a door, sprawled on the front stoop, or collapsed belly up once or twice under a tree in nearby Central Park—was, for the most part, a decent family man.

To answer Grandma Izzy's question, "Who do they think they are?" the Blanquitos knew exactly who they were. They were a family whose patriarch was too poor, too drunk, and too clueless to move his wife and kids away from a place they no longer belonged. That, of course, didn't stop Grandma Izzy from letting Mrs. Blanquito know, every chance she got, that even though meat hadn't passed the lips of most of the Barrio residents in months, and even though *she* came from *that* island, *her* family would be having turkey on Thanksgiving Day. "Don't worry," she must have said, "I'll make some extra *arroz con gandules* and give you some." The subtext being: unlike Mrs. Blanquito's shameless *sinvergüenza* of an *esposo*, *her* husband had provided for *her* family.

My father, Rodolfo Valentino (named after the silent film idol but God help you if you ever called him anything but Rudy) would soon turn twelve. His brothers, Freddy, Papo, and Junior, were thirteen, eight, and nine. The first operative mission of PETA, fifty years before it would become a household word, was about to begin.

People use the phrase "eat like a bird" to describe someone who picks at his or her food and eats very little. But in order for a bird to grow, unceasing amounts of nourishment must be continuously shoved down its eternally slavering, insatiable maw. At least that was the case with Señor Pavo. He needed to be fed day and night in order to (a) assuage his endless squawking and (b) gain enough weight ultimately to feed a family of soon-to-be seven, with, hopefully, some leftovers.

Where did this endless supply of turkey provender come from? The proud wartime tradition of child labor. My father and his three brothers woke up at 6:00 A.M. every morning, rain or shine, to trail behind the produce, ice, rag, seltzer, and knife-sharpening trucks— that were still horse drawn in those days—to collect stray manure to sell to the Victory Gardens. The gardens took up every available backyard, empty lot, courtyard, and fire escape (and were being replanted for the fourth year in a row). The boys would have just enough time to circle the neighborhood and exchange their load of fresh horsepoop for cash before heading off to school. After school, they would scour the streets for discarded tinfoil, another valuable commodity, provided by the Greatest Generation's chain-smoking gum chewers.

And so the daily chores went, until spring became summer, summer became autumn, and FDR was reelected to an unprecedented fourth term. My father and his brothers had helped Señor Pavo blossom from a scrawny pullet into a full-size Tom. Every morning Mr. Turkey would trill in recognition when he saw the boys. Not only had they taken turns feeding him over the past eight months, but also holding him in their laps as they stroked his feathers and sang:

Qué dicé Señor Pavo?
"Gublé gublé gublé!
Manaña es el dia por las gracias,
"Gublé, gublé gublé!"

(What does Mr. Turkey say?
"Gobble, gobble, gobble!"
Tomorrow is Thanksgiving Day.
"Gobble, gobble, gobble!")

On the other hand, whenever Señor Pavo saw my Grandma Izzy, he would leap up and try to nip a chunk out of whatever body part he could reach.

On the fourth Wednesday of November, I can only imagine my

grandmother whetting her long knife as she berated the boys for making a pet out of her dinner.

"*Mira*—Señor Pavo—he's going tomorrow. I told you not to name him."

The boys shed innocent tears as they climbed into their shared bed. My grandmother most likely dreamed sweet dreams of breast meat, drumsticks, and comeuppance as she paraded that turkey in front of the Blanquitos while she offered them her pot of *arroz con gandules*—a dream that turned into an open-mouthed nightmare when the next morning she found the rope coiled mockingly next to the kitchen steam pole and Señor Pavo gone.

My father would tell me this story three times, the last, a month before he died. The night before Thanksgiving Day, he woke up scared and breathless in his pitch-black room with an indescribable and unshakable sense of fear. He went into the kitchen to get a glass of milk and saw Señor Pavo on his mat next to the steam pole, his eyes glowing in the light from the icebox. My father got down on the floor to pet and sing to him one last time.

What does Mr. Turkey say?
"Gobble, gobble, gobble!"
Tomorrow is Thanksgiving Day.
"Gobble, gobble . . ."

Minutes later, my father returned from the front stoop and brushed the leaves off his bare feet as he crawled back into bed with his brothers. He woke up again that morning to the sound of my grandmother applying *cocotazos* to the backs of his brothers' heads. He knew he would be next, but he didn't care.

Grandpa Ezekiel came home from his shift in the middle of Hurricane Izzy wielding her *chancletas* in one hand and the *plancha* cord in the other. He looked at the steam pole and then at his sons, took a breath and said, "Isabel, there's nothing we can do. Just make some extra *arroz con gandules*. And save some for the kids downstairs."

So Grandma Izzy resigned herself. Gone was her chance to have a Real American Thanksgiving; her family would have to endure yet another holiday without meat. But as she tended her *caldero* of rice and pigeon peas, something even more astonishing than the disappearance of Mr. Turkey materialized—the unmistakable smell of roast beast wafting up the stairs. The Blanquitos had received a true Miracle on 106th Street: a freshly roasted turkey on their dinner table and a smile on all their eleven drawn faces.

Later that afternoon Mr. Blanquito told my father he swore he saw the Virgin Mary, or something like it. Upon waking up from his latest three-day bender on the apartment building's front stoop, he found a turkey curled up next to him. Tamed (and affectionate) from his short life of being hand-fed and petted by his adoring handlers, Señor Pavo didn't even squawk when Mr. Blanquito scooped him up and brought him inside. I can't say if he was silent when the knife fell.

Grandma Izzy followed her nose downstairs where two cultures, both known for their love of language and confrontation, came face-to-face. Accusations, insults, and ethnic slurs must have flared until both sides realized they were in the same boat and a truce was reached. There was a greater war going on, and they were each just a family struggling to survive the best way they knew how.

Grandma Izzy went upstairs to fetch her *arroz con gandules,* and in that late afternoon of the fourth Thursday of November 1944, eighteen people from two different cultures sat in the Blanquitos' apartment and gave thanks. Which in a neighborhood like Spanish Harlem in 1944 was somewhat of a miracle in itself.

And did they all eat . . . *it*? Of *course* they all ate it! There was no tolerance for alternative lifestyles back then. No grumbling about animal rights, food allergies, or growth hormones. There was a *war* going on.

At the end of the kids' table was twelve-year-old Elizabeth, "Betty" Blanquito, sucking the marrow out of a drumstick, inhaling Grandma Izzy's *arroz con gandules,* and batting the lashes of her big green eyes at my father as she listened to him tell (and retell) the story of "The Heroic Liberation and Sacrifice of Señor Pavo. At the grown-ups' table, Mr. Blanquito nodded in satisfaction—meat-drunk. He would, after this conversion, stay off the sauce for six months, long enough to hold a job and move his family, at last, the six blocks east to Pleasant Ave.

As for Betty Blanquito and Rudy, they kept what used to be called "company" on and off for the next eight years until one summer afternoon my father looked out a window and saw . . . my mother.

4

JACKIE O AND THE BOY FROM EAST 106TH STREET

It was a hot summer's day a year and a half after my mother had won her block's first TV. Daisy, a girl named Lydia, and she were walking along East 106th Street on their way to a party, when Daisy stopped the girls to chat up a group of boys hanging out on the front stoop of a three-story apartment building. On the second floor, lying on the sofa and listening to a New York Giants vs. Dodgers baseball game on the radio, was my father. He stuck his head out of the window when he heard Daisy's loud laughter and saw my mother. Years later he would tell me that he ran downstairs like hell because he was afraid if he didn't, she would disappear.

The person who made up the saying "Good things come in small packages" must have seen my mother at the age of twenty. When my father looked out of the window and saw her for the first time, she was petite and curvy, wearing tight but not too tight red Capri pants, a white-on-white, Swiss dot sleeveless blouse tied at her tiny waist, a black patent leather belt, and black patent leather wedge sandals. When he got downstairs for a closer look, he saw her liquid dark-brown eyes, flawless ivory complexion, and jet-black wavy hair. (He would later learn that she slept every night with her hair wrapped around orange juice cans in order to tame its tight curls and that there were other things she was equally rigid about.) That day he thought he could willingly drown in those eyes. His tongue filled up his mouth, and he, who had an answer for everything, could not think of a thing to say.

My mother looked at the boy standing in front of her. He was good-looking at five feet nine inches, with a slim, athletic build from years of recreational stickball, baseball, and dancing. He had brown wavy hair with a cowlick that fell in a curve over his forehead, a ruddy complexion, and a small cleft in his angular chin. (My mother would later learn just how often he relied on his good looks and charm to get him through tough situations.) That day she got butterflies waiting for him to talk to her. She was attracted to him, but would not chase him. Even at twenty, my mother was absolutely a lady.

Rudy didn't talk to Lucy that day. Instead, he talked to Daisy and Lydia and found out every place they were going to be for the rest of that summer. From Central Park to Orchard Beach to the Starlight Room's famous dances at the Waldorf Astoria hotel, Rudy appeared and tried to get my mother to notice him—but to no avail. He did become friends with Daisy and Lydia. He danced with them and introduced them to his other friends, while my mother remained a mystery.

That is, until the night Daisy got toasted. The girls usually had a cocktail or two on the nights they went dancing. My mother's signature drink was one classic martini with olives. It made her feel refined and in control. Daisy, on the other hand, liked whatever was sweet and fruity—and lots of it. Piña coladas, sidecars, and daiquiris all made her happy, and one night, Daisy became so *happy* that my mother thought it best if they immediately went home.

My mother looked around for Lydia to help her with Daisy, but Lydia had already left with her boyfriend. As my mother steered Daisy out of the hotel, trying not to draw attention, my father appeared. He immediately hailed a cab, but after Daisy got sick in the backseat, they were kicked out, still thirty blocks from their destination.

In the hour it took to walk to 99th Street and Lexington Avenue (where Daisy now lived), my father told every joke, story, and anecdote he knew to keep the girls entertained—and Daisy from barfing again. He told them about the pigeons he kept on different roofs, the horses he used to take care of at the West Side riding stables, and the turkey he and his brothers once had as a pet when he was a child.

Lucy saw there was another person besides Daisy who could make her laugh. She also saw that he had paid for the cab, argued with the driver when they were thrown out, and walked them both home without complaining or asking for anything in return. It was the first time a man had ever taken care of her so unselfishly, and by the time Rudy left her on her stoop with just a handshake and a "See you soon?" Lucy was in love.

Initially, neither one of their families was pleased about the relationship. Neither my mother nor my father was their parents' favorite child, and they both knew this. Grandma Izzy, a city person, thought my mother's family, coming from a small town in the mountains, were *jibaros*. But my mother's perfectly put together outfits; perfect manners; and soft, perfectly pitched voice—she was a "Jackie O" well before Jacqueline Bouvier ever met John F. Kennedy—won over Grandma Izzy's heart. She had to admit that my mother was a lady, and therefore almost *too* good for her son.

Papa Julio, the same man who had almost forced my mother to drop out of high school, didn't like it that my dad hadn't gone to school past ninth grade. But my father liked having money in his pocket and quit school to work anywhere. He sold beer at the Polo Grounds until he was fired for being underage; he made bread at an Italian bakery until he was fired for being Puerto Rican; and then he got his driver's license and got a job driving a forklift, which he kept.

When my father came to my mother's family's apartment to watch TV, he would "accidentally" leave change in the sofa cushions for Ofelia and Dulce to find. He even tried to fix the teenage Carmen up with his younger brother Papo, (which sadly didn't take). Eventually his charm and genuine goodwill touched my mother's family the way it had my mother, and Grandma Mari was glad her oldest daughter would finally be taken care of.

So Lucy took a chance and said yes for the second time in her life. She did love my father, but she also married him to get out of the house, which was not as cynical then as it would be today. In those days, in that culture, you needed a man in order to leave home. You needed to be rescued.

My father, who was sure from the first time he set eyes on my mother, married her in part because she was the most beautiful thing he'd ever seen. He also thought she'd give him the love and recognition he didn't get from his family.

They both wanted their lives together to be completely different from the way they had been when they were growing up. Their children would definitely have American names, and they would grow up speaking only English. There would be no societal stigma of bilingualism. No difficulty in school because of switching from one language to another at the age of six. No being teased or left back. There would be no language or any other cultural barrier. Nothing would keep their children from having the life they both felt they were denied. Rudy and Lucy would figuratively and literally keep my brother Kevin and me as far away from the *finca*, the *fogón*, and El Barrio as they could get.

5

LA MUÑECA

Mija,

Amor,

Mi muñeca,

    I love you. I love you with all my heart. I love you so much it hurts for me to write this to you. Even though I know you cannot read this yet, because you have just begun the escuela, still, I write this to you because I love you.

    I write to you because these are the things I cannot tell you. It is very complicada, mija, and you cannot understand. Not now. Maybe not ever. But I am writing this anyway because at least you will know that I did try to explain and maybe that will make a difference someday. Maybe it will make some things better for you.

    You, mi amor, are the only colorada in nuestra familia. You have the pecas of my mother of husband and the same big eyes that are questions, always questions for which there can never be an answer. And every time I look at you, I see the face, the skin, the eyes of Beltran, mi esposo verdad, the only man I loved. Will ever love. I also see him always, in your mother. And perhaps that is why I cannot. I did not. I have not.

    Yes, Papa Julio is not your grandfather. But you will probably never meet Beltran; he was lost to us, to your mother and me many years ago. But Papa Julio is a good man, an honest man, a hard-working man. He brought your mother and me to this country so we could have a better life. Because we were sola. We owe him a lot. We owe him our lives. But I must also say the truth, Papa Julio is not the padre of your mother, and maybe that is part of why she is not feeling well now.

She is not well, mija. Your mother is not well and she has to go to the doctor. She has to live with the doctors so they can make her be well, and that is why you and your brother are coming here to live with Papa Julio and me but you don't have to be afraid, in the name of ¡Gloria Jesus! you will not have to be afraid.

Life is complicado. So complicado. When you are older, you will see that life is hard for a woman. So hard. And you will see why certain things had to be a certain way. But now, you will be safe. I am your abuelita. I will watch you. I will protect you. I will do for you what I did not, could not do for your mother. And if you cannot forgive me, I hope you can at least understand.

No puedo escribir mas ahora. He is coming. Mija, yo te promeso, I will watch over you and project you. You are my muñecita, mi amor; I look at you and I remember.

Guárdenos, El Señor. Salmos 23, 27, 91, 121

Grandma Mari

6

LA VERGÜENZA Y LAS SINVERGÜENZAS
(The Shame and the Shameless)

There was never any explanation from Grandma Mari then or ever. It probably would not have made a difference if there had been.

I was five years old and lying on my stomach under a window and behind the couch in my grandmother's living room. I was drawing. Quietly. Very quietly. I had learned very quickly to be quiet in that apartment. If I wasn't, punishment—smacks, *cocotazos*, a whip from a belt snaking through my clothes, or, sometimes, against my bare bottom—would be swift and hard.

I would never be punished like that from my grandmother. Never from my *abuelita* who I knew adored me. And not from any of my *titis* either, not even from Titi Ofelia, whose sharp eyes, sharp chin, and even sharper tongue I instinctually kept far away from. It was my grandmother's husband I had to watch out for, Papa Julio. The man who told me never to call him *abuelo*, Grandfather, because although he was married to my *abuelita*, he was not my grandfather.

My mother was in a hospital. Today the illness she had then, postpartum depression, is recognized and treated with kindness, support groups, and patience and elicits empathy and sympathy from families and strangers. It's something one can recover from, or use as an excuse to get away with murder. In 1965, though, it was treated with seclusion, observation and medication. And it caused whispers and speculation everywhere your name was mentioned. It was considered a weakness, a character flaw, and a secret shame that would follow and define you for the rest of your days.

I remember the apartment was cold. My mother had been gone this time just a little over a week, but it felt like I had hardly seen her that year at all. I was copying a pair of kittens from an engraved copper plate onto a brown paper bag. My mother handmade the plate for me as a birthday gift, and even though my birthday had long passed, I had just received it the day before.

The two kittens were playing with a ball of yarn. I could easily draw the kittens, but no matter how many times I erased and started over, I could just not get the twists and turns in the yarn to come out right. I was going to give the finished drawing to my mother and wanted it to be perfect. As I struggled, familiar voices interrupted my concentration.

"The problem with Michele is . . . our sister brought her up to be white," Titi Ofelia said.

This wasn't the first time I had overheard a remark like that from my sanctuary behind the couch. My drawings and my Colorforms and my Barbies had helped me find out that my mother had twice been taken away to a hospital and that my father couldn't take care of my mother, my brother and me by himself, which was why we were living with *abuelita* and Papa Julio.

In Papa Julio's and his daughters' eyes, there was something wrong with my mother—something that made her so different from them that it made something wrong with me too. I always talked too loud; jumped too much; dropped, spilled, and broke things; and was caught where I wasn't supposed to be. I always was caught where I wasn't supposed to be.

The *titis* were sitting on a plastic-covered sectional couch in the large, bright, many-windowed living room with French doors, whose centerpiece was the huge wooden Philco TV/Hi-Fi/radio console my mother won in a St. Lucy's church lottery back in Spanish Harlem almost fifteen years before.

"Didn't you think Lucy looked better last week though? Didn't you? I mean, she was talking again," Titi Dulce said.

Titi Dulce was the youngest sister and the one who looked most like my mother: petite and shapely, with pale skin and almost-black hair. Dulce, who was about to turn twenty-one, had just gotten married and had just suffered her first miscarriage. She would play with me and give me extra hugs every time she came over, which was never often enough.

"I had Pastor Ramirez lead an intercession for Lucy last night. We don't want her to come home too soon again. Remember what happened last time."

That was Titi Carmen, the second oldest, the *jamona*. At just twenty-five she already appeared postmenopausal. She would never get married; her thick legs and squinty eyes would ensure that—as well as the oily black hair that ran rampant up her legs, down her arms, between her pancake breasts and occasionally sprouted from her brown double chin. She, like my *abuelita*, was very, very religious. It was good for her.

"Well, what are we going to do about Michele?" Titi Ofelia repeated.

Titi Ofelia was twenty-three, tall, slim, and too quick, with skin the color of a double cup of *café con leche* and a personality with a kick to match. Every other week she smoked a different brand of cigarettes, every other month she dyed her hair a different color, every couple of years she had a new husband. I'm sure if she was your friend, she was delightful to be around. Only, I wasn't her friend.

"I told you what she told Mami. As if our father would ever do such a thing. Who taught Michele how to lie like that? You know who: Lucy. That *princesa* of a sister of ours. Always fixing herself up as if she was the queen of Spain. Pretending she's not a *tregieña*—I don't care how *blanquita* she *thinks* she is . . ."

"Stop it, Ofelia," Dulce said. "And stop waving that cigarette at me. They smell like caca."

"Good, then maybe for once I can smoke a whole pack by myself.

Anyway, if you ask me that's what got our sister locked up. Lies. And Michele is going to turn out just the same if we don't teach her. Next time, I'm going to put some Tabasco on her tongue and no one is . . ."

"*Cállate*, both of you. *Dios mio*, she is here!" Titi Carmen warned.

My pencil had rolled to the end of the couch. The three of them turned around as I scrambled to retrieve it, and the conversation stopped.

"Michele! *Niñita*! What are you doing?" Titi Dulce asked.

"Oh look, she's drawing *dos gatititos*. Very nice, Michele. Very nice!" Titi Carmen affirmed.

"Drawing. Lying. Neither one will ever get her anywhere. *Mija*, why don't you go finish that in your room and let us talk, eh? Good girl."

Titi Ofelia didn't wait for an answer. She turned her back and they all continued speaking again—in Spanish. It was the mystery language grown-ups used for celebrations, lost tempers, and secrets. And since my mother and father had always only spoken English to Kevin and me, that meant I wouldn't find out when my mother was coming home, or what "being white" was, or most important, what I had been lying about. I couldn't think of anything, except the time I sneaked soap into the frying pan when Titi Ofelia was cooking and blamed it on a giant. But that had been a whole month ago.

I quietly, very quietly, left the living room and wandered down the long, dark hall past the kitchen and bathroom, the framed pictures of John F. Kennedy, Martin Luther King, and Jesus to the bedrooms; there were always two separate bedrooms for *abuelita* and Papa Julio for as long as I could remember. There was the bedroom I shared with *abuelita*, Papa Julio's room, and the back bedroom, where my brother Kevin was. He was kept in that room almost all the time *abuelita* wasn't home. And *abuelita* wasn't home a lot.

In the morning, she went out carrying containers of *sopa de pollo* and *arroz y habichuelas* to that other hospital where my great-grandmother was. In the afternoon, she'd put on her long-sleeved white blouse and dark purple skirt and go to church. Sometimes, she left after breakfast and didn't come home until it was time to cook for Papa Julio before he left for work.

I wasn't allowed to go into that back bedroom when *abuelita* wasn't there. There couldn't be noise in the daytime because Papa Julio worked nights and needed his sleep. There couldn't be any noise at all or he'd be very, *very* angry. I'd been told this many times, but I was five years old. I wanted to play with my brother.

I opened the door. Even though it was afternoon, the room was in shadow and the Venetian blinds were drawn. Kevin was standing in his playpen, holding its rail, jumping and gurgling. He was then two years old. He talked in sentences when we arrived at my grandmother's, but without my mother with him and with him being kept mostly in isolation, he had reverted to baby talk. He also didn't walk very well anymore either, and I couldn't chase him like I used to. One of Papa Julio's belts lay next to Kevin's bare feet. There was always a belt in the playpen.

I closed the door and we played until the door opened. I felt Papa Julio's large hand swing me by my ponytail and push me between him and the wall.

"I told you not to come in here. I told you I would punish you if I caught you. You are a bad girl, bad girl, bad girl, *mala, malissima,* just like your mother . . ."

He pressed me against him while he reached for the belt in the playpen. He pulled down my pants and spanked me with one hand like he usually did, but this time he rubbed the other against my behind and *pipi*. He didn't always do both. Sometimes he would just yell, but not this time. I didn't cry. I never did. I didn't have to. Kevin did the crying for both of us.

"You say nothing," Papa Julio said. "Just like your mother."

Then as quickly as it began, it was over. Both his hands retracted, and he pulled my pants back up and pushed me out of the room. I could still hear Kevin crying as the door closed. Papa Julio didn't look at or speak to me as he went back into his room.

I continued walking through the long hall back to the living room. Carmen and Ofelia had left; Dulce was still sitting on the couch and was now talking on the telephone. I tried to snuggle up to her, but then she heard Kevin, hung up, and left me to check on him. Everything would be okay for now. Dulce loved babies and Papa Julio wouldn't punish her.

When the apartment was quiet again, I went back to the only thing I could control—my drawing. It was the one thing that hadn't abandoned or betrayed me, and if something wasn't right, I could erase it and start over. I knew if only I kept trying I could get that yarn to come out right. The kittens would make my mother so happy that she would get well and come home.

I worked at the yarn until I erased a hole through the paper bag. The drawing was ruined. I went to crumple it, but the kittens looked too happy to give up. I smoothed out the bag and picked up my pencil. I had to keep trying.

7

IGLESIA CON POLLO

The very first time I was sure I was going to hell, I was five years old and sitting with my *abuelita* and Titi Carmen in church. It wasn't just any church; it was an *Iglesia Pentecostal*, one of the storefront churches that are part of every Latin neighborhood. It wasn't just any storefront either. It was on the second floor above a *vivero*, a live poultry butcher, one of the few left in Washington Heights.

My *abuelita* had been going to this church for years. In a neighborhood with an *iglesia* on every other block, she felt it was special, and not just because it was also right around the corner from her apartment.

When you ascended the stairs, plucked feathers stuck to the sides of your shoes like angel wings. When the congregation prayed in silence, it was underscored by the murmur of soft clucking. And the aroma of avian slaughter gave a whole new meaning to sermons about the redeeming blood of Jesus.

Of course, the sermons were in Spanish, so I barely understood them. My grandmother brought me there every Sunday anyway, though, perhaps in the hope that by absorbing the sound of enough *¡Gloria Allelujahs!* I would miraculously atone for the sin of not being a bilingual child.

It was almost Christmas, and this Sunday I was in the front row where children weren't usually allowed. It was reserved for deacons such as my grandmother, who throughout each service swayed, clapped, and took turns being "slain in the spirit," which meant falling on the floor and thrashing around until being revived by one of the nurses who sat off to the side.

The nurses smiled at me and gave a respectful nod to my grandmother. In a congregation teeming with pious women, she was known as one of the most devout.

One of the other deacons handed me a tambourine and told me in English I could play along with the music. And this, after a year of being told to "shush," "hush," "be quiet," and *"Cállate—coño, me lo dijo cállate o te voy pow-pow!"* made me very, very happy.

Each service always began with music, and we're not talking about any wheezy moth-eaten Catholic Church organ. This *iglesia* had electric guitars, horns, congas, and timbales, all played by men, some of whom looked as if they had stayed up all night (arriving straight from their Saturday night *salsa* gigs), and today I was to be their accompanist.

I banged and shook my tambourine in perfect 4/4 time. I moved from the row of chairs to the aisle where I jumped and swayed, my hands in the air, singing *"¡Gloria! Allelujah!"* just like everyone else. The deacons now smiled at me, and I played and sang even louder. It was so much fun, I was about to ask *abuelita* if I could start going to church with her on Wednesdays and Fridays too, when all of a sudden I was pulled to the front of the room.

All I could see were people's stomachs: rolls of flesh over belts pulled too tight, blouses badly tucked into waistbands, and a couple of missing buttons—until the crowd shifted and moved me into a line of people facing the pastor who was holding a little glass bottle.

The first man in line walked up to the pastor and tilted his head skyward. The pastor poured liquid from the bottle onto his thumb and pressed his thumb to the man's forehead. As the man bowed his head, my grandmother and the other deacons began praying in different, strange languages, in voices that were either higher or lower pitched than the ones they usually had. They were speaking in tongues.

I had seen this many times before, and it always fascinated me that each one of them sounded completely different every time. Speaking in tongues was considered a great gift. It was considered an even greater gift if you could interpret what you said, which was what my *abuelita* was preparing to do.

The deacons cleared a space for *abuelita*, and I turned to look for Titi Carmen. She was in a back row with her wide feet rooted to the linoleum and her deep-set eyes tightly shut. Her face had a look of such joy that she was almost truly beautiful.

The man up front screamed. I whirled around to see him throw his hands in the air as he fell to the floor. The nurses jumped up and dragged him over to the side. Soon there were seven bodies on that side of the room. I knew there were seven; I might not have been able to speak Spanish, but I could sure count. I also knew that I was about to be next, and as I turned to run, the largest deacon—the one I had heard some of the younger women call *La Gordita* or The Fat One, behind her back—grabbed me and carried me to the front of the line.

I felt a thick greasy liquid drip onto my head; it smelled like the Goya oil *abuelita* fried her *platanos* in. I struggled and *La Gordita* turned me around, crushing me against her bra; her blouse was the one with the missing buttons. It wasn't an undergarment as much as a device, with multiple straps, "cross your heart" stitching, smelly rubber, and bulky, cone-shaped cups. It mashed my face so completely that within seconds I felt as if I were suffocating.

I struggled harder, but she clutched me into her humongous smothering bosoms like a vise. With the last of my breath, I started crying, and as I did, I saw from far, far away, one of the kittens from my mother's etching. It whispered that I didn't have to be afraid . . . I could get away . . . if I wanted to . . .

With the last of my strength I bit, hard, right through the layers of stitching, rubber, and fabric and into pliant, living flesh. *La Gordita* yelled and dropped me to the floor where I sprawled, gasping, as the other deacons sprang to avenge her. One grabbed my legs. Another grabbed my arms. Another gripped me by the crown of my head. I heard another say in English, "The child has a demon!"

I closed my eyes and tried to find the kitten again but it had gone. I was fully awake and utterly trapped. No one would save me now. I wasn't sure what a demon was, but I was sure I was now going to hell, which I knew was where all Bad People went to get punished.

Was it because I couldn't speak their language? Was it my fault my mother had gone away? I didn't know what I'd done. As I awaited my fate, I smelled something familiar. It was my grandmother, the aroma of her perfume (which I'd much later learn was called Tigress) preceding her as she and Titi Carmen fought their way to me.

"What are you doing?" they yelled in Spanish and English. "She doesn't understand. She's only a child. You're the ones with the demons!"

La Gordita's minions released their death grip and I was set back on my feet. There was muttering, whispering, and then silence as *abuelita* took my hand. With Titi Carmen walking shotgun, the congregation parted to let us through. Some of the people we passed had been smiling and attentive to me just an hour before but were now looking at all three of us with angry faces. Others gave a look that said they felt bad, but didn't know what to do. A few others looked at the floor.

Just before we got to the door, I heard someone say in the first Spanish I ever fully understood, *"Vamos a resar por ti."* (We'll pray for you).

My *abuelita* turned, picked a chicken feather out of my hair, and said, "No *mi vida,* I will pray for you."

I thought I was going to be in trouble for getting *abuelita* and Titi Carmen kicked out of church, but they never said anything more to me about it. They just held their own "church" in *abuelita*'s bedroom while they looked for another *iglesia.* As it turned out, they would have had to anyway. A couple of weeks later the New York City

Health Department, acting on an anonymous tip, raided the poultry market, closing it down along with the church.

Abuelita and Titi Carmen eventually did find another *iglesia* a bit farther uptown, but I wouldn't be going there with them—and not because I had a demon or because I belonged in hell. Just the opposite: I was going home.

8

PIONEERS

Little Enough to Ride for Free, Little Enough to Ride Your Knee

I was sitting on a bus with my father. We were by ourselves, which was a treat for me. I hadn't seen him much in the last year, and when I did, he always looked worried or sad. Today he was happy.

We'd just left Grandma Izzy's, who I also hadn't seen for a while. She'd smothered me in kisses and stuffed me with *arroz dulce, dulce de coco,* and ice cream. Now my father was taking me somewhere else, to show me a surprise before dropping me back off at Grandma Mari's. He swung my hand and whistled as we walked to the bus stop. Being alone with my father for an entire day was fun enough, and I couldn't imagine where we were going or what was going to happen when we got there.

The bus ride to who knows where was long and boring. We sat across from the driver. I tried to kneel on the seat to look out the window, but my father told me to get back down. I swung my legs around and looked at the lady next to me as she opened her pocketbook and took out a *Photoplay* magazine.

In case you don't know, the cult of celebrity obsession was in full force long before *People* magazine, MTV, or TMZ. *Photoplay* was one of the first publications to cover celebrity gossip, exposing scandals and secrets from the dawn of the silent film era through 1980 when its staff was moved to *Us* magazine. I knew about it because before my mother got sick she would sit me on her lap while she was reading it and point out the words.

The magazine was open to a big picture of a man and woman. The man looked sleepy. The woman had a lot of blue eye makeup on, even more than Titi Ofelia or Dulce ever wore. Their faces were very close together. I pretended that instead of sitting next to my father, I was sitting on my mother's lap and looked closer to sound out the words.

"E-liz-a-beth Tay-lor . . . Ri-Ri-Rich-ard Bur-ton . . . Na-k-ed . . . Lust . . ."

The woman snapped the magazine shut and the bus driver whirled around. "Pay your fare!" he boomed.

"What?" my father said. "She ain't gonna be six till July, I swear."

"No five-year-old reads 'naked lust.' Shame on her. And shame on you. Pay your fare!"

I remember this entire conversation happened with the bus driver looking straight at my father and me. I only hope the bus was not also moving. My father didn't pay. It was the principle, after all. He slung me gently over his shoulder as we got off the bus, but not before getting one last swipe at the driver. "I bet your kids don't read."

But when he put me on my feet he said, "I told you, no reading on the bus! Now come on, before it gets dark."

We walked up a lot of stairs to a train. I ducked under the turnstile as my father dropped in his token. When we got up to the platform, he smiled and pointed to a sign. "You can read now if you want. What does that say?"

"Up-town. Pel-ham Bay . . . Park. Park?"

But there was no park when we got off the train, only the elevated train tracks, which we walked under for a couple of blocks. We passed an old-looking church that took up an entire block: a huge, weathered, gray stone building in between two gray graveyards with bare-limbed trees—everything gray in the late winter sun. It wasn't like the *iglesias* my *abuelita* and Titi Carmen had taken me to, not at all.

In fact, the entire neighborhood looked different. The streets didn't have as much garbage in them—especially dog doo-doo—and it was a lot quieter. There weren't as many people walking in the street, and no one was playing dominoes or leaning against the walls in front of the buildings, drinking out of brown paper bags.

We crossed the street and walked along a long block of apartment buildings lined up side by side. Where were we going? Were we going to visit someone? I went through my entire family in my head, but couldn't think of who it could be. I looked at my father. He'd stopped whistling and looked like he was thinking very hard about something. When we got to the building on the corner, he pushed open the door and we went in. There was a big open hallway with stairs going to the right and to the left. We went to the right and walked up more stairs. Now there was music, loud music coming from behind a few of the closed doors. Some of the floors smelled bad, like the time when *abuelita* had a tummyache and Titi Ofelia came over to cook, but the food had to be thrown out and we all had to eat Rice Krispies for dinner. Where were we going? Who lived here? My father had dropped my hand and started to go into his jacket pocket. He climbed faster and told me to hurry up.

Finally, we stopped in front of a door. It said 5C. My father fumbled in his jacket pockets again, then his shirt, and finally in his pants. Soon there was a small pile of stuff tossed onto the tile floor. I sat down to inspect everything: wallet, pack of Camels, lighter, hand-kerchief, a rubber band, half a roll of five-flavor LifeSavers, pepper-mint Chiclets, and, what I was hoping to find, Chuckles. I popped the sugar-sprinkled orange jelly candy in my mouth.

"Hold on . . . goddamnsonuvabitch," I heard him mutter. I knew grown-ups were allowed to say bad words when they lost things, but kids weren't.

A couple of more bad words later, he squatted down next to me turning over each object he'd tossed on the floor, looking at each thing again before he stuffed it back into a pocket. Had he lost something? His face was red, and he looked as if he was mad at something or someone, but I knew it wasn't me. He let out a long breath that was kind of like a whistle; only there was no music in it.

"Well . . ." he said. "The surprise is . . . we're getting ice cream."

We went back downstairs and down the block to an ice-cream parlor under the El. It was wide and bright, with dark polished wood, shiny green marble, and gleaming brass. We sat at the counter on red stools that twirled around, which I did until my father stopped me by gently placing one of his hands on the top of my head and shaking the index finger of his other. He looked as if he was about to tell me something, but a man wearing a white jacket and hat appeared and smiled at us. Then a train came by and my dad had to yell over it to be heard.

"This is my little girl I was telling you about. She don't go to school yet but she can read."

"Naw, really?" the counterman yelled back. He smiled again and handed me the menu.

My father let me order the black-and-white ice-cream sodas. When the man went off to make them, my father turned to me and said, "That building we were in . . . that's our new building. That apartment we were at . . . that's where we're going to live. Next week. But I wanted to show you first."

The ice-cream sodas came and I started mine right away. This was the second time I was having ice cream in one day, and I was going to finish it before my father realized it and took it away. He wasn't paying any attention though. He kept talking.

"I don't know what happened. I must have left the keys somewhere. Don't tell anyone I brought you here today. It's our secret, right?" And he started drinking his ice-cream soda.

My father had finally done it. Whether by hitting the number, finding a bag of cash that fell off a truck, or creating some other urban legend, my dad had finally managed to get Kevin and me out of *abuelita*'s. The apartment he'd misplaced the keys for was ours. That was so like him. He always tried to do stuff, but it hardly ever turned out right. But he'd always smile or make a joke and hardly anyone could stay mad at him. At least I couldn't. Not today anyway, when I had double ice creams in my belly. And this was a good secret. I could keep this and it wouldn't feel bad. Not at all.

As we finished our sodas, it was starting to get dark. We got back on the train and he took me back to Grandma Mari's, but it would be for the last time. My mother had finally come home for good. In exactly one week, we would all be together again—at last—on St. Peter's Avenue, in a no-name neighborhood between Parkchester and Pelham Bay Park, a few stops from the end of the number 6 train in The Bronx. It was a neighborhood I would call home for the next twenty-one years.

This wasn't going to be like living at *abuelita*'s. And this wasn't anywhere near the neighborhoods we'd lived before my mother became ill. One thing I'd noticed was that everyone spoke English. The other was—as I remembered the sparse orange scruff on top of the counterman's head—there were people who looked like me. Would I have friends? Would there be more ice cream? And what was my mother going to say? Was it going to be a surprise for her too? I hoped she would like it. I thought I would. I couldn't wait for us all to be together again. Like a real family.

9

KITTENWORLD

The girl was pulling my ponytail. She pulled it again and called me Whitey.

The girl did this to me a lot, every day in fact, in that kindergarten, that escuela I was going to, P.S. 28M on Amsterdam Avenue because I was living at 555 West 157th Street, apartment 6B, with my abuelita and Papa Julio.

I hated school. I wanted to stay home and draw and play with my brother Kevin, even though sometimes Papa Julio catches me. And he gets mad, always mad, and sometimes he yells at me and sometimes he hits me and sometimes he does something else which I'm not supposed to tell about and maybe someone has to hurt me, but not her. Not this girl.

So I whirled my head around and the three metal barrettes in my long, bushy ponytail whacked the girl in the mouth. I heard the crack of metal against tooth. I smelled blood.

I was brought into a room, an office, where there was an old lady like abuelita, but with a mean face, a "principal." She asked me where my mother was. I told her my mother was in Kittenworld. She went to play with the kittens.

"Don't you see the yarn? She's playing, we're all playing with the kittens. We smell good. We play nice. We have fun. No one ever gets hurt in Kittenworld." I want to go back there, I tell her. "I want to go home. I want to go home!"

I woke up. It was dark and I could hear my mother pacing the apartment talking under her breath. I am home, in the apartment my father had once lost the keys for, apartment 5C. Four rooms: two bedrooms, one medium sized with a false wall my father built to divide it in half. This is what my brother Kevin and I share. He has the side by the window; I have the side by the door. There is another, much smaller bedroom, where my father and mother sleep. There's also a bathroom, a large living room with two big windows, and a small, boxy foyer opposite a long narrow kitchen. That is where my mother stops pacing.

I don't know what she is going to say tonight. Sometimes it's from the Bible. Sometimes it's in Spanish. Sometimes it's something about a test, a parasite, and a plot. Sometimes it's just screaming out a window, "I hate you, I hate you, I haaaate yoooou!" over and over, and when someone yells at her to shut the hell up, she just speeches louder. Speeching. That's what she calls it.

The next day, Titi Dulce and Cousin Ray-Ray, who was just beginning to walk, came over. After three tries, Dulce had finally been able to produce a live baby, a sturdy little boy with almond-colored skin, straight brown hair, and hazel eyes. Her present, she calls him, since he was born just two days after her twenty-third birthday. I'm glad she has Ray-Ray to keep her from being lonely because Uncle Raymond is away again.

After we finished eating, my mother and Dulce sat in the kitchen having coffee. Kevin, Ray-Ray, and I were sitting on the floor in the living room watching *Batman*. Kevin had a Batmobile with action figures, and he and Ray-Ray were playing with them. Ray-Ray put one of the toys in his mouth; Kevin took it out. They both shrieked with laughter. Between them and the trains rumbling past, I could hardly hear my favorite villain, Catwoman, purr.

Then all of a sudden I heard Dulce say loudly, "*Como?* Lucy? I can't hear you. What? *Ay, por que* do you have to whisper to speak Spanish in your own house? So your 'I pretend I'm Italian' husband doesn't hear you?" My mother said something back I can't hear, and Dulce came into the living room, scooped up Ray-Ray, and left, slamming the door behind her. My mother and Dulce almost never fought, not like she and Ofelia. I wondered what started it, but my mother stayed in the kitchen and I knew better than to ask.

My family was the first and only Puerto Rican family ever to live in our building. "We're *Mayflower* Puerto Ricans," my father said. "Pioneers." But the Sabellis, Kirchbergers, and O'Gradys weren't exactly welcoming until they got to know my dad. He was St. Peter's Avenue's Jackie Robinson, the icebreaker, the "credit to his race"; the example that made it easier for those to come. Plus, he told everyone we were from the "Italian part" of Puerto Rico. And now they all greeted my father whenever we'd walk into the corner candy store or the ice-cream parlor.

"How about those Mets?" they'd say.

"They suck!" my father would say and talk about the rookie pitcher Tom Seaver, the *pheenom* who would one day make the Mets not suck. And then Kevin and I would get a free Chunky bar or extra ice cream in our black-and-white ice-cream sodas.

My father could go anywhere and make anyone like him. It was a gift. But my mother wasn't like him. She stayed in the apartment except for taking me to school or going shopping. Then she'd spend hours getting ready, putting on a full face of makeup, a dress, and her high-heeled shoes. She looked like one of the pictures in her movie magazines, even at home when she was wearing slacks and a sweater and her pink slippers with the little heels, *chancletas*, only she never called them that. She always looked perfect, but not like someone you could talk to or touch. She stared straight ahead when we walked, almost never answering if someone spoke to her. If Kevin or I ever stopped, she pulled us along and kept going.

We did have fun though, sometimes. I remember one day at the A&P, we were wheeling Kevin in a shopping cart and the Beatles "Fool on the Hill" started playing. My mother liked that song. I remember her smiling and softly singing along, wheeling the cart along with the music until another shopper passed us by, and she suddenly stopped and put her blank face back on. I wished that person had never come so she could have kept singing.

Besides her movie magazines, she also liked to read books by people with names like Carl Jung or José Ortega y Gassett. She'd get excited when she found something she liked, and she'd write stuff down on little index cards. I wanted to see what made her happy, so I tried to read those books too, but I couldn't understand them and put them back down as soon as I opened them. Most of the time, though, when she wasn't doing housework or physically taking care of Kevin or me, she'd pace the apartment until she found a comfortable spot to stop and speech.

When my father came home from work it was getting dark. He worked double shifts most days, sleeping for a few hours and then going back out to work again, but this day he was home early. Kevin and I were still watching TV, or trying to. My mother was yelling out the kitchen window while she reheated the pots of instant mashed potatoes, hot dogs, and frozen corn.

My father peeked into the kitchen, came back into the living room, and motioned me to follow him. He led me up the stairs to the roof and pushed open the unlatched creaking door. There were TV antennas whooshing and clotheslines flapping, and it was a little scary. I heard little pops of noise, then bigger hissing and booming ones. We walked over to the edge where there was a small wall and a rail even with my head. He picked me up and balanced me against him, my feet on the edge of the wall. He pointed into the growing darkness and said, "Look."

I followed his finger and saw little points of light streak through the night sky. Some of them trailed away. Others burst into flashes of colors and trickled down toward the ground. They were all very noisy, and I could smell smoke and burning, but I wasn't scared. I was with my father.

"You know what today is, little girl? It's July fourth and these are fireworks. They are for you. They know your birthday is coming. Six more days and you'll be seven."

He pointed out bottle rockets, four-ounce rockets, Roman candles, pinwheels, and fountains for a few more minutes before we walked back down to the apartment. He sent me back into the living room, then went into the kitchen again, and came right back out. He let out that same breath he always did when he didn't know what to do, the long whistle with no music in it. But when he looked at us, though, there was a smile on his face.

"Who wants ice cream?" he asked and took Kevin and me down to the parlor. I had a cherry-lime rickey—my new favorite. My dad and Kevin had black-and-white ice-cream sodas. When we got back to the apartment my mother was still speeching.

My father put us to bed that night, something he rarely ever did—and that was all he did: watched us brush our teeth, put our pajamas on, and climb into bed. No jokes, no reading. He had a strange, half-sad, half-mad look on his face as he told us good-night.

I could hear my mother pacing in the living room. She stopped by the window on the other side of the wall from my bed. I closed my eyes and waited for the kittens to come. They wouldn't always, but when they did, it was a place where no one was yelled at, no one was hit, no one ever cried. It was a place where your mother didn't take a lot of medicine that made her too tired to either play or talk or the exact opposite, running from room to room through the apartment, yelling out the window, threatening to get the "parasites, the scum of the earth, the filth . . ."

As my mother's voice rose, the kittens came. Sometimes they spoke to me, but tonight they just snuggled next to me on my pillow. As I lay between them breathing in their soft fur, listening to their purring, it drowned out her words and I fell asleep.

The next morning Kevin threw the entire Batman collection out of that same window, and my mother sent me down to the alley to pick them up. When I got there, I looked up and she was standing at the window watching me. As I climbed back up the five flights of stairs to the apartment, I remember thinking that even though we were now all together like a real family, something was still wrong. Even on the *Honeymooners*, it was Ralph who did all the yelling, not Alice.

10

BLOODSISTERS

One day I walked up to a group of kids in the playground next to my new school and said, "Hi, my name's Michele, what's yours?"

My father had picked me up from school after a half day because my mother was at the doctor with Kevin, who was having another ear infection. Instead of taking me home right away, he let me play in the playground next to the school, something my mother almost never let me do. I was excited. Some kids were playing with a small pink rubber ball called a Spaldeen, taking turns bouncing it against the brick wall of the "Parky House," the building where the New York City Department of Parks and Recreation employee, who was called the Parky, kept all the playground stuff.

The kids looked nice. I thought maybe I could make friends with them. I had been going to school there for what seemed like a long time, and I didn't really have any yet.

"Do you like Underdog?" I asked. "I like Underdog. Do you want to play Underdog?" Underdog was the quintessential Saturday morning cartoon back then, a takeoff of Superman about a mild-mannered dog with super powers.

"Freckle-Face Strawberry! Freckle-Face Strawberry!"

It was the fat boy with the hooded eyes. He yelled this at me every time he saw me, which was a lot: here at school and also in the other playground, which was down the block from our building.

I got quiet. Every time he yelled this at me, it made whomever I was trying to talk to run away. How was I supposed to make friends if the fat boy always spoiled it for me?

"Bwaaaaaah!" the fat boy yelled. Then he and the other kids ran to the other side of the playground. I slowly started to walk back to where my father was.

"I'll play with you."

It was a girl just my size, with pretty brown skin and three pigtails sticking up out of her head.

"My name's Darlinda and this is my sister Gigi," she said, pointing at an older, much bigger girl standing next to her who rolled her eyes at us.

"I ain't playing no baby games. You go ahead," Gigi said.

Darlinda and I climbed up the side of the monkey bars. When we got almost up to the top, I turned around and said, "It's just little old me, Underdog! Don't worry Sweet Polly, I'll save you!" and jumped off. I was surprised when I hit the ground. I was so happy finally to have someone to play with; I think I thought I could fly.

There was no padding under anything in playgrounds back then, just broken asphalt, broken glass, and occasionally, a broken hypodermic needle. My poor father, who had just looked down to light a cigarette, looked up to see me screaming and bloody with a piece of glass sticking out through the flesh under my lower lip. He ran to me, wrapped his handkerchief around my chin, picked me up, gently and carried me home to where my mother would pull out the glass, clean the cut, and yell at him for not watching me. I still have the scar, and I still remember being carried over my father's shoulder, looking back through my tears, seeing Darlinda waving after me.

From that day on Darlinda and I were friends. We were in the same class at school, and we were both in the Silver Reading Group (this meant that even though we were in second grade, we were reading at fourth grade level). We traded books: *The Shy Stegosaurus of Cricket Creek, Henry and Beezus,* and *Harriet The Spy.* We shared baloney sandwiches and Hostess Sno Balls at lunch. I showed her my kitten drawings. She drew too, a boy with a spotted pet dinosaur she called a Keebie.

One day Darlinda said, "Let's be Bloodsisters."

"What's that?"

"We get a razor blade and you cut your thumb and I cut my thumb and then we mix our blood together and swear we are best friends forever."

"Okay."

"You have to get the razor blade though."

"How come?"

"You have a father. Get the blade from inside the razor he shaves with."

Darlinda's father was dead. He died not long after we met. I told her that I didn't see mine once for almost a year, but she said it wasn't the same. I thought I was lucky I still had a father and I almost backed out, but I got the blade that night anyway. I'd gotten good at sneaking things at *abuelita*'s, like the time I put soap in the pan when Titi Ofelia was cooking and everyone thought she made a bad dinner and no one ever found out. I had to balance on the rim of the bathtub to get the razor out of the medicine cabinet and almost fell too, but I got it and stuck it in the new book I'd just finished, *Beezus and Ramona*. If I wrote a good book report for it that night, I'd be in the Gold Reading Group, the first one in the class.

The second they let us out in the schoolyard for lunchtime the next day, Darlinda and I raced across the concrete to the farthest corner and went behind a tree. I quickly took out the razor from inside the book and poked the end against the underside of my left thumb till a small red spot seeped out and trickled down my hand. It didn't hurt that much but looking at it made my stomach feel a little sick and I started to get afraid we were going to get caught. "Hurry up," Darlinda said as she grabbed at the blade, conveniently cutting herself as she did so. We looked at each other for a second, grabbed each other's hands, and then mashed our thumbs together while we jumped up and down.

"Bloodsisters! Bloodsisters! Forever and ever till we get married and die!"

A teacher heard us yelling and came over, but Darlinda had thrown the blade away so we didn't get caught with it, though we both were sent to the nurse. The nurse asked us what happened. "Nothing," we answered in unison. The nurse gave us a look of disbelief, daubed our wounds with Mercurochrome, put double Band-Aids on them, and sent us back to class. That was the only thing they really worried about in those days—that the cut was cleaned. If a child slit her thumb and mixed blood with anyone today, they'd both be kept under quarantine until they turned eighteen (or at least the next six months). But this was the early spring of 1968, the peak of the cultural and societal upheaval we now call "The Sixties" was just beginning.

While we were waiting for our book reports to be returned, I kept looking at my thumb. It hurt more now, but it was a good hurt, as if it had been for something. I never had a Bloodsister before. I wasn't sure what it meant; Darlinda and I already played together all the time. Maybe it meant that the fat boy wouldn't bother me anymore. While I was thinking about all this, I got my book report back and on top was a gold star. I was in Gold Reading Group. It was the best day of my life. I couldn't remember ever being so happy.

After school though, Darlinda had to go right on the school bus and my mother and Kevin weren't waiting for me out front like they usually did, so I had to stay behind the fence in front of the school doors, where you were supposed to wait if your parent was late. I went down to the gate to look for my mother, but heard someone breathe behind me and turned around. It was the fat boy. He was in third grade, but his class barely got up to the Green Reading Group. I knew because all the names of the kids who had gotten their colored stars were put up on the walls outside their classrooms. The fat boy kicked *Beezus and Ramona* out of my hands and my thumb started to throb.

"Goldie-star! Smarty-pants! Freckle-Face Strawberry!"

A few kids and teachers were at the top of the stairs, but none of them were looking at us. I tried to go around the fat boy but he blocked me. I bent down to pick *Beezus* up. He pulled my ponytail and said, "Go back to Ireland, Ketchup Head!"

"Ireland?" I said, puzzled. "I'm not Irish."

"Yeah, well, what are you?"

"My family is from Puerto Rico, but I was born in Manhattan. We live on St. Peter's and . . ."

"Puerto Rican! No wonder you play with niggers . . . spic."

I didn't know what to say. I didn't know what a "nigger" was. I knew the words *negro* and *negrito*, but they weren't bad. Titis Dulce and Ofelia called Titi Carmen *negrita* all the time. Did he mean Darlinda? She was brown like Titi Carmen. But the fat boy wasn't smiling. He meant it to be a bad name. I could tell by the way he looked and sounded when he said it. I did know what a spic was though. That was another bad word to call what my family was. Some people in our building used to call us spics until my father made friends with them. Maybe I could make friends with this fat boy, and he wouldn't say bad names anymore.

"My name's Michele. Do you watch Batman? I like . . ."

"Your name is Spic. Nah, you're too small to be a Spic. You're a Speck." He spit on the floor between us as if to point out just how small I was.

"Pasquale! Get *ovah* here right now! Where's *Ant'ny*?" A tall woman like Titi Ofelia, with the same tan skin and black hair but a different way of speaking, was yelling from halfway down the block.

"Aw ma!" Pasquale wailed

"Don't 'aw ma' me! *Getcha brudduh* and get *ovah* here . . . now!"

Right behind the woman was my mother. She was wearing a pink tweed spring coat and a short pink dress with dark red suede high heels. There was a flowered scarf tied around her head; she hadn't wrapped her hair. Kevin was clutching one of her hands; I could see the other was balled up into a fist. The tall woman, who was wearing dungarees and a plain shirt and long sweater stopped to look at my mother. She smiled and I thought she was about to say something, but my mother brushed past her and went straight inside the gate to me. As she passed, I noticed she barely came up to the woman's shoulders. My mother took my hand and we started walking home, going past the tall woman, the fat boy, and his *brudduh*. I could feel eyes in my back—they—or someone was watching us. I wished my mother had smiled back at the lady. Why was it so hard for people to be friends? I wondered if grown-ups ever did Bloodsisters.

"What happened to your thumb?" my mother asked. She walked fast, her heels going clickity-click as Kevin and I struggled to keep up.

"Nothing," I said.

It had been the happiest day ever and now it was ruined. My book was gone, my thumb hurt, I was called bad names, . . . and I was confused. I looked like the kids at school, but that wasn't good enough. I was smart, but that wasn't good enough. I even had a Bloodsister, but that still wasn't good enough—she was called names too. No matter what, it was never good enough. I wanted to tell someone all this, but who? Not my mother. How could she listen when all she did was talk?

I cried that night. "*Pleasepleasepleasepleasepleasepleaseplease*," I thought, "let me wake up with a regular family where no one talked out windows and everyone looked the same and I would have regular straight brown hair and no freckles—a normal family."

The next morning when I woke up, my mother was speeching. My hair was still red and curly; my face was still spotted. When I got to school, Darlinda was playing with a group of girls from her school bus who were all brown like she was. I wondered what would have happened if they'd heard the fat boy Pasquale saying those bad names. I started to run over to Darlinda, but stopped. What if those other girls didn't want me there? What if they started calling me names? But when Darlinda saw me, she ran over. She stuck out her bandaged thumb and I bumped it with mine. We played "Giant Steps" until the bell rang, and we went into school. No matter what'd happened, we were still best friends. Bloodsisters.

In June Darlinda and I were skipped. That meant we weren't going to third grade, but straight into fourth. And when we did, Pasquale Baleena, the fat boy, would be there.

11

TITI DULCE'S REVOLUTION

Dear Michele,

I just wanted to say I'm sorry for the way I left your mother's house the other day. It's just that I get so frustrated because she won't talk to me. Well, she'll tell me what she's making for dinner or what good grades you're getting or what new dress she bought, but she will never talk to me about the things that really matter, like peace and what is happening in the world. But then, the other day, well, I just couldn't believe it.

I knew something was wrong. And not just from when your mother was sick, from way before that. I can see it in her face every time you come to Mami's, your grandmother's house.

But what she said? No. It can't be. It's not possible. It's just impossible. But I wanted you to know I'm not angry with you. And I'm not angry with your mother either. I just think it's best if your mother and I don't see each other for a little while.

You are almost nine years old. Your whole life is ahead of you. You have nothing to regret. Nothing to wish you could do over. But I want you to know that sometimes things happen that are no one's fault and no one knows why. Sometimes you love the wrong person, but you can't help it. Sometimes life is not the way we wish it to be.

Don't let someone else's past be your future, Michele. If there is something you ever need to tell me, you can, you know. I love you. I love your mother, too, even though she doesn't think so right now.

Love,

❀ ❤ ☮

Titi Dulce

12

SPANISH ON SUNDAY (part 2)

There never was a letter like this from Titi Dulce. This time, it might have made a difference if there had been.

Until I was nine, Titi Dulce was my idol. She was twenty-four and everything I wanted to be when I grew up. Not that I wanted to be married, like she was or have babies like she did. What I wanted was to be was as beautiful and loving and universally loved as she was. Everything she said, did, or touched seemed to get nothing but praise, smiles, and attention. Everything I wanted to have.

It was Sunday afternoon. I hated Sundays. It was the day I had to pretend to be Puerto Rican, as opposed to the other six days of the week when I had to pretend I wasn't. It was the hardest, scariest day of all. I was always afraid something bad was going to happen and my mother would have to go away again.

My *abuelita*, Ofelia, and Carmen were in the kitchen finishing enough *pollo guisado*, chicken stew, to feed five armies. Papa Julio walked in to complain that the food was taking too long and walked back out. My father and Titi Ofelia's husband were in the living room watching the Mets game while Kevin and our cousins Benny and Ray-Ray played with G.I. Joes. I was sitting at the table in *abuelita's* dining room, drawing.

I had a new obsession. I was drawing books with fashion models wearing beautiful clothes like on *Rowan & Martin's Laugh-In*, the comedy show that launched the careers of Goldie Hawn and Lily Tomlin. I was allowed to stay up for it; Kevin wasn't, even though he was in love with the "Sock It to Me" girl and always tried to sneak out of bed to see her. I loved watching that show. It was one of the only times my mother would laugh for real, instead of with that bitter screech that would make me put a pillow over my head and call for the kittens.

Titi Dulce came into the room. She was very, very pregnant. She had been pregnant twice before Cousin Ray-Ray was born and once after. She had cut off all her dark brown hair into a pixie haircut and frosted it platinum blond. She looked like the *"Boricua* Mia Farrow," which I only knew because I had heard Titi Ofelia say that. Under the frosted hair and swirl-printed minidress, her face was pale, but she still smiled and hugged me.

"What are you drawing?"

"I'm making a book," I said and showed her the cover for *Book One: The Mod-Mod World of the Go-Go Girls.*

She picked up a drawing of a girl wearing long dangly earrings, a midriff blouse with a big peace-sign medallion and hip-hugger bell-bottoms.

"I wish I could wear that." She pointed to her huge stomach and smiled again.

My mother was in the dining room with Titi Dulce and me, but she was staring out the big window that faced the Hudson River, from where you could see Palisades Amusement Park. At night it was beautiful; everything was all lit up, and you could even count the cars on the Ferris wheel as it spun around. I used to do that all the time when I lived there. My mother looked perfect, as always, but she also looked tired. She spent the morning screaming, releasing some of the hurt, anger, and fury that swirled inside her like a whirlpool. But like a whirlpool, no matter how much poured out, it always filled right back up.

Then *abuelita* said, *"Ven acá!"* and everyone came in to eat. Five-year-old Cousin Benny (who was Titi Ofelia's son from the first husband whose name no one ever mentioned anymore) switches from English to Spanish flawlessly. "Grandma! I'm hungry! *Damé un poco de algo, por favor.*" Even Ray-Ray at two-and-a-half, squirming in his high chair, speaks more Spanish than I do as I struggle to ask for another glass of *refresco*. My brother Kevin, who is a year older than Benny, doesn't even try. It's hard enough for him to speak English sometimes. He has to go to a special speech class in school.

The dishes were passed. Ray-Ray, Benny, and Kevin all slurped down their chicken stew with big smiles on their faces. I didn't. I carefully picked all the capers, pimento-stuffed olives, and bits of *recao* off my plate and every bean off my rice before I started to eat.

Titi Ofelia looked at me with her lip curled up the entire time I inspected my food. She was now on Husband Number Three, a quiet, bespectacled man with thinning hair wearing a powder blue jacket with a Nehru collar. He started to say something, but she cut him off with *that look* and he went back to eating. Of course he had to be quiet. He's married to Titi Ofelia.

"You know, Lucy," Ofelia starts, "maybe the reason why Michele is so difficult is because you don't teach her about our food. What do you cook at home anyway? She's becoming a chubby little *gordiflona.*"

My mother stiffened, her ivory skin blanched yet another shade lighter, setting off the contrast between it and her black hair and even more contrast with the beige and brown faces of her family. But before she could answer, Titi Dulce cut in. Dulce looked at my mother and then at Benny shoveling in rice and beans and said to Ofelia, "Oh, but it's okay that your son is fat because he is eating what you want him to eat?"

Titi Ofelia turned bright red and retorted, "When is Raymond coming back? It must be hard to be living back here with *mami* and *papi* again. You must miss him."

They both started arguing in Spanish until *abuelita* made them stop.

After dinner everyone went into the living room where the couch, my old listening spot, was now pushed firmly against the wall. The TV went back on, the G.I. Joes came back out for Kevin and Benny, and Ray-Ray was put down for a nap. My father took off upstairs to the roof with Ofelia's husband for a cigarette, even though Ofelia and Dulce both smoked in the apartment. I walked into *abuelita*'s room to draw until it was time to go home.

I looked up when I heard music. Titi Dulce had come in and turned the radio on. She was dancing to Sly and the Family Stone's "Everyday People" and singing along.

"Come on," she said, "I'll teach you the Mashed Potato."

She tried to teach me the dance, but I was as stiff as a seventy-pound bag of frozen lard. I quickly gave up and flopped onto the bed. Dulce continued dancing. Her tiny feet were a blur, and even though she was huge, she still seemed to float over the floor.

Benny waddled into the room and jumped up and down. Then Kevin came in. My little brother was a better dancer than I was. I left them and went to the back bedroom to get Ray-Ray. "Let's see how good he can dance," I thought. But as I reached into the playpen, I sensed something and turned around. Papa Julio had come into the room. He started to close the door.

For almost a year I had lived in that apartment like a vole, hiding in shadows, never knowing if or when the weasel would strike, and when it did, I'd go back into darkness to lick my wounds alone. I knew what a vole and a weasel were. I had read *The Wind in the Willows*. But I didn't have to live there anymore. Instead of backing up as I always had, I ran toward Papa Julio. It surprised the both of us for the instant I needed to squeeze between him and the door.

I ran down the hall until I saw the breakfront at the end near the kitchen. In it were all of *abuelita*'s good dishes, the ones that came all the way from Great-Grandma's house back in Corozal. But Papa Julio was right behind me, and I was afraid of what would happen if he caught me. Before I knew what I was doing, I took off one of my shoes and threw it at the breakfront. It shattered the glass like an explosion.

"Don't touch me!" I screamed.

Everyone immediately came into the hall and stared at the glass sparkling the floor and me sitting in the midst of it. Feet came running down the stairs and into the apartment. It was my father and Titi Ofelia's husband. There was a flurry of Spanish, and my father picked me up and said, "Why did you do that for?" I could tell he didn't really want to spank me—he never did, actually—but I knew I was going to have to be punished for this. I couldn't say what had happened to make me do this. If I did, I was sure my mother would have to go back to the hospital, and I would have to live in that apartment again. I started crying.

My mother was standing behind *abuelita*, Carmen, and Ofelia. They didn't see her. No one could see my mother but me; my father's back was to her and everyone else was in front of her. Her face went white and then still. All of a sudden I heard a voice say, "Don't hit her, Rudy!"

My father said, "What?"

It was my mother. "It was an accident. I saw it. Michele was skipping down the hall and slipped and fell into the breakfront. It was an accident. We should be glad she didn't get hurt." I saw her eyes searching the hall. Was she looking for Papa Julio? I turned around. He had disappeared. When I turned back, so had she.

"*Gloria al Señor!* Praise the Lord!" Titi Carmen said. "It's a miracle. *Si, un milagro.*" She squinted and raised her arms skyward with the framed photos of John F. Kennedy, Martin Luther King, and the blond, blue-eyed Jesus in agreement behind her.

I started to relax. Maybe everything was going to be okay. Except Titi Ofelia started saying "Accident my ass . . ." But before she could finish her thought, Dulce, who had been looking at my mother and me the entire time, grabbed at her stomach. *Abuelita* leaped toward her, "*Mija,* you must lie down," she said and shot Ofelia a look that produced another *milagro*: it closed her mouth.

The grown-ups started to clean up the glass, and I ran into the dining room. I had a feeling my mother would be there. She was there, back at the window, and I could tell she was watching the Ferris wheel. It was all lit up from its lights and the setting sun, spinning and going nowhere like the whirlpool I could see she was trying with

all her strength to control. My father came in and got me. It was time
to go home.

We took a Checker Cab back to The Bronx: my mother and Kevin
staring out of one window, my father staring out of the other. I lay
across the folding seats and went to Kittenworld right in front of
them. I had to. The entire day had just been too much for me.

It had been too much for my mother too. When we got home,
she wouldn't stop speeching and wouldn't take any of the pills my
father tried to give her. After a while he gave up and spent the rest of
the night on the phone. I was sure she would go away again, and it
would be my fault, but my mother didn't go back into the hospital.
Instead, *abuelita* came and stayed with us on the days my mother
went to a day clinic and my father was at work. Titi Carmen, Titi
Dulce, and Titi Ofelia took turns coming over too.

I remember going into the kitchen soon after that Sunday and
seeing Titi Dulce with my mother. Although I didn't hear what they
had been talking about, Titi Dulce's face reminded me of Sunday
school when we learned about Lot's wife who turned into a pillar of
salt because she had seen something she wasn't supposed to. Suddenly Dulce got up and put on a sweater that couldn't close over her
belly. But before she left, she handed me a bag. Inside were a new
Twist-and-Turn Barbie, a Skipper, and an extra outfit for both.

"You can draw them for your next book," she said. "You're getting good at it."

I was happy to get the presents, but I didn't know why Dulce
was leaving, so I hugged her. She hugged me back.

I can't be sure, but I think I know now what Titi Dulce and my
mother were talking about. I think my mother told her what Papa Julio did to her. And I can understand Dulce thinking that was treason.
Horror beyond belief. It was, after all, her father. How do you get
your mind around the fact that your own father could do something
horrible? It goes against everything you know to be right. It goes
against love.

I always wondered if my mother stuck up for me because she
knew I was running away from Papa Julio. But she never asked me

and I never told her. I wouldn't see Titi Dulce again for a long while. She didn't go back to live at *abuelita*'s, instead she and Ray-Ray moved in with her mother-in-law, Uncle Raymond's mother. They would stay there until Cousin Evie was born and Uncle Raymond came home. But by that time, I found something else to admire.

13

JUST ANOTHER DAY IN THE PARK

"Hey, look, it's the Speck!" Another slight; another summer.

For two years now, we had lived on St. Peter's Avenue in that Italian/Irish/German/Polish neighborhood where we had been the first Latin family ever to live there and where they had once complained to my father every chance they got that our food stank, our music was too loud, and my brother Kevin and I ran wild through the halls. It didn't matter that my mother fed us Wonder Bread, instant mashed potatoes, and Stove Top stuffing, that the only music we ever listened to was Hugh Maskela, the Fifth Dimension, and 77 WABC Music Radio's *Cousin Brucie's Top Ten Countdown*, and that Kevin and I were not allowed to play in the hallways *at all*. I suppose someone had to be blamed for the relentless rock music (when everyone knew Puerto Ricans listened to Santana, thank you very much), the stench of burnt garlic (not all Italians can cook), and the junkyard of broken Tonka trucks and half-melted Crawly Creepers abandoned on the stairs (a pig wearing lipstick is still . . .).

Maybe some kids did play inside their buildings, but once summer came, all the neighborhood kids were encouraged, persuaded, or forced out of their houses or apartments to the playground up the block every day, starting immediately after breakfast until dinnertime at 6:00 P.M.

Welcome to the summer of 1969, when telephones were in the

kitchen and water came from faucets; video games and cable TV had yet to be invented; hippies were getting ready for their legendary three-day music and mud-fest; and children actually played outside for eight or ten hours a day—tender, innocent, wholesome games . . .

Marijuana, marijuana, LSD, LSD!
Rockefeller makes it, Mayor Lindsay takes it,
Why can't we, why can't we . . ."

It was ten-thirty, maybe eleven o'clock in the morning. I was nine years old and standing in the middle of St. Peter's playground. I was watching a group of kids on what we called a sliding pond (a slide) play a game I really, really, really hope no child anywhere plays at all, anymore, ever, called "Nigger on the Bus."

"Hey, Speck, you wanna play? You can be our nigger. Bwaaaaah!"

To play this game three kids would first go down the slide, each alternately swinging their legs over the opposite sides when they reached the bottom and staying put. But the game didn't "officially" start until a fourth kid slid down. Everyone would start the chant again as the fourth kid slid down as hard as he or she could with the sole intention of trying to knock as many of the bottom kids off the slide as possible. As more kids joined in the game, the stakes increased exponentially. Soon there were a dozen kids running and climbing, screaming, sliding, and falling.

"Oh no, here comes Fat Pat! Fat Pat, Fat Pat, the Sewer Rat!"

Fat Pat, a.k.a. Pasquale Baleena, was black of hair, swarthy of skin. Ten years old and the unofficial despot ruler of St. Peter's Park, he seemed not to notice his name's prefix as he lumbered up the steps. He was the boy who had branded me as "The Speck" back when I was in second grade because, as he told everyone, "She's too small to be a regular spic."

As Fat Pat reached the top, he took a moment to catch his breath, savoring the mounting unease from the squirming bodies below, and then he yelled, "Nigger on the bus! Nigger on the bus!" and flung himself down the shiny silver path of ruin. The irrefutable laws of physics and gravity took over, and as his mammoth haunches collided with the spindly frames of the next-closest children, a sort of domino effect took over. Five, six, seven kids were catapulted off and over the slide, landing on the concrete below.

"Ow! Ow! Owwwwwwwww!" the kids yelled as they assessed their damages: a scraped knee, a twisted finger, a shard of glass sticking out of a calf. Make no mistake, in our minds these were war wounds, just as much as were the tallies of the Viet Cong and U.S. dead and wounded we heard about each night as our parents watched the *Huntley/Brinkley Report*. Yes, St. Peter's Park was a playground battlefield. And as always, I was on the wrong side.

"Speck!" Fat Pat flung at me as he went around to start the game again.

The first irony was that Fat Pat, like many of the other kids of Southern Italian heritage in my neighborhood, were two, three, even four shades darker than I was, but that didn't matter. Since I *was* a spic, I was The Speck.

The second irony was, from my days behind *abuelita*'s couch, I knew there were five different words to differentiate the color of one's skin. There were *moreno* and *negrito*: brown and black, which depending on one's tonality and prior relationship, were also terms of endearment. Then, there were *prieto* and *tregieño*, which have no direct English translation and at the time seemed to me to be nothing more than mildly insulting descriptions much like ugly or stupid. And finally, there was *cocolo*, which loosely translates to "coconut head." By no means could *cocolo* ever be considered nonoffensive. You did not ever call someone a cocolo unless you wanted to start a fistfight.

And the third and most shameful irony? Once I had actually wished that someone, somewhere, would call me a spic—just once—so I would know what it was like to feel that righteous indignation, that justified anger created by that nasty ethnic slur. I had even begged Kittenworld for it. I had imagined I was walking down a street when someone stopped and said, "Look at that spic." And I said, "What did you say? Spice? Stick? Oh, spic? You think I look Spanish, you think I look Puerto Rican? Yay! Goody! Yippie!" And then Titi Ofelia clapped. It was not one of my finer imaginary moments.

But when it did happen and Fat Pat named me The Speck, I had cried and cried. Because that was the first time I realized I was a double outcast: I didn't fit in with my family and I didn't fit in anywhere. And even though not every kid in the neighborhood called me that and even though some of the kids did play with me—when Fat Pat wasn't around—it still hurt . . . a lot.

Mister Softee arrived at two o'clock, just in time for lunch. I dug into my culotte's pocket for the quarter my mother gave me and sat on a side bench with my Blue Gelati Italian ice and wooden spoon, digging at the vaguely lemony stickiness that would turn my tongue a psychedelic turquoise blue.

"Hey, you wanna play jump rope?"

It was a small group of also-misfit girls, Dawn, Nicole and Janey, who the cool kids called faggots, which didn't mean a homosexual—not at all. Instead, it meant that by your physicality (too thin: Nicole), appendages (glasses, braces or both: Dawn,), or general doofiness (your mother made you wear "skips," the cheap sneakers that weren't Keds or PF Flyers: Janey), you, too, were just not cool enough to play Nigger on the Bus.

As for me, I was a bit chubby but wore no appendages and was dressed better than most. My mother took us a few times a year on marathon shopping excursions downtown, to Ohrbach's and Bloomingdale's where she'd spend hours scouring the sale and clearance racks for her pastel minidresses, white knee boots, swirly scarves, and clothes for Kevin and me. So no, I did not wear skips.

"We need an end. Donna had to go home."

"Okay."

I took one end of the rope, a long piece of dirty clothesline, and the smallest girl, Janey, took the other. We started turning as the metal-mouthed Dawn and splinter-thin Nicole took turns jumping.

Miss Lucy had a baby, she named it Tiny Tim,
She put him in the bathtub to see if he could swim.
He swam to the bottom, he swam to the top,
Miss Lucy got excited and pulled him out by his cock—tail, ginger ale,

five cents a glass, and if you don't like it, I'll shove it up your ass—me
no more questions,
I'll tell you no more lies,
A man got hit with a bowl of shit . . . How many times?
One, two, three . . .

This was where little Janey and I started turning the rope as fast as we could because if we could get Dawn and Nicole out before they got to ten, they would have to take the rope. Then, it would be our turn to jump.

"Hey, let's play Junkie Tag!" Fat Pat yelled from across the park.

This game was based on the popular schoolyard game Freeze Tag—except St. Peter's Park was three blocks away from a Daytop Village methadone clinic, whose patients were almost exclusively Vietnam War veterans in their early twenties. They would get their doses, then go back to the park and sit on the back benches, where they smoked cigarettes, cursed the U.S. government, and nodded out. But eventually they'd need to go to the store for another pack, and when one or more of them would stand up to attempt the trek across the street to the deli, that was where the game began. Because, being junkies, they couldn't travel more than a few feet without stopping for a few minutes, tilting forward or sideways like a troop of bandannaed, army-jacketed-even-in-the-summer Leaning Towers of Pissers.

Whenever they were spotted, the call for Junkie Tag would go out. The most daring child would pick a junkie and run as close to him as possible, with the intention of tapping him and then running back to home base. You got extra points if you could knock the cigarette out of his hand without getting hit back.

"Get the fuck outta here! I catch you, I fuck you up . . . Aw shiiiit!"

Crazy Vinny, leader of the St. Peter's Junkie/Vet Association, had swatted at me as I—who had not been invited to join the game but who had run out anyway—knocked the half-smoked Kool cigarette out of his hand as he toppled over. He sprawled on the concrete groping for it.

"Fucking kids. Fucking fuck. Aw shiiiiiiit."

Why had I done it? I couldn't tell you for certain. Maybe it was because even though I knew saying nigger was wrong; even though I knew that if Darlinda, my Bloodsister, my best school friend had been here, she would have first cried and then fought them, all of them; and even though I really didn't want to play that stupid, stupid game—still—I wanted to be invited, allowed, welcomed to play *with* them and not *be* their nigger—or Speck. I ran back to my new girlfriends, unsure what was going to happen next.

"Hey, watch me," Janey said. And she ran up to Crazy Vinny and snatched the cigarette off the ground—a bare inch away from his clawing fingers—then ran back to us and took a triumphant puff.

"Want some?" she asked, offering it around. Nicole, Dawn, and I stared at her, half in admiration, half in disgust.

"Ew! Cooties! No wait. Let me get some," Fat Pat demanded. And he grabbed the nearly burned-out Kool from Janey's hand.

None of us thought that was strange. Those were the days where two kids would share a cigarette, three would share an RC Cola, four would share a piece of gum. We called it ABC, or already been chewed. But no one got sick. Kids back then never were sick except for maybe sometimes when your mother would make you climb into bed with your cousins who had the German measles in hopes that you would get it and get it over with so they wouldn't have to pay for the shot.

"The Parky just set up the Nok-Hockey! Who *wantsta* play? Come on!"

Fat Pat stuck the cigarette butt in his mouth and waddled to the front of the Park House, where the Parky had set up a Nok-Hockey board on the battered, splintered, lone picnic table, shooing off a couple of junkies who had decided to recline there.

Nok-Hockey was the precursor to air hockey and foosball. It was a wide rectangular board divided by red goal lines, with open slots at each end, and a diamond-shaped wooden block in the center. A kid would use an angled stick or her thumb to bounce the round wooden puck off the sides of the box and through the opponent's slot to score a point. The first person to score eleven points won; seven-nothing was a shutout. First Janey, then Dawn, and Nicole, and then finally I ran to the group, hoping without hope they'd let me play with them. They did. I was thrilled. And I beat both Janey and Dawn, but lost to Fat Pat, mostly because he terrified me too much to shoot straight.

Clang! Clang! Clang! Clang! Clang! . . . Clang.

The bells of St. Peter's Church across Westchester Avenue announced the changing of the guard. *Clang! Clang! Clang! Clang! Clang! . . . Clang.*

It was six o'clock in the evening. Time for us smaller kids to go home. The teenagers, wearing their fringed and torn bell-bottom jeans, were just starting to come out for the night. They clustered around the swings, opening quarts of Schaefer beer and rolling joints. The junkies had all retreated to their back benches. Yes, God was in his heaven and all was right with the park.

As I left, the song the teenagers had been singing stuck in my mind:

I'm a juvenile delinquent, marijuana do or die,
I smoke with the sailors and I drink with the bums
I wait on the corner till my pickup comes . . .
Oh I'm a juvenile delinquent . . .

It all became perfectly clear to me—as clear as the early fingernail moon rising above the roof of my building as I said good-bye to my new friends. Maybe I had to be a Speck, but I had been the one to knock the cigarette out of Crazy Vinny's hand; that had to count for something. Yes, maybe there was a way to fit in after all.

That night my mother went to her window and speeched. Who knew what had happened that day to set her off? Maybe she had an argument with *abuelita* or one of my *titis*. Maybe the cashier at Mary's Market stared too long at her. I had given up trying to figure it out. I tossed and turned as I tried to get to Kittenworld, but it didn't come that night or the next. It would be a full month before I realized the kittens would never return.

14

LA PIRATA

Dear Mee-chele,

I hope that when you get this letter, you and your brother Kevin, your mother, and your father are in the best of health. We are all fine here in Florida.

We are very busy getting the new house ready for everyone to come next month. Uncle Freddy and Uncle Junior will be coming too. Uncle Papo and Frankie and your cousins Isabel, Damaris, and Willy will be happy to see you. I hear your mother is staying home. I hope she changes her mind. I have two banana trees, a lime tree, an avocado tree, and a big mango tree in my new backyard. You will love the mangoes. They are very good. The only bad thing about here is there are no subways or guaguas, so now for the first time, your grandfather has a car.

There is one thing I wanted to tell you before you come to Hollywood. That day you came over before we moved, I heard you ask your father where did he come from. I don't know what your father told you, but you are a big girl now and it is time you know the truth. We are not los jibaros like where your mother's family comes from, even though your Grandma Mari and your mother are very nice.

Here is one dollar for you to buy stamps with. Tell your father I sent it so he doesn't let you spend it on ice cream. Be careful with ice cream. You eat too much and you get the diabetes like me. Tell your father to stop eating ice cream too.

See you in Agusto.
Love,
Grandma Isabel

15

SPANISH ON SUNDAY (part 3)

If Grandma Izzy had really asked me what I meant the day I asked my father where he came from, I'd have told her that I meant if he came from work or home. I had left my drawing notebook at home and wanted him to bring it to me. Grandma Izzy was right about one thing though. Until I was ten years old, I thought my father's family came from the "Italian part" of Puerto Rico. That's what I'd always heard my father say to the people in our neighborhood, so that's what I always believed.

The first thing Grandma Izzy did when I got to her new house was take me to see her mango tree. It looked even better than she had said in her letter. It was a sprawling green canopy, heavy with ripe red-orange fruit. As I ran to pick one, Grandma Izzy asked me first to bring her the milk crate from underneath the tree. As I bent down and lifted the slatted wooden box a nest of what looked like huge armored brown cockroaches swarmed out and took flight around the tree in protest after having been disturbed from their afternoon nap. I dropped the box and ran screaming back to the patio where Grandma Izzy stood in a halo of Salem Lights.

"*Eets* only palmetto bugs." Grandma Izzy chuckled. "*Joo* have to get used to them when you live here." She smiled and patted me on the head. "Come on, *eets* time to eat."

Another Sunday at another *abuela*'s house. Only this house was in Hollywood, Florida, on a long, flat stretch of road with palm trees, croton, and hibiscus lining the sidewalks and on a corner where, if the wind was right, you could smell the Atlantic Ocean two miles away. This was where my uncles Frankie and Papo, and finally Grandma Izzy and Grandpa Ezekiel had all moved by 1970, leaving behind burning buildings, cold winters, and cockroaches for faux haciendas, eternal summers, and flying bugs. Outside on a back patio shaded by banana, lime, and avocado trees was a table laden with enough food to feed an entire neighborhood (just like my New York grandmother's), and just like in New York, food I didn't want to eat.

I found a strange triangular object in my beans. I picked it up and my fingers crushed through its gelatinous middle as a hard pointy object came squirting out. "Eeew!" I said. "What's this?" and threw it at Kevin right before he flung a forkful of rice at me. My cousins Isabel, Damaris, and Willy, who I hadn't seen for a couple of years, giggled.

"*Eets peegs* feet," Grandma Izzy said. "They add *sabór* to the *sofrito*."

For emphasis, she picked one off her plate, sucked it between her teeth, and smacked her lips. "*Joo* don't know what is good."

After that dinner, my grandfather, who sported an occasional wiry reddish hair among his gray stubble and who spoke perfect English, slapped his knee for me to come and sit. He bounced all eighty pounds of me as he told me a story. Although he was only five feet five inches tall and never weighed more than 140 pounds, he had been a merchant seaman and traveled the world, always bringing back gifts: Kachina dolls for me, carved animal figures for Kevin, silk scarves and perfume for my mother. (He also had another family, a fact that was confirmed when he died six years later.) Finally, he had retired, learned to drive (at sixty), and moved to a place where he and my grandmother could pick ripe fruit from their own backyard and walk again on a beach. South Florida was almost like the island home they had left as teenagers over forty years before.

"You know where your red hair comes from, right, *muñeca?*" he started. "The name Carlo comes from Italy, from Genoa. We helped to make the boats for Cristobal Columbus, but we had trouble with the queen and we became prisoners of the Spaniards. They took us to *La Princesa* prison in Old San Juan and threw us in with the pirates, but we escaped and made our way to Cabo Rojo. It was called something else before we came, but once we were there, they called it Cabo Rojo because we were *pelo rojos, colorados,* redheads. For four hundred years, the red hair skips every other generation and that is how, if we go to Cabo Rojo, they will know you and I are Carlos!"

"Ezekiel, stop putting stories into *Mee-chele's* head," Grandma Izzy said. For all Grandma Izzy's love of practical jokes, she had little patience for what she considered *"fantasia,"* unless it was her own. *"Joo* know we all came from *Majorca en España. Una gente muy importante,* they chased us out for *una poco de desacuerdo* with the queen's shipwrights. They sent us to Puerto Rico to die, but we were strong and we lived!"

"Bah, that's a lot of *mojón!*" Uncle Junior cut in.

Uncle Junior had been silently drinking beer at the end of the table and stood up to talk about the Caribbean Indian tribes: the Taíno, Arawak, and Caribé. "These indigenous people who were raped and slaughtered by the Europeans and enslaved with the Africans and indentured Irish are our brothers . . . Never forget that we are a mix of the conquered and the conquerors, because then at least, the conquered would not have died in vain . . ." He went on for a while, but no one listened, so he sat back down and opened another beer.

Uncle Junior was the family's black sheep. He lived in downtown Manhattan in "The Village" with his Japanese "wife" and her son. He had a first wife once, but I don't remember what happened to her. He painted, wrote poems, and played music. He'd also been on heroin on and off since he was a teenager in the 1950s, a poorly kept family secret. I knew because my father brought me to his apartment once, and I heard them fight about it.

The apartment had brick walls. Along one was a bookcase that ran from the floor to the ceiling and held more books and records than I had ever seen in anyone's house before. I looked through the books, and the Japanese wife's son, who was fat and had pimples, stared at me while my father and Uncle Junior argued in the back-yard. When we were leaving, Uncle Junior tried to give me a record, but my father made me give it back. Whenever my father saw me drawing, he warned me not to end up like Uncle Junior.

Later that afternoon when I was by myself in the front yard try-ing to catch lizards, I saw Uncle Junior come out, banging the screen door behind him. I immediately ran back inside for my notebook and then back out to the yard to show him my drawings. I'm not sure why I wanted to. Maybe I wanted him to know I could draw too.

"You have talent. Maybe they will let you do something about it," he said as his eyes looked at something far away. The next day he flew back to New York alone, and I wondered why he came to Florida at all.

But before our secret moment together, back on the patio at lunch, I looked at my uncle's brown hair and beige skin and tried to picture him as a ruddy, redheaded, Indian chief with a shield made out of palmetto bugs. Grandma Izzy had gone to sit in a lawn chair under one of the banana trees. She was smoking and watching him too.

I walked over to Grandma Izzy and asked, "Are we Indians?"

She took my freckled face in her hands and said, "*No te preocupes.* (It doesn't matter.) *Joo, Mee-chele,* are a very pretty girl."

Just then, Uncle Freddy arrived with his family, including my other cousins Nelly and Evelyn. It was also their first time in Florida. They ran up to ambush Grandma Izzy with hugs, but she stopped them before they could and asked, "*Esperate, mi vidas,* can you go out to the mango tree and get something for me first?"

Nelly and Evelyn ran out to the tree, and Grandma Izzy looked sideways at me, squinting and smoking. I was about to warn Nelly and Evelyn of the flying bugs, but I closed my mouth and returned to the dinner table under the trees where my grandfather, father, and uncles (minus Uncle Junior who was no longer in the backyard), were all lifting Welch's jelly glasses with the Flintstones cartoon characters on them, half full of Fundador brandy, toasting "*La Pirata*" (The Pi-rate.)

But before I could ask why they were doing that, Nelly and

Evelyn screamed as the palmetto bugs once again flew out from under their tree. Once they had settled down, we all ate mango slices with vanilla ice cream for dessert.

Two weeks later, I sat in my grandfather's brand-new used Dodge Dart with my father and brother. My grandfather and Grandma Izzy were driving us to the airport in Fort Lauderdale. My father yelled at my grandfather to slow down and look where he's going. Grandpa Ezekiel had a small cigar clutched between his teeth and was hunched over the steering wheel like one of the humpbacked lizards I had spent my vacation trying to catch. His response was to drive even faster. Grandma Izzy laughed and held her cigarette out the window, and I watched the smoke trail behind us.

My brother was asleep on my shoulder. I looked at his straight dark brown hair and pink sunburned skin and then up at my reflection in the rearview mirror. After two weeks in the tropical sun, I had the first real suntan of my life and it was hideous. Instead of burning like my brother or turning a rich, nutty brown like my father, I'd become a sickly yellowish-almond color that only served to underscore the hundreds of brown freckles that had popped out all over my face. And my hair had lightened to the shade of a new copper penny.

I remembered what Grandma Izzy told me that first day under the mango tree before she convinced my cousins Nelly and Evelyn that it was safe to pick the mangoes. "See those *pecas* on your face, *Meechele*? God couldn't figure out whether he wanted you to be dark or light, so he made you both." She laughed, patted me on the head, and took a long drag on her cigarette. "*Mira*, what's that buzzing around your head?"

August was over and we were going home. Back to The Bronx. Back to school. Back to trying to figure it out all over again.

We were from Spain, Africa, Ireland, and Italy, we were Taínos, Indians, shipwrights, aristocrats, slaves, and maybe, pirates. How could they all be so sure about being from other places when it was so long ago? And why didn't anyone ever actually say we were Puerto Rican? Was there something wrong with it? How could I be Spanish or Italian or whatever with them, but when I was with kids who also said they were Italian, they said I was a spic? How could that be? How could I be one thing one place and another thing elsewhere? Who was I? What was I? What was the truth? Why was everything such a secret in this family?

16

SECRET SUMMER

Every family has its own ritual for celebrating summer. Some go to the mountains; some go to the beach. My family had its own private club my father named after the July birthstone, "The Ruby Club." Through some freak of synchronized conception on my father's side of the family, my Grandpa Ezekiel, four of my seven cousins, and three of my five uncles were all born in July. Every year we'd pick a day to celebrate all our birthdays together, pile into Uncle Freddy's old green VW bus or Uncle Papo's blue Chevy Impala with the bobble-headed Dalmatian on the dashboard, and head "upstate"— upstate meaning to a park or a lake outside of the five boroughs. We had done this every year that I could remember.

Each member of my father's side of the family had a job in the Ruby Club. My immediate family brought Coppertone, blankets, a jug of lemonade, and a transistor radio for the Mets game; Grandma Izzy and the other women brought pots of *arroz con gandules*, trays of *tostones* and *maduros*, homemade potato and macaroni salads, and a big bowl of sliced avocados, red onions, and tomatoes; Uncle Freddy brought the beer (although I never remembered seeing him drink any); and Uncle Papo and Frankie brought the *pernil*, the roast baby pig that was the official Ruby Club birthday meal. Uncle Papo and Frankie would get up at 4 A.M. to drive up, dig the pit, and start roasting.

The Ruby Club was extra special this year. It was the first one since half the family had moved to Florida, so it was a reunion *and* it was happening on the same day as my eleventh birthday. As the oldest cousin, my job was to keep the younger ones entertained and out of trouble. I took this responsibility seriously and had thought up a new, fun car game to play on the drive up to Lake Welch called "Let's Give the Finger to All the Cars from New Jersey."

Uncle Freddy and his wife, my aunt Gloria, picked up my family at 8 A.M. Their daughters Nelly and Evelyn sat in the back along with Uncle Papo's kids, my cousins Isabel, Damaris, and Willy. Grandma Izzy and Grandpa had already gone up with Papo and Frankie and their wives, so with my mother, father, Kevin, and me, that made eleven of us on the bus.

As soon as we got onto the highway, I had a feeling that the Ruby Club was going to be different this year—and not just because everyone was together again. For one thing, the grown-ups were whispering in Spanish, which, of course, was the signal that something was going on that we kids were not supposed to know about. For another, we were going in the wrong direction.

"Why are we going to Staten Island?" I asked.

"You're going to meet someone special today," Uncle Freddy said.

Once we were on Staten Island, we drove to a group of buildings and all got out to stretch our legs. The buildings looked a little like the hospital where my great-grandma Mari used to be, except here the grass was long—in some places it came up to my knees.

Uncle Freddy went into one of the buildings and came out after a few minutes with a tall, skinny boy, who, even to my eleven-year-old eyes, didn't look right. His eyes looked weird, his pants were too big, and the bulge above his waistband showed that underneath his pants he was wearing a diaper.

"Say hello to your Cousin Tony," Uncle Freddy said. "He turned twelve years old last week, and we're taking him to the Ruby Club with us."

Twelve? I was supposed to be the oldest. Birthday? Today is *my* birthday. I ran over to my father and whispered, "Why is he wearing a diaper? Is he a retard?"

"You look out for your Cousin Tony," my father said. "He's . . . slow. Make sure everyone plays nice."

Back on the bus, I tried to get my brother and cousins to play the Finger New Jersey game, but they just stared at Cousin Tony rocking back and forth—everyone, that is, except Nelly and Evelyn, who sat huddled together as far away from the rest of us as they could. Finally, I gave up and got a soda out of the cooler, which Tony grabbed out of my hand and sprayed all over the bus.

"What did I tell you, Michele?" my father said, "Stop fooling around and play nice!"

I was so angry I had gotten blamed for spilling the soda, I thought up a new game to get back at Cousin Tony: "Let's Throw the Retard's Diaper out the Window." I convinced my brother, Willy, and Isabel to hold Tony down while Damaris and I ripped his (thankfully empty) diaper off. Nelly and Evelyn watched in silence as I flung it out the back window, where it flew over the roof and landed on the driver's side windshield. Uncle Freddy skidded across three (thankfully empty) lanes, and we ended up on the highway shoulder with a New York State trooper's car pulling up right behind us.

It doesn't matter where your family comes from—you do not want a New York State trooper to stop your car. Uncle Freddy and my father went with the trooper to his car, and I could see them pointing to the back of the bus. I ducked behind the cooler. A minute later we were on the road again. I peeked out and saw the trooper standing by the side of the road holding his hat. He was shaking his head, and I could swear he was trying hard not to laugh.

My father didn't think it was funny though. When we got to the lake, he grabbed me and took me over behind some trees, away from everyone, and ordered me to make up with Cousin Tony and tell him I was sorry. But I wasn't.

"He can't even talk," I said. "Why do I have to share my birthday with a retard?"

I didn't mean for it to come out like that, but it did, and I had never seen my father so angry. He almost ripped his pants getting his belt off, and I was scared because that would have been the first time he ever really hit me.

But instead of hitting me, he threw his belt on the ground and did something worse. He told me he was ashamed of me. Cousin Tony didn't know how to act any better, but I did. Then he walked away. I almost wished he had hit me instead.

I went back to the Ruby Club, but for me, it was ruined. My cousins had been told to keep away from me, and I could hear them all playing and swimming. Nelly and Evelyn sneaked dirt onto my food more than once. Uncle Freddy and Tony stayed on one blanket with my mother and father and the other grown-ups. Even my Grandpa Ezekiel ignored me. Eventually, I just went and sat on the edge of a quilt until it was time to go home. I wished I hadn't done what I did. I wished I'd never seen Cousin Tony.

The ride home was the quietest trip the Ruby Club ever had. After we got home, my father sat me down and told me about Cousin Tony. His mother was Uncle Freddy's first wife who had died having him. Uncle Freddy couldn't take care of Tony by himself, so he put him in a special school where they could take care of him. And that was why he had gotten so angry with me. Because if I was bigger, if I was stronger, and if I was smarter than someone, then I was supposed to look out for and not exploit them. Because even though I wasn't really the oldest now, I still was supposed to set an example.

"Exploit? I don't understand," I said.

"Make them feel bad," my father said. "Don't pretend you don't know. And how do you think Nelly and Evelyn felt with you making fun of their brother?"

I hadn't thought of it that way before.

The next time I saw my cousin Tony, he was on TV. My mother always left the TV on to Channel 7 news while she was cooking dinner. Back then, there was a young, idealistic reporter who specialized in investigative news, risking his life to fight social injustice. You may remember him; his name was Geraldo Rivera.

He had spent months secretly filming the horrible conditions in a home for the mentally disabled on Staten Island, called Willowbrook. Now I don't know what made me look up from my homework at that exact moment, but even though I had only seen him that one day, I swore that right there in living color was my oldest cousin chained to a chair wearing nothing but a diaper.

"Mom? Mom! Look, it's Cousin Tony!" My mother ran into the living room and looked at the TV. Her eyes went huge and she quickly shut it off.

"Aw, mom," Kevin said.

"It's not him," she said. "Finish your homework."

When my father came home from work, I told him what I had seen, and he too said, "It wasn't him."

But the next couple of days were full of whispered phone calls and Spanish. Then late one night, soon after the TV-spotting incident, I woke up to the sound of Uncle Freddy and my father leaving the house. I could hear Uncle Freddy was crying.

The following day, when I came back from school, my father was already home. He told me that Cousin Tony was now in a place where no one would ever hurt him again and that he and Uncle Freddy were very, very proud of me because by speaking up about what I had seen, I had looked out for Cousin Tony when no one else could. We never spoke another word about it. I've only seen Cousin Tony twice since that day at the lake—at my dad's funeral and again at Uncle Freddy's. I don't even know if he is still alive.

That last Ruby Club was almost forty years ago, but if I close my eyes, I can still see us at Lake Welch. My mother, father, and grandparents eating and squinting in the sun; my cousins splashing in the water; Uncle Freddy feeding Cousin Tony; Cousin Tony clapping his hands and laughing; and two of my aunts, both six and seven months pregnant, sitting together picking at a plate of roast pig, one holding a can of Rheingold and the other a cigarette. It was truly a more innocent time back then, the end of an era—for everyone.

17

BUHRE AVENUE SUCKS!

"Run!" Darlinda said.

I sprinted through the number 6 train as it careened down the elevated tracks. Darlinda was right behind me. Just as I leapt between two cars, the train lurched, swinging me into the triple row of rubber-coated chains that kept me from falling into the whizzing tracks below. The train screeched and so did Darlinda as we both dashed into the next car.

By the time the train pulled into the next station, Darlinda and I were in the front car. The doors opened and we stood—absolutely still—in front of them. As they began to close, Darlinda grabbed my arm and we leapt onto the station's platform, leaving the man who had been chasing us behind.

We looked to see where we were and yelled loud enough for the man to hear, "Buhre Avenue sucks!" The train pulled away with the man glowering at the doors. We turned away and took out our markers. We had one more station to hit before our afternoon's work was done. The man was most likely the infamous early 1970s NYPD undercover cop, "Officer Schwartz," whose job was to stop kids like us—graffiti writers.

In seventh grade, I gave up drawing peace-sign-wearing Hippie Girls for my "tag"; my new nickname, Shell 194. I chose Shell because it was already part of my name and the letters looked nice together. Darlinda's tag was "Grape" because they were fun to draw. The 194 was an afterthought. Most people's tags were suffixed with the number of the street they lived on, but there were no numbered streets where I lived, so I took 194 from a street near our new favorite stop on the number 6 train, Buhre Avenue.

The two of us had an unspoken rule of yelling "Buhre Avenue sucks!" at the top of our lungs every time we visited the station, which was a lot. We wrote our tags on it and every other station stop on the number 6 line with markers and spray paint—along with the insides of subway cars, bus seats, and brick walls. We did this on every unmarked surface we could find, every chance we got.

We were far from the only two kids doing this. An entire subculture had formed seemingly overnight. Many credit a young messenger from Washington Heights, Taki 183, as one of the first "writers," but whatever its source, graffiti, or graf, spread quickly citywide.

Some writers were black and Latino, such as Stay High 149, Super Kool 223, and RayB 954. Others were white, like Pistol, Tracy 168, and Zephyr. Most were boys, although there were a few girls, such as Barbara and Eva 62, and later, Lady Pink.* These writers, and some others, were "up," which meant their tags could be seen throughout the city, and they were considered among the Kings and Queens of their time.

There were also the Toys, or Toy writers, the group I belonged to. We were writers who may have tagged a lot where we lived, but didn't have real train fame. A "Toy" was a derogatory term, the equivalent to being on someone's D-List today. Even though I'd hit up lots of the insides of subway cars, I hadn't yet hit a car's outside—*the* rite of passage for a writer.

You could hit the outside of a subway car with one of the follow-

---

* There were so many more writers than I could have possibly named here, so if you wrote back then and your name was left out, my apologies. You were most likely immortalized in Grape's tagbook.

ing: a throw up, a quickly filled-in bubble letter rendition of your tag; a piece, a more elaborate tag with designs such as stars, swirls, and force fields; or a top to bottom, the most ambitious and respected of all that covered *at least* an entire third of a subway car, from its roof to below its doors, including the windows, with the writer's master-piece.

To hit the outside of a subway car, you needed three things: an uninterrupted block of time with a nonmoving train, a lot of spray paint, and Fat Caps. A nonmoving empty train, or a layup, was easi-est to pin down at night or on weekends when trains would park on the dormant stretches of express tracks. I could see the number 6 layups from my bathroom window at home. An alternative was to sneak into the yards where trains were kept for cleaning and mainte-nance. There was such a yard on Middletown Road, walking distance from where I lived—but I hadn't yet had the courage to go.

Pearl Paint, an artist's supply store on Canal Street in Manhat-tan, was the best place to buy spray paint. Most writers, though, couldn't afford to buy ten or more cans at a time, so they "racked up"—shoplifted them.

Finally, Fat Caps were the nozzles on cans of Easy-On Spray Starch and some other cleaning products. The wider openings on their caps allowed for a more diffused spray, which was essential for covering large areas quickly and evenly. Writers would go into supermarkets, delis, and bodegas to rack the caps—sometimes deci-mating an entire shipment at one time. If your mother ever had to bring a can of Easy-On back to the store because it came home with no cap, now you know why.

After school, Darlinda and I would go to the 149th Street/Grand Concourse subway station where the number 2, 4, and 5 trains con-verged. The 149th Street station was both a subway platform and a clubhouse. Writers would use it as a meeting spot before going off to tag, as a conference room to plan their next pieces, and as a theater, watching the trains as they rolled by. Whenever a piece passed by or stopped at the station, the writers would assess it, giving praise where it was due and scorn where it was deserved. There was a distinct code of honor among writers: you had to come up with your own tag, style, and designs. If you were caught copying someone who had become known before you, you were called a Biter, and other writers could slam you by scribbling HOT 110 over your tags. It even became a catchphrase, "When writers are biters, they soon will be fighters."

At 149th, it didn't matter if you were black, white, Latino, or a mixture of the three. And it didn't matter if you were a girl or boy. Writing culture was achievement driven and egalitarian. What mattered was your tag. Some people tried to overintellectualize writing as a product of the post–Civil Rights, post–Hippie/Vietnam era, or dismiss us as disenfranchised children of the oppressed whose voices needed to be heard or, in this case, seen. I just knew that the act of writing was exciting, forbidden, dangerous, and, therefore, cool. It was a society where, if I did the work, I could belong.

One afternoon after school at 149th Street, Darlinda was getting autographs in a sketchbook that she kept as a tagbook. (If she still has that book today, it's a slice of history and is definitely worth a lot.) I had scored a seat on the bench and was about to pull out my notebook when I heard someone yell "Grape!" I looked up and saw a train with a masterpiece on half the car. It looked amazing. It had Darlinda's character made from a bunch of grapes and a force field. Darlinda stood on the platform smiling and receiving congratulations from the other writers. She was now officially up and could sign W.A.R., Writers Already Respected, with all her future tags.

Upon seeing Darlinda's masterpiece, a few questions raced through my mind, "When, where, and with whom had she done this? And why wasn't I invited?" I realized that the only way I could be completely accepted and respected by the writers—and keep my best friend—was no longer to be a Toy. I had to have my own masterpiece.

Darlinda and I were also friends with a small group of writers who'd hit up a few trains, but weren't as up as the 149th Street crew. While hitting the insides of the number 6 alone one afternoon, I ran into three of them, Mad Mark and Rod 15, twin brothers from

Parkchester who wrote TFT: The Fantastic Twins and their friend Gabe 177. They were going to the Zerega Avenue layups that weekend—the ones outside my bathroom window—and wanted me to be their lookout. "Only if I can do a piece," I said.

"Sure," they said. "Just get your own paint." And with that, I was invited to do my first piece.

The nerves kicked in before I even had paint. I was hesitant to buy the cans from my neighborhood's hardware store because I was afraid the owner would tell my father what I was up to. And I was too chicken to go to Pearl Paint in Manhattan alone. So I racked the cans from a different store up by Buhre Avenue: two red for the fill-ins, one black for the outline, and a silver can for designs. I stashed the cans in the bottom of my closet, went to the A&P, and breezed out with four Fat Caps in my hand, then proudly made my way back home to sketch my piece. Luckily for me, no one was tracking my artistic path from kittens to fashion design to vandalism.

That Saturday, toting my completed sketch, I hopped or sneaked onto the train at the Zerega Avenue stop. The token clerk scolded me without looking up from his newspaper. Mark, Rod, and Gabe were already at the station, and after giving me a quick overview of my duties, climbed down to the tracks to start their work. My job as the lookout was to stand at the end of the platform pretending to wait for a train. When I saw someone come up onto the platform, I had to whistle to cue them to duck between the cars. And when a train was at the next station, I had to let them know. It was nerve racking. Every passerby in black lace-up shoes looked like Officer Schwartz.

An hour and a few false alarms later, the boys returned to the platform, thanked me, and said, "Let's go."

"Wait! It's my turn."

"Aw, you sure you want to do this, Shell?" Rod said. "It's dangerous. I would have hit you up, but now I'm out of paint."

"I have my own paint for my own piece."

They reluctantly promised to look out for me, and I climbed onto the tracks.

"Shell, wait!" Gabe yelled. "Look out for the third rail! Be careful when you stand on top, some of the wood is broke."

Third rail? Broken? You have to stand *on* it? I knew that trains ran on electricity and that the middle rails held the juice, but I hadn't thought about the reality of doing a piece out in the open, in the middle of live tracks—at all. I suddenly remembered another writer's kid brother who recently died. He was hanging off the side of a train and fell. But the train was moving too slow for the fall to kill him. In a daze crawling along the tracks, he touched a third rail and was electrocuted.

I stopped and looked down at the tracks. Once you were past the platform, there were spaces—big enough to fall through—between the wood planks. Since the boys hit up the choice spots close by, I had to walk farther out between the stations.

I forced myself to keep going until Gabe yelled, "TRAIN!" I was so startled that I ran between the closest layup cars—stepping on the wooden beam on top of the third rail. Luckily, that one wasn't broken and the train wasn't that close. Gabe was always a jumpy kid. I was terrified to move, but more than anything, I was determined to do my piece.

About thirty minutes later I was done. I walked back to the boys—this time along the side walkway the track workers used, which wasn't nearly as dangerous. They'd all stayed and watched out for me. I climbed up onto the platform, and Mark said, "That was quick," then, "What happened to you?" In my rush I had pointed a can of red the wrong way and sprayed the front of my shirt. It looked as if I had been shot.

When I got home, I threw the shirt out the bathroom window and spotted Mad Mark's, Rod's, and Gabe's pieces, but not mine. I looked for it every chance I had over the next few days, but never saw it.

A couple of weeks later, Darlinda and I got off at 149th and watched a train pull into the station with—my piece! I never expected to see it there. I didn't know trains could and did switch lines. I looked at my creation and saw it was a sad-looking piece . . . a disaster. It barely reached the windows. The outline was crooked and the different-sized letters reflected my shaky nerves on the layup that afternoon. The last *l* in Shell hardly had any fill-in as I had run out of red, and I had failed to do any designs, as I had forgotten to bring the silver paint with me. But I had done it. I had my piece.

I wasn't the only one who'd noticed it. Some of the other writers had seen it too. They laughed, "Who is that Toy?" I don't think any of them realized it was me, and now I wasn't going to admit to it. I wanted to cry. All that work, all that fright, all that everything—for nothing. Darlinda had seen the piece too. She turned to me and said, "You wanna go hit the number 6?"

So Darlinda and I went along the number 6 line just the way we used to, hitting up an entire train car by car and then getting out and waiting for the next to come. We even got off at Buhre Avenue where we unscrewed some lightbulbs and threw them off the platform yelling, "Buhre Avenue sucks!" just as we used to, but my heart wasn't in it. Finally, it was time to go home. We didn't even go up the extra stop to Pelham Bay, just crossed over to the downtown platform.

On the way back Darlinda said, "Fuck them. You did it. So what if it didn't come out so good. It never does the first time. You'll do better later—oh snap, it's Schwartz—run!"

Officer Schwartz never would catch Darlinda . . . or me. I would do a couple of more pieces before I quit writing, but what was more important was that Darlinda and I were still friends. We had gone a long way together—from Gold Reading Group in second grade to the second-smartest class in our entire junior high school, 7E2. That was all about to change.

18

8-BC

"Your daughter is a very angry little girl, Mrs. Carlo," the guidance counselors said. "We don't understand what keeps Michele from achieving her potential. We have no choice but to put her into a Behavior Control class."

In just six months I had gone from a special progress (SP) honors class for gifted kids to sticking lit firecrackers in erasers and throwing them out of the window—when I wasn't throwing chairs or writing graffiti. My parents were called into school every other week, but no matter what threat they used, what privilege they took away, I wouldn't listen to them. I wouldn't listen to anyone. I hated that SP class with its stuck-up kids who made fun of you when you got less than a 90 percent on a test and was glad when they threw me out. Labeled an academic and social failure at the ripe old age of twelve and a half, I was now in 8-4, Behavior Control (BC), or as its denizens said with misplaced pride, "B-a-a-a-d Class."

This class was considered even worse than being in 8-18 where the recent immigrants, borderline slow, and truly illiterate were dumped. Some of the kids in 8-4 had been left back—twice. Some smoked cigarettes and drank Boone's Farm Wild Mountain in the back of the classroom. Some had Youth Delinquency (YD) or even Juvenile Delinquency (JD) cards, which meant they had been picked up by the cops for shoplifting, trespassing, or truancy. But they all ganged up together on the misfit among misfits: a pimply-faced, squeak-voiced gargantuan bag of uselessness named Pasquale Baleena, aka Fat Pat the Sewer Rat.

This was the same Fat Pat who had bullied me for years in grade school and in my neighborhood park, the same Fat Pat who had told kids not to play with me and who spit on me, and the same Fat Pat who had named me The Speck. I would never know how he ended up in BC, but it was here, in eighth grade, that the tables were finally turned on him. Always heavy, he now wore glasses and had developed acne. This combination in a class full of kids from different neighborhoods—some pretty tough—was lethal. They didn't know him from before and owed no fealty to a self-styled bully who they correctly sensed was as timid and insecure as the kids he had once terrorized, which made him the class human sacrifice.

One morning Fat Pat was lured into an empty classroom with a Clark Bar and Donna Nunzio's Teenform bra and ended up depantsed with his naked bottom glued to a chair where he stayed, mewling, until the boys' gym teacher, Mr. Glick, finally found him. No matter how hard Mr. Glick tried to make him say who had done it, Fat Pat wouldn't rat, which made Mr. Glick so mad, he finally dragged him, chair, and all, down the hall to the principal's office. But come on, who was Fat Pat gonna obey? Some transient so-called authority figure who was going to be gone in a week? Or the kids who really ran the show, and with whom he would have to deal for the rest of the school year?

All over TV, on the radio, and in the newspapers that year were the death rattles of what had once been the Revolution. Nixon had promised to end the Vietnam War and the hippies had run out of things to protest. Some turned to the false peace promised by plentiful and cheap heroin. Some put their energies into other causes, such as Women's Lib or the environment. Others would become Moonies or end up in Jonestown. But in our little corner of Junior High School 127, the spirit of anarchy ruled—not that any of us really knew what that meant.

When the Moratorium happened, that nationwide demonstration where all the high school kids walked out of school with black armbands on, protesting the Vietnam War, we fourth graders just stared out the windows at them until the teacher called us back to our seats. Three and a half years later, when Darlinda and I threw a window pole like a javelin out of our classroom's second-floor window, we'd no idea we were, in essence, rebelling against authority too. And speaking of authority, almost every other week, we'd have a new teacher who'd do absolutely nothing but stand at the front of the room, frozen faced, praying for the bell to ring. Or one who'd spend the day yelling at the top of his or her lungs and was lucky if nothing worse happened than getting hit on the forehead with a lit cigarette.

There was one teacher, though, Mrs. Golden, who lasted almost a month. Just from the sheer fact that she had stuck it out for that long, she was at the cusp of getting everyone's respect. But then Joey Lamonica and David Stein jerked off on her chair one morning, and she didn't notice it until she sat down, felt it, and sprang up. When all the kids saw the wet spot on the back of her dress, they started calling her Crotch Rot, singing it in unison to the tune of the old Wonderama song, "Does Anybody Here Have an Aardvark?" She ran from the room and never came back.

Such complete and utter sociopathic disregard, disrespect, and depravity from those whose bosoms had barely sprouted and whose balls had barely dropped was incredible. The collective adrenaline rush that came from knowing you had even one small part in contributing to it was truly addictive. Perhaps this is what it felt like to be a gladiator. Yes, this class was an arena and I loved it. 8-4 was a place I felt I could truly belong.

There was Mabel and Neethi, who came from The Bronx River Projects and who were fascinated with my thick frizzy hair. They'd pet it and braid it and say, "Look, it's almost like ours!" I accepted their caresses because some kids said Mabel kept a razor blade in her Afro. Even though I didn't agree with them, I just smiled and said, "Thank you."

There was Linda and Antoinette, identical twins from the Italian part of Morris Park, who were in BC for their second tour of duty.

They compared my freckles with theirs and said, "Look, they're almost like ours!" They then told me how on their last summer vacation, they had both "got eaten" by the same boy at the same time. They were almost fifteen. I was twelve and a half, still surreptitiously playing Barbie dolls, and had no idea what they were talking about. I remembered what happened to Fat Pat, though, so I just smiled and said, "Cool, no, I mean, outrageous!" Even though once again I was almost like everybody and exactly like nobody, I felt I had found a home.

The thing that drove all the teachers, guidance counselors, and parents crazy was that some of us were really smart. Even among those with YD cards, there were several at college-reading levels and some, although left back twice, had math or music gifts. Others, like Darlinda and me, spent their days drawing, when they weren't playing hooky and tagging trains. Were we bad seeds? Misunderstood? Simply bored? Today they'd just make up an acronym, wring their hands, and throw some Adderall at us. But the guidance counselors were right: I was a very angry little girl.

My mother still spent much of her days and nights screaming out of a window. My father was still always working. My brother was still just a kid. I didn't have a lot of friends besides Darlinda. I was overweight. I was ugly. And to make it all worse, I was smart. Smart enough to know all this, but not yet smart enough to know how to fix any of it.

Soon after New Year's the tests came: the Specialized High School Admission tests, otherwise known back then as the Co-Ops. These were tests for the special high schools such as Stuyvesant, Brooklyn Tech, Fashion Industries, the High School of Performing Arts (what would later be known as the "Fame" school), Art and Design (A&D), and The Bronx High School of Science. Darlinda and I, who had been Bloodsisters since second grade, made another pact: we were going to go to A&D and get famous doing comic books together. We would find cute boys and get married and make more comic books while they cooked and took care of the babies. Of course, we thought that could happen, this was 1973—probably the last year people really believed any type of utopia was possible.

Back then, the test for each school was on one day and one day only. I had already taken the test for The Bronx High School of Science because my parents made me, but I was going to take the test for A&D because I wanted to. I lay in bed at night imagining being all grown up, with a house full of drawings and people telling me how good they were.

The night before the test, I made sure my manila envelope of cartoons, fashion designs, and graffiti tags was right next to my bed, but I couldn't sleep that night. Not because of nerves, but because my brother Kevin had the mumps as did almost his entire fourth grade class that week. His fever was very high, and he moaned and cried all night while my mother stayed up with him. It was really sad and I feel sorry for him now. But then? It just made me—guess what?— angry. How dare he be sick and ruin the night before the most important day of my life? If I missed that test for whatever reason, there would be no makeup.

In the morning I woke up not feeling so well. I went to the bathroom, threw up, and looked in the mirror. The entire right side of my face and neck looked like I had swallowed a lemon that had gotten stuck. My forehead burned, but I was freezing cold. I didn't need to be Marcus Welby, MD, to know I had caught the mumps. Nothing, though, was going to stop me from taking the test for A&D. Nothing was going to stop me from being a famous artist.

I got dressed and went to Kevin's side of the room and threw open the window. It had snowed some during the night, but I figured going down the fire escape wouldn't be so bad if I was careful. So what if it was five flights up and slippery—I'd walked down subway tracks—the rest of my life was at stake today!

I started out. Kevin stirred. "Shush!" I said. "You gave me mumps and I hate you!"

"You can't climb out the window. Mommy's gonna catch you."

"Shut up, doofus—it's your fault!"

I was almost down to the fourth floor when I realized I had forgotten to take the manila envelope. As I climbed back into the still-open window, Kevin started yelling, "Ma! Ma! Michele's going out the window!" I ran back in, got the envelope, and smacked him on the mumpy side of his head with it to shut him up, which, of course, only made him yell louder. I made a desperate swing back to the window and was caught by my father's iron fists. Only the manila envelope was successful in its escape. I watched my shattered dreams flutter five flights down to the alley below, coming to rest on an already yellow stained patch of snow.

That spring, Darlinda found out she had made A&D. Then Darlinda and I both found out we had made The Bronx High School of Science, along with a couple of kids from my old class, the SPs. So two kids from just about the worst class in our junior high had been accepted to the city's two best high schools.

Darlinda, of course, chose A&D and would go there that September. My father wanted me to go to Bronx Science even though it was two bus transfers and an hour and a half ride away. Getting into such a prestigious school must have made him and my mother really proud, but I didn't care. I didn't want to go to Bronx Science. I wanted to be an artist, not a scientist. I wanted to draw, not do math. I told my parents if I couldn't go to A&D, I wasn't going anywhere. And nothing they said or threatened me with could make me change my mind. I didn't yell or throw things—I just refused. I turned from anarchy and became a conscientious objector. Only it didn't last very long.

Three days later I was sitting on a bench in the 43rd Precinct waiting for my father to get me. I had been out tagging with some new writers I had met, and they asked if I would be their lookout while they tagged the Glebe Avenue library, and then they'd look out for me. I stupidly said yes. When it was my turn to tag, they all disappeared and I was caught.

The cops put me into the back of their car. There was a mesh gate between the driver's and passenger's seats and no handles for the doors or windows, but that didn't frighten me. They took me into the precinct, sat me on a bench in a hall, and asked me my name, my parents' names, where I lived, and my phone number. I told them everything, but that didn't frighten me. They left me on the bench and went to a desk nearby to call my parents. The hall stank. The walls were puke green and the floor had grimy tiles. The bench was hard and dirty and covered with carved names and scrawled tags. I wanted to add to it with my "mop," the Pilot marker I had converted by picking apart the nib until it was a mass of strings (hence, the mop), which I then filled with fresh ink. I went for the marker, but remembered the cops had, of course, taken it, but that still hadn't frightened me.

I wasn't handcuffed or otherwise restrained, so I guess I could've tried to escape. If I was more hardcore, I probably would've, but the fact was, Shell was a Toy, so I stayed put. One of the cops brought me a paper cup of cold tea and a baloney sandwich with mold on it. I was hungry, so I took it, but when I saw the mold I dropped it, and the cop said, "This is all you get to eat in jail." That was what finally scared me and I started crying. If that officer is still alive, he must still be laughing about that today. Like I said, Shell was a Toy.

My father came to the precinct furious. He told me I was lucky they didn't give me a YD card and put me in Spofford, the Bronx detention home. He asked me why I had done this. Why I had to break his heart like this. He asked me what he needed to do for me to behave. What did I need?

What did I need? I needed not to be me. But of course I didn't know that. And so, of course, I didn't say that.

When June came, I found out academic excellence outweighed antisocial behavior, and in September I'd be back to quasirespectability in a solid, "normal" ninth grade class. The Revolution may have been over, but in my little corner of The Bronx, I continued my rebellion. I was still a very angry little girl who was determined to be an artist somehow. I just didn't know how—or why.

19

WHEN THE WIZARD WALKED BY

I later learned that Darlinda had her own run-in with the law, coincidentally the day after mine. There had been an after-school incident on the number 36 bus, resulting in a "police action" where the bus was sealed off and Darlinda had been nabbed climbing out a back window. She had kicked the officer, called him a "pig," and was taken to her precinct where her mother and older sister, Gigi, had to retrieve her. She hadn't cried. Darlinda was always more hardcore than I was. Luckily, she didn't get a YD card either.

That had all been at the end of eighth grade. In September, Darlinda and I would be in different schools. And although our relationship would change, we remained friends and we still tagged. She, Pistol, and FJC IV took me to the underground layups at New Lots Avenue where I produced my one and only "passable" piece. And we shortly became crazy Mets fans—playing hooky to sneak into Shea Stadium and cheering from the empty box seats during the dismal Nino Espinosa/Dave Kingman/Lee Mazzilli era. We even stayed in touch after high school when she joined the Army, became a communications specialist, and traveled the world. We were in each other's weddings, and twice a year, on birthdays and Christmas, there was a card saying, "Miss you." So that much of being Bloodsisters did come true.

But it would never again be the same as it was when we saw each other every day. And as was or is natural for kids of our age (going on thirteen), we, or at least I, developed other interests.

I had never seen Darlinda much in the summers between grades anyway and slowly became friends with Janey, Nicole (now Nikki, with double hearts over the *i*'s), and Dawn, whom I had met in St. Peter's Park playing jump rope years before. Nikki and I became the closest, and I now considered her my second best friend after Darlinda.

Nikki Cleary lived with her mother, grandmother, and two older brothers in a big ground-floor apartment a couple of blocks from the park. She was half Irish and half Italian, and her Italian grandmother, Nana, who lived with them used to make us pizza bread when I would go over there after school. Nikki's and my birthday were only three days apart, and although she was a year older than I was, we were in the same grade since I had been skipped back in grade school.

Nikki and I had a secret we didn't tell Janey, Dawn, or anyone. We would sometimes play Barbies together, even though we were way too old. Nikki had just graduated from Sacred Heart, a neighborhood Catholic school in a neighborhood that had four Catholic schools and would be going into ninth grade at St. Catherine's Academy in September. I, too, would soon be in ninth grade, but every once in a while, we'd take out her collection of Barbies, Skippers, and Kens, and we'd play.

But instead of playing the dress-up or house games we would have played even two years before, we cut off Barbie's and Skipper's hair, took off their clothes, drew on their bodies, and mashed them up and down on Ken and each other. We called this "banging," or having sex—which, of course, we could both only guess at what that actually entailed.

Perhaps Nikki's oldest brother, Ralphy, influenced us. Ralphy was eighteen and just out of high school. His birthday had been one of the first called in the last Vietnam War draft lottery, and even though that had been two years before and he was always too young to have gone, he remembered it and celebrated anyway by locking himself in his bedroom with his girlfriend Cheryl, playing albums, smoking pot, and having sex—lots of it.

Nikki and I didn't know what actual sex looked like, but we knew what it sounded like. Nikki's mother would be at work. Nana would be either cooking or sleeping. Nikki's other brother, Scotty, who was sixteen, would be in his room also smoking pot and playing albums (sadly for him, no girlfriend at that time). Nikki and I would be sitting in the hall between them, breathing and listening. In between the smoke, squeaks, and moans came a life-defining moment.

Scotty liked hippie music and played a lot of the Grateful Dead and the Eagles—whom we both hated. Ralphy liked hard rock and played Jimi Hendrix, Cream, Led Zeppelin, and Black Sabbath. We always took our Barbies closer to Ralphy's room whenever we heard Black Sabbath coming from behind his door. I knew all their albums: *Black Sabbath, Paranoid, Master of Reality*, and *Black Sabbath Vol. 4*, our favorite. Nikki liked the song "Changes," but I loved "Tomorrow's Dream." There was just something about that song. When I closed my eyes it took me to a place I couldn't describe but wanted to stay. Maybe it was just a contact high from breathing in all the second-hand smoke, but every time I went to Nikki's house, I hoped Ralphy would play that album.

One afternoon Ralphy and Cheryl ran into the apartment screaming, "We got tickets! We're gonna see Black Sabbath!" Nikki and I had been camped outside Ralphy's door for a half hour waiting for the music to start (neither one of us had thought he wouldn't be there). We didn't know he and Cheryl had gone to Ticketmaster to get Black Sabbath tickets. I didn't even know you could actually go and see them play.

Nikki did. "Michele and I want to come!" she said.

"Are you nuts?" Ralphy jeered. "Yeah, I got four tickets, but no way am I taking you or your stupid friend."

"Oh yes you are, or you're not going." That was Ralphy, Scotty, and Nikki's mother, Peggy, or Mrs. Cleary, who had come home from work early and walked in right behind them. She worked very hard as a single parent raising her children, and she believed that they should do things together, perhaps to make up for the fact that she couldn't always be around. That the last thing her eighteen-year-old son wanted to do was take his thirteen-year-old sister to a rock concert never crossed her mind. Or, perhaps, it did.

"But MA!" Ralphy whined. "We were going to take James and Terry."

"Where's this concert?" She asked for the ticket and Ralphy handed it to her.

"Nassau Coliseum? Out on Long Island? You are definitely taking Nikki, or you are not going," she said.

I can only imagine that Mrs. Cleary's motive for glomming us onto Ralphy and Cheryl was the hope that by tagging along, we would act as reverse chaperones and would keep them from getting into more trouble than they might have otherwise. Now, of course, Ralphy, being eighteen, technically didn't *have* to listen to his mother. He could have told her to fuck off and did what he wanted.

But Ralphy was a bit of a momma's boy. He was the oldest and therefore the man of the house. He also lived rent free (even though he had a job at the Hess station), had Italian home cooking, had his laundry done, and had the use of his mother's car—and the Nassau Coliseum wasn't easy to get to without one. Ralphy wasn't stupid. The concert was months away. He'd figure a way out of having to take us.

"Okay," he said. "Sure, Ma. Nikki can come."

As Nikki jumped up and down whooping, Mrs. Cleary asked, "Michele, would you like to go too?"

Would I? Go to a real rock concert to see my favorite band in the world? Hear my favorite song in the world with my new best friend in the world? Would I? The question really was, could I?

"Umm . . . I don't know," I lamely said.

"Well let me call your mother and ask her. It's not that far. You should be home by eleven."

Mrs. Cleary went right to the phone and called my mother who, incredibly, said yes. I couldn't believe my mother was actually going to let me go. I don't know what she was thinking. Maybe she was like

Ralphy and thought, "I'll just say yes and then she'll forget about it."
My mother didn't know what Black Sabbath was. How could she?
She wasn't there sitting outside Ralphy's door.

The months passed. Nikki and I went into our respective ninth
grades and stayed friends, and as it turned out Mrs. Cleary didn't
forget about the concert—and neither did I. I was lucky, the only reason I got to go at all was that the concert had first been cancelled, then
rescheduled, and was now on a Friday instead of a school night.

When Ralphy, Nikki, and Cheryl came to pick me up, I didn't
even recognize Nikki. Her hair was pinkish and broken and hadn't
been like that the day before. She told me she had wanted to bleach
the front blond for the concert, but her mother said she was only fourteen and too young to dye her hair, so Nikki put her bangs in Clorox
instead. The entire way to Long Island, we sit-jumped up and down
in the backseat of Mrs. Cleary's Buick station wagon, saying, "We're
gonna see Black Sabbath! We're gonna see Black Sabbath!" Ralphy
turned around, told us to shut the fuck up, and said if we went anywhere near him once we got to the Coliseum, he would murder us.
Cheryl turned around and said, "Yeah!" And as soon as we got there,
he gave us our tickets and flat left us right outside the doors.

Our tickets were way up in the top section, and as Nikki and
I made our way up stairs and more stairs, I noticed three things: One,
was that nearly everyone was smoking, even the ushers. And some
of those cigarettes smelled like what came out from Ralphy's door
when his mother wasn't home. Two, Nikki and I were the only two
people who were actually walking. Everyone else was either bouncing off the walls or stumbling. And three, Nikki had taken her coat
off. She was wearing a white halter even though (a) it was still winter
and (b) she was a skinny stick who really didn't have anything on top
to show at all. But that and her pink hair got us a lot of attention.

Everyone was offering us stuff: regular cigarettes, "funny" cigarettes, and things I knew were pills. I was like, "No, no thank you,
I'm thirteen," but Nikki grabbed them all. We saw a boy who was
passed out on the floor with his zipper open, clutching a bottle of

Blackberry Brandy. Nikki ran up to him, snatched the bottle out of his hand, and we ran to our seats with it.

I couldn't see a thing. The arena was just one huge drift of smoke, and the glow from people flicking lighters and striking matches was everywhere you looked. I stood there watching the brief flashes of light, which kind of put me into a trance. Nikki passed me the bottle of Blackberry Brandy. I took a sip and spit it out; it was nasty. "Hey, don't waste it," Nikki said and took it back. Then I heard it—my favorite song in the world, "Tomorrow's Dream." It was nothing like hearing it outside of Ralphy's door or in the car on the way to the concert. That guitar, . . . I could feel it behind my eyes, inside my head, my heart, and my stomach. And Ozzy Osbourne's voice, . . . high pitched, yet aiming low, straight into the one place on my body I hadn't really begun to think about yet because I was still only thirteen. I closed my eyes and went with the song. Then Nikki poked me. She decided we needed to get down to the bottom nearer to the stage, so we started sneaking our way back down.

It took awhile, but we did finally get to the bottom, only we couldn't get near the front of the stage, so we decided to try to go around the back. We wandered into a hall area where a man was looking into a small plastic bag. He saw us and called us over saying, "Girls! Girls! Over here!" Nikki started going over to him.

Another man, carrying what looked like a cage, which I thought was really strange, came out, took one look at skinny Nikki in her halter, another at me in my baby blue Pro-Keds with jingle bells on the laces, and said, "No! Run, girls, run. Run while you can!" I went and grabbed Nikki, and we ran out the first door I saw, which unfortunately led us outside the arena and we couldn't get back in.

We didn't see the end of the concert, so we don't know if any animals were harmed during the show (Ozzy did have an infamous "bird act" around that time). We also didn't get to hear if they played Nikki's favorite song, "Changes," but by that time, she wouldn't have noticed. She was now staggering like the kids we'd seen at the beginning of the night and basically falling asleep standing up.

They say God protects drunks, fools, and children, and that night It protected all three. Somehow outside we ran right into Ralphy and Cheryl, and if I didn't get home by exactly eleven, at least I got home in one piece, which was more than I could say for Nikki.

When Mrs. Cleary saw the condition Nikki arrived home in, she yelled at Ralphy for not watching us properly (for the record, to the best of my knowledge Ralphy, who was driving, was substance free that evening). I wouldn't see her again for a month. If Mrs. Cleary had known the whole truth, Nikki would have been grounded until she was eighteen.

I wasn't punished. I saved my allowance for the next couple of weeks, and when I had enough, I went to the Head Shop record store in Westchester Square and bought my first whole album, Black Sabbath *Master of Reality*, because they were out of *Vol 4*. Soon I had a new favorite Black Sabbath song, "Sweet Leaf," but I had no idea what they were singing about. Yet . . .

20

MY FUNDILLO

Meanwhile, back in my half bedroom in a top-floor tenement walk-up in The Bronx, I was waiting for the 1970s and high school to be over. Earlier that day, my best friend, Nikki Cleary, had vogued through the girls' locker room before our first gym class wearing a brand-new, double-D cup, black lace bra as if it was a trophy.

I had just started real high school in tenth grade at Herbert H. Lehman High. Lehman was a newish building straddling the Hutchinson River Parkway just past Westchester Square that all the kids called Lehman State Prison because that's exactly what it looked like. I still have one of the bus passes I wrote that on to prove it. Nikki had transferred into Lehman, a public school, after being asked to leave St. Catherine's for non-Catholic behavior: she'd been caught playing hooky, smoking cigarettes, and making out with boys from Cardinal Spellman too many times.

I hadn't seen Nikki that summer. I'd been sent to Florida to stay with Grandma Izzy and Uncle Papo, in my father's words, to "get straightened out." But together, my cousin Isabel and I were just as volatile a combination as Darlinda and I had been, but in a different way. After we sang "19th Nervous Breakdown" (you had to be there) at her father (Uncle Papo) when he caught us in a state of public drunkenness at the Broward Mall, I was sent home in disgrace. I'd never even had beer before. Cousin Maritza, the eighteen-year-old granddaughter of Grandma Izzy's sister, Titi Marialuisa (or as we called her behind her back, Titi Gran Vieja) had bought it for us. That didn't matter. I was the city cousin and therefore blamed for everything. I was sent home.

Nikki had been away too. I don't remember where. When she came back, though, I barely recognized her. It was almost like the day we had gone to see Black Sabbath, only worse—or better—depending on your point of view. Always skinny Nikki had gone away the flat-as-a-board president of St. Peter's Park's I.B.T.C., "Itty Bitty Titty Committee" (I, sadly, was the vice-president) and came back the newly endowed Nikki "Boom-Boom," her old wardrobe of baggy Huckapoo shirts replaced with formfitting V-neck Danskin bodysuits and tube tops.

Believe it or not, I wasn't impressed. I know for most people, the female rite of passage is getting your boobs. When you're Latin, though, your body part of choice is the buttocks.

This is the cheeky skeleton in our Latino closet, the five happy words we have to describe one's bottom: *culo, nalgas, fundillo, cheechos,* and *delicioso!* Yes, I know, everyone has a bottom, and, of course, they do. It's just not the perfect Latin bottom: not too wide in the hips, yet full and meaty across the beam. Not as high as a bubble butt, but completely lifted off the back of the thighs. Picture two teardrop-shaped globes of firm, pliant, undimpled muscle, with built-in rack-and-pinion steering that allows each cheek to undulate separately from the other even when its proud owner stands completely still.

There was no escaping this perfect posterior in my family. In every house I went to, every *salsa* album cover had one (and every *merengue* album had two). Every *novia* on every *novela* on Channel 47 had one. My sixty-five-year-old *abuelita* had one. My five-year-old cousin Evie had one. Every Latin woman in New York City had one—except me. And this was a problem. To the women in my family, this was a disaster that needed to be prevented, a catastrophe that needed to be averted, a disease that needed to be cured. And so, my Titis held what I like to call the Cheecho Council of 1975.

Titi Carmen said, "Pray for her!"

Titi Ofelia said, "Stop feeding her," and after I walked by, "Forget that, hide her till she's twenty-one."

And then, a voice in the background, "Listen to me all of you, no daughter of mine is going to be *una gordita.*"

That, of course, was my mother, the former Jackie O of East 103rd Street. The woman who never raised her voice (unless she was speeching), who never cursed in public, and who never was seen without full, age-appropriate makeup and outfit, high heels, and perfect hairdo. I had to give credit where credit was due. After twenty years of marriage and two babies, she still weighed the same as the day she walked down the aisle: 108 pounds—70 of which was butt. And she was convinced that with the right diet, makeup, and foundation garments, the little *gordiflona* would be transformed into *una gran mamichula.*

This was something my mother understood, and she paid attention to me now as (to my mind) never before. Not that she'd been a bad mother. Kevin and I were always clean. We were fed. Our clothes were washed. We had toys. When we had school, she made sure our homework was done. But something had always been amiss with us. I'd been in enough people's houses by now to know that there were mothers who didn't speech, fathers who didn't always work or sleep, and families who actually . . . talked. They didn't yell, whisper . . . scold, or blame, but talked. And now my mother and I were talking. And that couldn't be a bad thing, could it?

Although I was a little chunky, I wasn't really fat. They all just thought I was, because I didn't have a shape. Their shape: a pear shape. I tried it my mother's way. I ate plain broiled chicken and salad, with no rice or beans, no bread or soda, no Marathon bars or pizza, no crunchy Cheez Doodles, and, absolutely, no French fries with extra salt (my favorite snack). I tried out for the gymnastics team at school and actually made it. All that careful walking and ducking on the layups made balancing and tumbling easy for me. I even let my mother buy me control-top panties and they hurt! Still, after one month, no butt.

I was sure there was something else wrong with me. Maybe I was really adopted. That would explain a lot. But I looked too much like both my parents for that to be so. Maybe I was really a hermaphrodite, like we were learning about in health class. But I'd finally started having regular periods, so to my mind that couldn't be so either. Or maybe I should've gone to talk to someone who really knew about such things. But instead of asking my mother, I went to see my best friend, Nikki Boom-Boom.

Safe in the sanctuary of Nikki's room, I immediately babbled everything I had gone through for the past month while I squeezed her Pet Rock as if I could somehow turn it into a diamond. She paid no attention to me but just stood twirling in front of a full-length mirror, wearing a brand-new, tie-dyed, V-neck Danskin bodysuit, only pausing when I stopped sniffling to say, "Oh grow up Michele. You'll grow. Someday." Then she giggled as she went back to admiring her twin proofs of womanhood.

I slunk off to the bathroom, closed the door, and was confronted by yet another full-length mirror. This time I was the one who twirled and twisted, trying to see my back view, . . . and all I saw was nothing. I was convinced I'd be at least thirty by the time I looked like a woman, and by then, why bother? I walked back to Nikki's room to say good-bye, and through the open door saw her still reflected in the mirror. Only now the bodysuit was pulled down to her waist and she was stuffing wad after wad of tissues into each double-D cup of her black lace bra. And believe it or not, I didn't feel betrayed. I just thought, if she could stuff her bra, why couldn't I stuff my butt? I laughed. Nikki turned around.

"Hey! How long have you been standing there?"

"Me? I just got here. Wanna go to Wetson's and get French fries?"

And so for the rest of the weekend, I finally had something behind me I could be proud of. Well, sort of. It shifted around a lot, and I couldn't really sit down or it would flatten out. On Sunday, we went to Titi Dulce's, and I walked around the apartment as if I were holding a dime between my butt cheeks, just like my mother said a real *mujer* walked. But no matter how much I shimmied and swayed in front of everyone, no one noticed. These were women who could spot an unplucked eyebrow at thirty paces, and I couldn't believe they couldn't see the total and complete transformation of my body. But that was okay because the next day at school all my friends would.

Everything was fine until gym class, when I realized I would have to get undressed. I tried to hide in a corner, but of course Nikki saw me and came over. I turned around with my back toward the lockers and Nikki said, "Hey, Michele, you got something weird hanging out of your . . . oh my Gawd!"

As Nikki pulled a long trail of Charmin out of my underwear and into the cold fluorescent light of the locker room, she said, "What are you, stuffing your butt?"

Everyone in the locker room froze as Nikki pulled and pulled yelling, "Hey everyone, look! Michele stuffs her butt! Michele stuffs her butt!"

I knew the rules. This was high school and my life was now over. There was only one thing left I could do. I pushed Nikki over a bench, and as she fell, her double-D cup black lace bra popped open and out flew enough pink Kleenex for every Ortiz Funeral Parlor in The Bronx and half of Brooklyn. As the entire locker room howled, Nikki leapt on top of me. She pulled my hair and I tried to strangle her with what was left of my toilet paper tail. Finally, a teacher pulled us apart. I didn't go back to school for two days.

The Cheecho Council didn't take it very well.

Titi Carmen said, "Take her to church."

Titi Ofelia said, "Forget that. Send her to jail."

My mother just softly said, "How could you?" I wasn't sure if she meant the stuffing or the fight.

While everyone around me argued, I grew three inches over the next year, and the extra ten pounds around my middle somehow migrated just the right distance. And if I may say so, it produced some of the finest *nalgas* in my entire *familia*. Except that still, no one noticed. I finally had a Latin butt, but it didn't make a damn bit of difference. My classmates thought I was a fake. My family thought I was a loser. I was left in my half bedroom on the top floor of that five-story tenement walk-up thinking about . . . my mother. I wouldn't notice it for quite a while longer, but she'd begun to speech less and less and to reach out to me more and more. It was okay, . . . but it'd been too long. I was too used to interacting with friends and using them for emotional support, and besides, I was fifteen now. I didn't really need her anymore.

Nikki and I would soon make up. It would be the night Janey introduced us to something I'd sneak down to Florida on my trip the next summer. Something even Cousin Maritza hadn't had yet—and this time we wouldn't get caught. It was something that beat gymnastics, that was better than graffiti, and that made even the kittens seem exactly like what they'd been, a distant, childish escape. It was something I became really, really good at and somewhat known for. I now knew what the Sweet Leaf was. I'd discovered weed.

21

SEMILLA MALO
(Bad Seed)

Dear Michele,

Your mother is very worried about you. She says you have become a bad girl. She says you don't listen. She says sometimes you don't go to school. She says you play that rock music in the house, and when she tells you to take it off, you put it up louder. She says you come home sleepy, and you don't want to get up in the morning for school.

You are a big girl now. You are going to high school. Now is the time for you to make choices. You don't see it now, but the things you do or don't do today will come back to you later when you are older. I know right now you don't think about that, but you will get older and then you will know.

The last time I saw you, you told me to shut up. That was not nice. I was just trying to help you. I know your Titi Ofelia sometimes says things in a funny way, but she means well. She loves you. We all love you, your brother, and your mother, although I do not think you believe that.

I talked about choices before. I know your mother made her choice, and you and your brother don't speak Spanish and you don't really like our food or our music. And to me, that is okay. Just remember things can change. Just because you see me now as a jamona doesn't mean I never had another life. I don't judge you by your choices, and you don't have the right to judge mine. Only God can judge.

You must stay in school. You must be a good girl. If not for your sake, then for your mother's and father's. Your father loves you. This I know is the absolute truth.

One thing I also notice is you are not respectful to your grandfather either. Read the Bible. Pray to God. It will help you to be good.

I will see you at Titi Ofelia's on Thanksgiving.

Love,
Titi Carmen
James 4:7

22

SPANISH ON SUNDAY (part 4)
El Cuco, la Chupra Cabra y la Baina (The Bogeyman, the Bloodsucker, and the Whatchamacallit)

Titi Carmen was right about one thing. We all have choices to make. And we all have to live with them.

Abuelita's house: Thanksgiving Day 1975. The family had changed little over the years, except Titi Ofelia had temporarily sworn off husbands, and Uncle Raymond had gone away for good. He was one of the unfortunates who'd be busted right after the passage of the extremely punitive and draconian Rockefeller Drug Law that demanded mandatory twenty-five-year jail terms for possession of small amounts of heroin. Did he deserve that? He deserved help: help kicking a habit and help learning how to live without drugs. It was really sad that my cousins Ray-Ray and Evie had to grow up without their father, and that my once beautiful and carefree Titi Dulce slowly became melancholy and rigid. But who was I to talk about drugs? I was now smoking weed every chance I could and had discovered a new favorite pastime: tripping and listening to Pink Floyd. I sometimes think the only thing that kept me from burning out like Syd Barrett was that acid was expensive, and I wasn't yet old enough to have a real job. Plus, I was too afraid to deal like my friend Janey did. Once a Toy, always a Toy.

It was just another holiday at *abuelita's*, same apartment, same food, same family talking about the same things. For my father, it was baseball, or it would have been if he was there ("How about those Mets and that 82–80 season!"), but he had traded with a co-worker who had just had a baby and was working his shift that day. With Titi Ofelia, it was politics. She worked for the Legal Aid Society and read three newspapers: *The Daily News*, the *New York Post*, and *Newsday*, every day, a fact she would announce loudly and often. "Can you believe that President Ford? First, he falls down and then he tells us to drop dead? Bah! That's what happens when you don't vote for your leaders."

Titi Carmen and *abuelita* talked about the missionary work they had been doing. They were now going to Riker's Island twice a week to work with the prisoners who were in the infirmary. Titi Dulce and my mother chatted about the mundane everyday things they both did so well, talking, yet never really saying anything. My cousins were all competing for attention, gabbing about what they were doing in school. Even Evie, the youngest, was in kindergarten. I heard the boys, my brother Kevin, Benny, and Ray-Ray (who were twelve, eleven, and nine, respectively), complain about book reports, math tests, girls who won't look at them, and girls who won't leave them alone. I was the only one who was being quiet and uncharacteristically so. Maybe, I thought, I should say something before someone noticed and asked me about things I didn't want to talk about, like school. But somehow, when I did open my mouth what came out was, "There was a race riot at my school. I got stabbed."

It had been Kill Black and Puerto Rican Day, a day where the white gangs had war with the black and Latin gangs, and every high school was caught in the middle. Two Italian boys from Waterbury Park had cornered me in a back staircase when I was going downstairs to gym class and asked what I was. I'd thought I'd be safe because of how I looked, and I didn't think anyone I knew would actually try to hurt me. But I didn't know these boys, and before I could answer with the lie I'd prepared, Fat Pat, or what used to be Fat Pat, appeared behind them. He'd lost at least forty pounds in the two years since eighth grade, and his skin had cleared up. Many of the girls in school thought he was "dark and handsome." I knew better—I knew him—and all he was to me was dark. He looked at me and he had a chance, he really did. He could've told the boys to leave me alone. He could've said I know her. Let her go. But what he said was, "I know her. She's a spic."

One of the boys held me; the other poked my right shoulder with an ice pick while Fat Pat watched. Then they all ran off. At least, I think it was an ice pick. It could have been a letter opener or a stiletto. All I remember was I ran as well, out of school all the way back to the park holding my arm the entire way.

The wound wasn't very big or very deep. It was more of a puncture, like an animal bite, so I suppose I was lucky. It didn't get infected and it healed up pretty well and quickly. It only left a small raised scar, kind of like a vaccination mark. I didn't say anything about it at home, especially not to my father. If I'd told him, I was afraid he'd have gone down to the park and hurt someone, but only because they'd hurt me.

That wasn't the worst of it. Worse was, Pat and I hung out in the same place—the same park. Even though I stayed on one side and he stayed on the other, sometimes the groups would come together, and I would just keep as far away from him as I could. I was trapped, but had nowhere else to go. The park was where Nikki, Janey, Dawn, and other girls who had become part of the crowd—Jeana-Ray, Ruthie, Big Lisa, Little Lisa, Sometime Sue, and Crazy May-ree—were. They were my friends, and so I had to stand being around *him*.

I didn't say all this at *abuelita*'s Thanksgiving table. I just said I had been stabbed because I was Puerto Rican. They all looked at me as if they didn't believe me, as if they thought I had just made that up to get attention. I could tell even my mother thought that.

Papa Julio, who was sitting at the head of the table as he always did, wiped his mouth and said, "Well that is your fault for being stupid. If I looked like you, I would pass myself off for the rest of my life."

"If I looked like you," I answered. "I would kill myself."

It took a second for what was said to sink in. Everyone's jaws dropped down to the burnt orange shag carpeting. Titi Ofelia almost choked on a mouthful of *arroz con gandules*. Titi Dulce tried to tell me Papa Julio didn't mean that the way it came out. Titi Carmen and *abuelita* immediately got up and started carrying dishes into the kitchen. My brother and cousins all stared for a moment, but when nothing else happened, they went back to their grade-school one-up-manship. The only one who didn't outwardly react was my mother. She just looked very, very sad. I was very, very glad my father wasn't there.

Later that afternoon, I was walking down that long hallway to get my coat from my grandmother's bedroom. I had a cigarette hidden in the pocket and was planning on sneaking up to the roof to smoke, but Papa Julio came into the room and tried to push me up against the wall. He hadn't tried to do that in years, and I didn't know why he was doing it now. I wasn't the same girl as the one who had smashed *abuelita*'s breakfront as a child. I had walked into subway tunnels. I had taken acid. I had been stabbed. Every day I had to figure out a new way to survive, and it was all I could do not to become crazy because there were so many things going through my head, thoughts and feelings I didn't recognize and couldn't control and didn't know why. But this I did recognize, and I could control it.

I had a knife, a 007, in the back pocket of my Faded Glory jeans, and I pulled it out. I wanted to say my father gave it to me to protect myself because of the riots at school, but that couldn't be. First of all, he didn't know what'd happened. Second, he would never have given me a knife even if he had known. So a friend must have given it to me. Maybe it was Janey who was now a pot dealer and needed protection, or maybe it was Crazy May-ree, the new girl at the park who everyone was half afraid of. It doesn't matter. I had the knife, and I took it out and very softly told Papa Julio if he ever tried to touch me again, I'd cut his balls off. He saw the knife. He looked into my eyes. He knew I would have, or at least tried. He backed off. He never said anything about it and never touched me again.

Sometime after that, my *abuelita*'s decades of prayers finally worked. Papa Julio got religion. He started going to church, became a deacon, and carried his *Santa Biblia* everywhere he went, quoting the gospel and blessing people. The air about him looked and felt different, so I do believe his transformation could have been a true one.

Maybe coincidentally, maybe not, *abuelita* also announced she was moving out of their apartment on 157th Street, where they had lived for almost thirty years, to a senior citizen building around the corner Titi Dulce had helped her get into. She and Papa Julio weren't getting divorced, they were just not going to live together anymore, and in the words of my Grandma Mari, "I want some peace while I still have some life left." She moved into a cheery little one bedroom on Amsterdam Avenue with her plants and her photo albums and her knickknacks . . . and railings in the bathroom . . . and an intercom buzzer in every room. For the first time, I could see *abuelita* was getting old.

Papa Julio would go over there every day after breakfast and go back to his now empty apartment after dinner. Whenever I'd visit, I'd always bring a box of pastries from Veniero's in the East Village, *bizcochos*, they called them. Papa Julio especially liked the cannolis.

Papa Julio would end up getting Alzheimer's and eventually he only remembered me as the girl who brought the *bizcochos*. When he finally went into the nursing home, everyone except my mother asked me why I never went to visit him. I was a full adult then, and Titi Carmen and my father were already gone, so I told Titis Dulce and Ofelia the truth, at least what I could remember. They both went into shock and denied it, but of course they would. "He was a holy man, a Christian man," they said. I didn't dispute that that's what he'd become, but it didn't change what he'd been. Of course, he'd never have done what he did to them or to *their* kids. But he wasn't my grandfather. And that's all I have to remember. He wasn't my grandfather.

Except for one last time, Pat Baleena was never again as mean to me as he had been on that Kill Black and Puerto Rican Day. Inexplicably over the next couple of years, he became, if not friendly, then at least nonadversarial. I still don't know what triggered him ratting me out like that. Maybe it was payback for eighth grade when on my way back from the bathroom, I walked past the empty classroom when Joey Lamonica and David Stein were gluing his butt to the chair and I said nothing. Maybe. Or maybe eight years was long enough to hate somebody, and it just played out. Whatever it was, I didn't care. I had other things to worry about.

For one thing, I'd had a secret crush on a boy for the first time in my life, and I didn't dare tell a soul. For another, the next time I was on my way to the park, I took the 007 and threw it down a sewer. I didn't want to have it anymore. I was afraid if I continued to have something like that, the next time something happened to me I'd use it. That I hadn't used it yet was at least one choice I could be thankful for.

23

THE GIFT

It was just a regular Tuesday, a couple of days before Christmas. As usual, right after school I went straight to my room and pretended to do my homework while making mix tapes off 95.5 WPLJ *Pass the J*, the "cool" rock station. The station I could somehow only get if I put my cassette/radio out on the fire escape and aimed the antenna at the Whitestone Bridge, which of course connected to Queens, the total opposite direction from Manhattan.

It had begun to snow and between trying to sneak a cigarette and brushing the snowflakes off the radio, I didn't hear my mom come in and tell me that I had to go to the store. Now! Aw man! The last thing I wanted to do was truck all the way to Castle Hill Avenue. And the last thing I wanted to get was what she needed: Kotex. The big box. The big purple box with the bright yellow letters that said "Super." The box that never fit into any size bag so that the top always stuck out and everyone who looked at you knew you must be bleeding. Lots.

I stomped through the streets and into the drugstore where the four-eyed, pimple-encrusted cashier drooled as he took my money. I swore that if I ever had a daughter, I would never, ever make her buy my menstrual supplies, and as I tried to stuff the bag under my jacket, I heard someone call, "Hey, Shell!" Two boys whizzed by me, one grabbing the bag from my hands as they both slid down the block.

It was Dennis and Louie of the Overing Boys. That meant that they hung out at the P.S. 600 Schoolyard, smoked weed, and knew all the girls on the block wanted to make out with them. Except me. Well, not really. I actually had a raging crush on Dennis—along with thirty other girls in the neighborhood—but because I knew it would never be reciprocated (I wasn't blond, blue-eyed or big bosomed) I hated him in the way only another teenager could understand.

Dennis and Louie were taunting me with a Salugi game, throwing the bag back and forth between them like a football, and I was so terrified that one of them would realize what was in it, my shame made me run faster than they could. "Hey! What the fuck!" I yelled, and I tackled Dennis, only to see the big purple box with the bright yellow letters spring from his hands onto Westchester Avenue where it was immediately run over by a number 4 bus. I pushed Dennis, then Louie, not caring if they beat me up.

"Hey Shell, it's only a box of cookies, you can get another one," Louie said.

"Cookies?"

Dennis grabbed my hands and looked at me. He knew, but he didn't tell. "C'mon, Shell, we'll walk ya home."

The snow was really coming down now. It looked like it was almost a foot deep, all in the half hour since I had left home. The three of us walked past all the houses done up for the holidays—homes of working people with small budgets and big imaginations. And somewhere between the dancing Rudolphs, talking Baby Jesuses, and competing soundtracks (Andy Williams vs. Donna Summer), we started sticking out our tongues to catch the flakes before they fell on each other's sleeves.

Then we ran, scooping snow off the hoods of cars and throwing it at each other. Louie skidded into a parked car, Dennis and I both jumped on him and bounced up and down (no car alarms back then) until we all fell into a drift. Every time one of us got up, the other would push that person down until we were all covered in snow.

We got up and ran again, slipping, sliding, and laughing down Tratman Avenue until we fell, got up, and fell again, rolling like a giant teenage snowball. At the end of the block, a streetlamp broke our descent and somehow the three of us were standing up holding hands.

A car backfired. The spell was broken, and we dropped our hands at the same instant. We stood twinkling under the streetlamp, frosted with snow, and glowing red in the December twilight, not knowing what had happened or what to do next.

Finally, Dennis asked me if I was home. I nodded yes and then both Dennis and Louie stood on either side of me. They each kissed me on my wet, frostbitten lips and ran back up the block. "See ya, Shell. Merry Christmas!"

I floated upstairs and told my mother a bus ran over her box. She made me pay her back out of my own money and sent my father out to get her supplies. He wasn't happy either.

Soon after Christmas, Dennis and Louie were murdered. They and another friend, Billy Gizmo, were walking out of the McDonald's on Silver Street when a car drove by and threw a beer can at them. Louie threw it back and called them douche bags. The car drove around the block and the boys inside shot them down as they were crossing the street. Billy somehow saw the gun out of the corner of his eye and threw himself to the pavement a split second before the shots rang out. He didn't even have time to yell a warning, but it saved his life.

Ever been to a teenager's funeral? It's kind of like when your grandfather dies, except your friend didn't have bushy white eyebrows and a cough from smoking for sixty years. I remember crying in front of Dennis's closed casket and then feeling rather than seeing his mom kneel down next to me.

She looked very old for a mom; at first, I thought she was his grandmother: gray hair, gray skin, red eyes, alone. She asked me if I had known Dennis well. I wanted to tell her about that night in the snow, but to say anything felt like a betrayal, a breach of trust, an admission of something I didn't yet have words for. All I said was, "Yeah, kind of."

She looked into me. When I didn't say anything more, she put her hand on my shoulder and got up to comfort someone else.

I don't remember seeing anyone else from Dennis's family at his funeral, not a father or grandparents or any brothers or sisters. Just his mom all alone. I realize now what a gift it would have been for me to be able to tell her about the night in the snow: that her son was a gentleman, that he didn't betray my secret—and that his kiss was my first. Now I wish I had told her.

Day blends into twilight. Dusk melts into black. We were fifteen, sixteen, maybe seventeen. The years have faded. Some are beyond memory. But I'll never forget what the wind, the snow, and the colored lights gave to Dennis and Louie and me that one Tuesday night so long ago. The last pure night of our childhood.

24

KILL WHITEY DAY

I was standing in the basement of Macy's Parkchester in The Bronx, in a line of what seemed like a thousand teenagers, smoking both cigarettes and weed, chanting, cheering, and waiting for Ticketmaster to open. Adult shoppers were nonexistent, and salespeople had abandoned their posts either in foreknowledge or in fear, except for the lone Ticketmaster employee at the window, way beyond where I could see. All around me were kids I knew, but I acknowledged no one. I was on a mission.

It was a little past ten o'clock on a weekday morning. You might be thinking that we all should have been in school. Yes, we should have, and maybe some of us would have, except for one thing: Led Zeppelin was coming to Madison Square Garden, and tickets were about to go on sale. Because in those primitive analog days before cable TV, cell phones, and the Internet, you listened to your favorite FM radio station (95.5 WPLJ) day and night, nonstop, waiting for the DJ to announce the day and time concert tickets would go on sale. And then you lined up at the nearest Ticketmaster and you waited. If it was a weekday, fuck school. Who in their right mind would go to school when for seven dollars and fifty cents, you could see "Kashmir."

I didn't get a ticket that morning. Not because they'd sold out, but because I didn't have enough money. Even the blue nosebleed seats were now $5.50—a whole dollar more than the year before—and I wasn't the only one who was disappointed. Some of the kids were so disappointed, they started tearing up the selling floor, tagging graffiti, throwing mannequins around, and cursing. I was having none of that. I had spent an hour in the 43rd Precinct for graffiti writing and vandalism once and wasn't eager to repeat the experience. So at ten thirty, I left Macy's with my five crumpled one-dollar bills and walked back to school, figuring the day wasn't a total loss as I'd only missed three periods. I arrived at school a little past eleven and right away saw something was up. For one thing there was a phalanx of cop cars around the Westchester Square train station. For another, I heard the yelling from all the way up the hill. Then I remembered—today was "Kill Whitey Day."

I know that in some alternate universe one's high school days were a halcyon, carefree time, with fond, gauzy memories of homecoming days, pep rallies, and proms. But at my high school, fondly referred to in those days as Lehman State Prison, the pivotal events we had to look forward to each year were Kill Whitey Day and Kill Black and Puerto Rican Day.

It's said that gangs are cyclical in New York City. There were gangs in the 1950s. There are gangs today. But in the mid to late 1970s, teenage New York was a city divided and ruled from Parkchester out to Morris Park and up to Throgs Neck by the white gangs the Bronx Aliens and Bronx Ministers. Their black and Latino counterparts, the Savage Skulls, Savage Nomads, Mongol Brothers, and biker gang the Ching-a-Lings, claimed everywhere south of Soundview Avenue and west, past Yankee Stadium and Fordham Road all the way to the Harlem River.

Every year, each high school would have its couple of times a year when it would be at war. As in any war, any unfortunate civilians who found themselves behind the front lines would just have to get by as best they could.

The messed-up thing about it was you knew exactly when it was all going to go down. The information crossed gang, race, and ethnic lines and flashed through your entire school faster than group text messaging locks down a campus today. You *knew* when your Kill Day was going to be. Not going to school that day was not an option. Everyone would know you had punked out, and your own neighborhood would make you a pariah for being a faggot and a pussy, for not having enough heart to risk getting a beatdown with everyone else.

Lehman High School, being in a mostly Italian neighborhood, was Bronx Ministers' territory. But by some fate of late 1960s decentralization, half the student population was various ethnicities of white, the other, black, or Latino (from the South Bronx neighborhoods my parents had succeeded in escaping ten years before). So Lehman was a school doubly "blessed" as it observed both Kill Days. This year, Kill Black and Puerto Rican Day had been the previous week, and luckily, I had escaped unscathed.

Not so the year before, when two Italian boys had stabbed me in the shoulder with an ice pick. Not because they specifically hated me, as I later found out, but because a couple of Savage Skulls had whipped them with a car antenna. And since they weren't motivated (i.e., brave/stupid) enough to go down to the Bronx River Projects to extract revenge, the next best thing was to attack me. They both actually apologized to me later and hoped I understood it wasn't personal. As I mentioned earlier, I still have the scar.

Since it wasn't an option, I had to go into school. I went around the back way, where I knew (and security amazingly didn't) a door was always propped open. Fourth period was about to begin, and something told me not to try to sneak a cigarette before entering the relative safety of health class. But I was nervous, so I took a chance. I peeked into the girls' bathroom and seeing no one, ducked into the last stall and immediately assumed the smoker's position: crouching on the toilet seat so someone bending down to check the stalls wouldn't see my feet and waving my right arm back and forth constantly so the curling smoke wouldn't give me away either. After a few minutes, though, the Newport Light just wasn't doing it for me, but I decided there was still time for one more drag. Famous last words.

I was about to flush the cigarette when the door opened and four black girls came in. I knew they were black because of their names. Keishas and Tawandas were in utero or just being born. Girls my age were the last of a generation who were still named after jewels and desirable attributes: Crystal, Ruby, Precious, and Unity. Delicate flowers who stashed razor blades in their Afros and carried rolls of pennies balled up in their bandannas.

I knew who they were because of their reputations. They were finely tuned, Black Pride lionesses who hunted their prey with particular savagery: what they caught, they would not release. I knew that if they caught me, I was a goner. None of them would stop to ask a light-skinned, freckle-faced redhead where her family was from before they beat the living hell out of her.

"Dag, Ruby, you see that blond bitch face when we knocked her toof out?"

"Yeah, but shoo, my hand cut up. Precious, watch the door. Oh shit, you smell something? Who in here?"

I had neglected to do the one thing that could have saved me, which was to douse the cigarette and keep still. There wasn't a thing I could do except wait as the stalls were opened one by one until they found me. It was pointless to fight back—one definitely, two . . . maybe. But there were four of them. And it would have been suicide to try to tell them they were making a mistake.

The year before, an olive-skinned Irish girl named Ellen something or other had tried to say she was half Puerto Rican, and she ended up being held down and raped with an umbrella. That was not going to happen to me.

They pulled me off the toilet and threw me on the floor. I rolled up in a ball and tried to protect my face as they punched, kicked, and penny rolled me. How long? Too long. And then, the door opened.

"Yo, Nan-cee, we got another white girl, you want some?"

I looked up through one swollen, tear-and-Afrosheen-clouded eye and saw Nancy Jimenez walk in. Nancy, who really was half Puerto Rican and half Irish, was one of those anomalies in our little world: a blessed creature who moved seamlessly between the races, befriending everyone, beat up by none. She came over to look at me. "Dag, man, that girl ain't white, she's Puerto Rican."

"Whut?"

"She's Puerto Rican. That's Shell, I know her from homeroom. She's from St. Peter's, but she's Puerto Rican. She just looks white."

The punches stopped. A razor blade whizzed by my left cheek and clattered onto the tiles. The one called Unity said, "She's Puerto Rican?" and prodded me with her Pro-Ked.

"I axed you, you Puerto Rican?"

I spit out a trail of blood and snot and croaked out the only thing I could think of, "Si."

"See, I told you. Stoopid!" And Nancy, having secured her eternal place in heaven, left the bathroom.

Four pairs of eyes saw me as a person for the first time. "Oh man! We sorry. . . . Oh man, we sorry. . . . Shoo! Why didn't she say something? . . . Why didn't you say nothing? . . . Come on, help that girl up." That was Unity, their leader, talking.

Crystal, Ruby, and Precious picked me up off the floor, patted my hair, and tried to rearrange my clothes. "Get some water, clean her up," Unity commanded. The girls ran to the sink, wet their bandannas, and daubed at my face. I took Ruby's pink bandanna and walked to the mirror to clean myself. She didn't protest.

"This ain't right," Unity said. "We sorry. We didn't know. . . . Why didn't you say nothing? . . . You're not gonna tell, right? . . . We gonna make it up to you. . . . C'mon. Give her your weed."

Crystal, Precious, and Ruby all looked down at their sneakers.

"I said, give her your weed," Unity yelled. "Give it up!"

One by one, the girls reached into their Afros and their tube socks and pulled out crooked joints rolled in banana, chocolate, and strawberry E-Z Widers. Mutely, with averted eyes, they handed them to me. "We sorry," Crystal mumbled.

"Yeah, man, we sorry," Ruby said.

But Precious didn't reach for anything. She'd been standing on the other side of the bathroom and was now trying to sidle her way toward the door, but she couldn't get away from Unity's watchful eye. Unity's fist shot out: *Biff!* and punched the side of Precious's head so hard her Afro pick flew into the sink, clattering in front of me.

"I said, give her your weed, Bitch!" Unity commanded. Precious's hand trembled as she dug around her bra and finally handed me a crumpled, sweat-stained, half-full nickel bag.

"Look, we sorry. It was a mistake, right?" Unity asked. "You're not gonna tell right? . . . I mean, like we did you a solid and all. Come on, let's go kick some real white ass."

Just like that, they left. I stood in the bathroom for a moment and totally accepted what had just happened as just the way things were. I still couldn't quite believe my luck in escaping with only a slightly cut lip and black eye. Then I looked at what was balled up in my clenched fist—and I did believe it. I walked right out of school and over to Zappa's Corner where I sold all the pot, then ran back to Macy's, getting there just before Ticketmaster closed at 4:00 P.M.

The day wasn't a total waste after all. I was going to see "Kashmir."

25

NIGHT OF THE BLACK CHRYSANTHEMUM

We were living around the corner from St. Peter's Church in The Bronx, one of the oldest buildings in all New York City, dating back to the 1600s. A large part of my childhood was spent in that church graveyard reading faded tombstones, trying to catch praying mantises or looking around fresh graves for a fat wallet because my cousin Benny once found a $50 bill near one. Kids always played there, probably because it was the only place with trees and grass for blocks that wasn't an abandoned lot.

I felt totally comfortable there. The spirit world didn't bother me. I'd been aware of it my entire life. When you grow up Latin, traditions from hundreds of years of varied forms of worship color your everyday life. For instance, Titi Ofelia kept a glass of holy water behind her door so if anything evil followed her into the house, it would fall in and drown. Titi Carmen had a special plant she'd break out to make a tea whenever someone couldn't sleep. And my mother had a rosary with multicolored glass beads, and when she sat praying next to a window and the light was right, it looked as if she counted rainbows in her hands. But no holy water, no *tilo* leaves, and no Our Fathers could've prepared any of us for the Great Voodoo War of 1976.

Over ten years before, my family had been the first Latin family to move into our building and for a time endured the Italian and Irish families complaining that our food stank, our music was too loud, and we kids ran wild through the halls. Like Italians are quiet, the Irish are peaceful, and garlic doesn't stink—right.

So when two more Latin families moved onto our floor, we thought we'd have new allies. But both the Garcia and the Morales families kept to themselves. The adults didn't speak much English and the teenagers didn't listen to Led Zeppelin or Black Sabbath and were therefore useless. My mother found out the two new families came from the same town back in Puerto Rico, and there was bad blood between them, to which my father said, "If they didn't like each other there, why the hell did they move in together here?"

After a couple of weeks we found out. We never knew what started this installment of their war, but it was obvious it'd been going on far longer than even they could remember. First, there was cursing. Not the usual "Screw you, you mo-fo son of a bitch" kind of cursing, but proclamations: threats for barren wombs, incurable diarrhea and brain tumors, unemployment, insanity, and more diarrhea. It actually would have been funny if they hadn't sounded so serious.

One day I came home from school to find three pennies in a triangle in front of the Morales's door with some white powder sprinkled around them. I picked them up and showed them to my mother, and she threw them out of the window, made me wash my hands with Lava soap, C-N, and alcohol, and told me not even to look at anything near either of their apartments.

Every couple of days though, there was something else not to look at, like kernels of corn, dead black flowers, or strange-looking candles. The arguments got worse too. Almost every night we'd hear them in the hall, only now I couldn't understand what they were saying because it was all in Spanish, and these were words my family didn't use. My brother and I would look up from our homework at my mother or father, and they'd just turn the TV up louder.

One afternoon I did something I hadn't done in years—I went to St. Peter's graveyard to be alone. I had just found out another boy I had a total crush on said I had a nice ass . . . but an ugly face. I sat down under a tree to cry and saw a piece of mail addressed to the

Garcias smeared in what looked like blood, and worse, a pair of what looked like freshly cut chicken feet was neatly tied around them with red string.

I ran home and told my mother what I had seen, and she went straight to the Garcias' door and knocked. When no one answered, she said, "I know you're in there and I know what you're doing. You have to stop. It's not sanitary. Children play in that graveyard!" A voice behind the door told my mother in heavily accented English to mind her business or she'd be next. The next day, there was a skinned, crucified mouse taped to the Morales's door. They moved out late that night. We could hear them screaming and crying, hurling generation upon generation of curses upon the Garcias and everyone else in the building.

My mother was beyond furious. "This isn't right. Somebody's got to do something."

Kevin said, "What're you gonna do, get Titi Carmen's plant after them?"

"No," she said, "worse." And she went into her bedroom and shut the door.

What had once been a simple clash between the Puerto Rican Hatfields and McCoys had now become Armaggedon. Because when my mother went into the bedroom, she opened her Bible and read it out the window, out loud, nonstop the remainder of that night and into the next day.

Did I say nonstop? When my brother and I left for school in the morning, she was at the window. When we came back, she was at the window. When my father almost burned down the kitchen trying to make us dinner, she was at the window. Every once in a while, one of the Garcias would yell something at her, and that only served to make her read even louder and now—solely in Spanish.

My father tried reasoning with her, but when she started reading at him too, he suddenly decided he needed to work a triple shift, abandoning my brother and me on the front lines. We tried to launch a counterattack by blasting late-night reruns of the *Honeymooners* and *Rat Patrol* on our little twelve-inch TV, but we were no match for the

Almighty Word of God. How so? Because not only did neither of us get a minute of sleep, but we found out the next morning the Garcias had moved out sometime in the middle of the night and, what's more, silently.

As I was about to leave bleary eyed for school, my mother, looking as fresh as ever, asked me to take out the garbage. When I got to the alleyway, I saw a pile of house stuff with pieces of paper among them. I looked closer and realized they were pages torn from the Bible. I looked up and saw our windows between what had been the Morales's and Garcias' windows. Not only had my mother spoken the Word of God, she hurled it at them.

And so, the Great Voodoo War of 1976 was stopped with the one weapon no curse on this earth has any power against: the righteous fury of a Latina mother scorned. Even though my mother later said she needed to repent for tearing up the Word of God, I didn't think so. Yeah, it might have been crazy, but she was also ahead of her time. She had Sinéad O'Connor beat by a whole sixteen years.

26

KEEP ME SEARCHING FOR AN
OUNCE OF GOLD

There was a year and a half where Nikki, Dawn, Janey, and I were as inseparable as only a quartet of sixteen- and seventeen-year-old girls can be. We shared everything: our makeup, our record albums, our secret crushes, our clothes—and our weed.

Let me rephrase lest you write us off as an idle group of stoners—we went places and did things with our weed. We went to Orchard Beach (Section 13, of course); to the movies: *Tommy*, *The Rocky Horror Picture Show*, *The Song Remains the Same*; and to a Star Trek convention (my idea) where we were denied entry (I wonder why?). But Nikki and I found a back elevator that the four of us ran into, not checking if it was going up or down, and who was standing inside but Mr. Spock, Leonard Nimoy himself! The four of us stared as he stood in Vulcan silence. I was about to ask him for his autograph—for my brother Kevin, of course—when Dawn woke up and screamed, "It's Spock! Oh my God, it's Spock!"

Needless to say, Mr. Nimoy got off at the next floor, tempted, no doubt, to have given the Vulcan neck pinch to all of us.

The four of us sashayed along St. Peter's Avenue in our Lee jackets and Landlubber jeans with huge safety pins and fringed suede pouches hanging from our belt loops. We stumbled along cracked pavement on our Buffalo sandals. We all double pierced our left ears. I was the only one with no ear piercings—quite unusual, having been born into a culture where six-month-old girls sported gold-studded earlobes. My mother didn't believe in it. She said God had given me all the holes I needed.

One evening Nikki took her Nana's piercing earrings: fourteen-carat yellow gold instruments of torture imported straight from Sicily, with gold balls on one end and miniature ice picks on the other. Nikki rubbed ice on my ears, then she swabbed them with Bactine, and we shared a bottle of Tango as Dawn and Janey held down my arms while Nikki stuck the earrings into the carefully marked pen dots she drew on my earlobes. Since I hadn't had any piercings at all, I had to endure triple pain that night, but it was worth it. A month later I walked into Titi Ofelia's Easter dinner wearing a three-inch-long purple feather, a cross, and a skull and watched my mother ignore Ofelia's outburst. I've gotten my ears pierced four more times since then, but Nikki's piercings were the ones that healed the fastest and gave me the least trouble.

Yes, Shell, Nikki (who over the past year had naturally grown into and now deserved the name "Boom-Boom"), Dizzy Dawn (who had outgrown both her glasses and braces and become a real beauty), and Baby Janey (still tiny except for her huge hazel eyes, and still the most daring out of all of us) were the self-described Fly Four, and when Nikki, our leader, was about to turn eighteen, legal, we knew we had to do something special for her. But a set of Bonne Bell lip glosses or Love's Baby Soft wasn't going to cut it. Neither was Pink Floyd's *Animals* or a Fudgie the Whale cake. No. Only weed would do. Specifically, an ounce of pure Acapulco Gold.

"So yeah, Shell, how're we gonna get that?" Dawn asked at a pre-birthday powwow at Janey's house.

Good question as I was the only one of us with an actual job. I was now working twenty hours a week at Macy's Parkchester for $2.35 an hour—half of which I had to give to my parents. This left me with about $15 a week, which left me—uh—us over $40 short of our ounce of Gold.

It was the middle of June. We had a little less than a month as Nikki's birthday was three days after mine, on July 13. Dawn thought we should try to do a kissing booth in the lunchroom at school. "It's summer," she said. "Everyone wants to make out."

"Who's gonna pay to kiss you when they can get it for free?" Janey asked, and while she and Dawn good-naturedly bickered, I, as usual, started thinking about myself. I complained how I had bought a hit of windowpane acid for the Led Zeppelin concert I had gone to the week before and how it was beat. A dud. No trip. Not one little bit. Three dollars out of my precious $15 wasted. I was going on and on how Zeppelin just wasn't the same when you only had two beers, when Janey interrupted, "That's it!"

"Huh?" Dawn and I both asked.

Janey repeated, "That's it—we sell beat acid and that's how we get the money."

"Yeah, right." Dawn jeered. "I'm gonna go to Woolworth's and five-finger (shoplift) Nikki some Love's Baby Soft. You two can take it on the hop. See ya!"

"Faggot!" Janey called after her. "Right, Shell?"

The scary thing was I actually thought we could get away with it, even though the only time I had ever attempted anything close to dealing was once, when I sold some loose joints to get money for a concert ticket. But that had been a consolation gift for enduring a mistaken-identity beatdown, and was, therefore, totally different. There were only two weeks left of school though, so we had to think fast. I gave Janey $10. She put in the rest and bought as many different types of acid as she could. She always knew where to get drugs.

Two days later, we looked at her purchases side by side on her night table. There was one hit each of windowpane and blotter acid, chocolate and strawberry mescaline, and a half hit of orange, double-barrel sunshine. The fruit flavors were out as they were actual pills and could no way be imitated. So was the windowpane, which looked like a piece of compressed dry-cleaning bag. But the "blotter"—the blotter acid was just a small square of slightly stained paper. Janey picked it up.

"No eating the sample!" I said and grabbed it. We split up the rest.

After the weekend, when our brain synapses were normal again, we met back in her room to make the beat acid. On observation, I had discovered that the square of blotter was pretty much close to the graph paper we used in art class, so I stuck a few sheets in my notebook. I also five-fingered an X-Acto knife. Janey had an eyedropper she had taken from her grandmother's medicine cabinet and two cans of soda: RC Cola and Fanta Orange. We figured we wouldn't be greedy and only do the exact amount we needed: forty tabs, since we agreed we would both chip in $10 each.

"You got money now? Where'd you get a job?" I asked Janey.

"Not really," Janey said. "I've been helping Jackie Scungilli at the Huntington." Jackie Scungilli was a major pot dealer who hung out at the end of Ampere Avenue in a clearing just inside Pelham Bay Park called the Huntington—a place real hard-core pot and pill-heads hung out.

It was even rumored that a few of the boys had fed some acid to a stray dog and laughed as it chased its tail until it collapsed. I didn't think that was cool to do to a dumb animal and said so.

"Chill! I wasn't there when they did that," Janey said.

We got to work. My job was to cut and Janey's was to stain. It took awhile to make the forty tabs. Some of them didn't come out straight and some had too much color or too little. I cut my knee when the X-Acto knife slipped out of my hand and jabbed me right through my jeans, but finally, we had our forty tabs of blotter, which we put into an envelope. I decorated it with the Zofo symbols from *Led Zeppelin IV* for luck. We were all set to open up shop in school the next day.

We didn't think about what would happen if we were caught. We didn't think about what would happen to us when people found out it didn't work. We didn't think. Period.

We had decided to sell them at the deep discount price of $1 each. We figured that they would sell quicker and that no one would complain much if they didn't get off since it only cost a dollar. It wasn't all that uncommon to have a tab of beat acid from time to time, so we were counting on that to save us from any retribution.

Business sucked. That first week we only sold five. We started to panic. School would be over soon, and we couldn't sell it to the people we actually hung out with. At least, I wasn't going to. But then a miracle happened. Pink Floyd was going to play a bunch of concerts at Madison Square Garden in the beginning of July, so we sold five more. And then . . . we got a couple of repeat customers from the first wave. They said things like "Well, it took a long time to get off and it only lasted ten minutes, but hey, it's only a dollar, so what the fuck." Or "That last tab was beat, but hey, it was only a dollar so lemme try another one."

This is when I started having bad dreams. Dreams about Diane Linkletter, who had taken acid back in the 1960s and jumped out of a window, and Karen Quinlan, who took Quaaludes and drank vodka and was now a vegetable. I woke up gasping for breath. I thought "What if they thought they actually got off and thought they were a bird and jumped off a roof ? Wouldn't that be our fault?"

But when I mentioned this to Janey, she said, "Stop being such a faggot, Shell. Look, I sold another two hits!"

I tried confiding in Dawn, but she said, "I told you not to do it. I don't know what's up with Janey lately; she's getting to be a real burnout."

School ended. Janey and I met up again in her room the day after my birthday. Nikki's birthday was that Wednesday, and we had only sold fifteen tabs. I felt guilty about not helping after I started having the bad dreams and gave Janey $20, the extra $10 coming from part of my birthday money. That still only made $35, but Janey said not to worry. "I'll go to the Huntington," she said. "I know people."

I hoped she did. Janey, Dawn, and I had gone to every park, schoolyard, and corner hangout in three neighborhoods inviting kids to Nikki's party—we had to deliver. But I didn't want to go with Janey to cop and said so.

"That's cool," she said. "I'll take Dawn." I was surprised that Dawn would go with her, but I said nothing. The night of Nikki's party, I passed the park on the way to her apartment and saw kids were starting to congregate behind the pool, drinking beer and waiting. Janey and Dawn had gone up to Pelham Bay at six and said they'd be back in an hour. My job was to stall Nikki until seven. After we had done our makeup, blown out our hair, and listened to most of *Quadrophenia*, Nikki finally said, "Come on Shell, let's go, I gotta be home by one." I could see there were some advantages to being eighteen.

We got to the park a little after seven and Janey and Dawn weren't there. But there were a group of maybe forty kids yelling "Happy Birthday Nikki Boom-Boom!" and in minutes she was surrounded with presents: a quart of Schaefer beer, a bottle of Yago Sangria, a gift set of Love's Baby Soft, and a copy of Pink Floyd's *Animals*.

"Where's Janey and Dawn?" she asked.

"They're coming," I said. But seven thirty, eight, eight thirty came and went and no Janey, no weed. People were starting to get antsy. Most of the girls had to be home by eleven or eleven thirty, and no one yet had a buzz.

At nine o'clock Janey and Dawn finally burst in. "Sorry, man, the 'man' was following us," Janey said and reached down the front of her jean shorts. "Happy birthday, Boom-Boom! This is from Dawn and me."

Everyone cheered. Nikki hugged them both. I was stunned. *Dawn* and her? Wait a second. I was the one who gave Janey the idea. I was the one who still had a piece of scab on her knee. I was the one who had the bad dreams. I was the one who put in $20 of her own friggin' money! I opened my mouth to tell Nikki that Janey was full of it, when she opened a brown envelope and took out a baggie stuffed with what looked like the purest Acapulco Gold ever. Everyone cheered again. Someone pulled out a huge piece of rolling paper they said came from Cheech & Chong's *Big Bambú* album.

"Let's roll the biggest bone in The Bronx and then we can do a coconut!"

As everyone crowded around Nikki, and Janey and Dawn started rolling, I hung back. Suddenly I wasn't in a party mood anymore.

I sneaked away and started walking out of the park to go home. As I climbed through a hole in the fence on one side, I saw a cop car pull up to the other. I got scared but couldn't go back to warn them, even though I knew the cops hadn't seen me. Was Nikki's party going to be busted? I had to know, so I ducked into Artie's Deli and bought a bag of crunchy Cheez Doodles to stall for time. But as I was leaving the deli, all the streetlights on the block suddenly went dim. They went really bright for an instant. And then they went out. I didn't know what else to do, so I went straight home as people in the buildings above opened their windows and yelled to each other. It was the night of the infamous New York City Blackout of 1977.

I later found out that when the cops came, half the kids ran through the fence I had just gone through. The other half hid under the pool. Janey, Dawn, and Nikki were literally left holding the bag. One of the cops grabbed the baggie, opened it, sniffed it, and cracked up. "Stoopid girls smoking catnip!" But then the lights went out, and the cops had a lot more to worry about than three teenage girls with beat pot.

Fordham Road, among many other New York City neighborhoods, was completely looted that night. I heard from Jeana-Ray, who was at P.S. 14 up in Throgs Neck with her boyfriend, that they caught the last number 40 bus going to Westchester Square, and when they got off, they saw men with shotguns in front of several stores. I walked up the five flights of stairs to my family's apartment in the dark. My mother had just gotten off the phone with my father when the lights went out. He was in Florida with Kevin. Grandma Izzy was really, really sick. I had wanted to go down with them, but couldn't get off work. My mother put the police lock on the door and jammed a mop and a broom against the two windows that led to the fire escape. We went to bed in silence. The lights wouldn't come back on till the next evening.

The cops had let Janey, Dawn, and Nikki go, but things weren't quite the same with us afterward. Nikki and Dawn wouldn't speak to Janey for the rest of the summer, and even though her friends at the Huntington sold her beat weed, she started hanging out there more and more. She now had a new nickname: Janey-the-Waste. As for me, I luckily didn't get blamed for anything. Nikki even said it was the thought that counted. And I never, ever was tempted to deal drugs again. Janey asked me to help her out once or twice, but I said no. I saw what had happened. It was like that old commercial for Battling Tops: "For every action, there's an equal and opposite reaction." Beat someone and get beat in return. Besides, it was nice to be able to sleep in peace again.

27

HEAT

(Escape from CBGB's, part 1)

The year 1977 had been a pivotal year for New York City. We had survived a blackout, Son of Sam finally was caught, Reggie Jackson, a.k.a. Mr. October, became a candy bar, and to top the year off, right before Christmas the boiler in my family's apartment building exploded. It burned out the ground-floor apartment directly above and left the rest of the double building without heat or hot water for the entire winter, precipitating a grassroots tenant's organization, a rent strike, and a spike maybe in the building's birth rate the following September. To me that was the least of it. Unless you grew up so far north that living in a five-story igloo was considered normal, you cannot imagine the multitude of misery entailed with living through a no heat and no hot water New York City winter.

The indignity of taking sponge baths in the kitchen behind a makeshift curtain and watching the ice *inside* the window melt while your father and brother hollered at you to hurry up was horrible— and then you get your period. Or imagine the smell a four-room apartment takes on after the oven has been on at 400 degrees every single day for over a month—and then you get your period again.

And while Kevin and I were going to bed each night looking like refugees, wearing every sweater we had, three pairs of socks, and these fingerless gloves my father had made us, my mother tooled around in shorts and a T-shirt. She had her own personal combustion system keeping her warm that year—a continuous hot flash that lasted basically the entire winter. You could actually stand next to her and feel it.

Not only did she not complain, but she was not fazed one bit at being at least five years too young for this middle-age milestone. Mother declared it was God's Will that gave her the Change of Life that year as opposed to any other. And since she seemed so cool with it, Kevin and I gave her an orange T-shirt for Valentine's Day. It was from the neighborhood head shop, and it had a lightning bolt iron-on on the front that said Hot Mama. She didn't think it was funny. And, of course, it was all my fault. "Wait until this happens to you," she said as she threw her *chancletas* at me. "You think you're going to be young forever? Get out of my sight!"

Well, yeah, I was almost eighteen—well, seventeen and a half—and at that point in my life, I did actually think I was going to be young forever. And I didn't mind going out since it was actually warmer at the park than it was in the apartment.

When I got there, my friends were crowded around the neighborhood nut job, Crazy May-ree. None of us really liked May-ree, but she had started hanging out at the park a couple of years before, and we let her because everyone was kind of afraid of her. She had bleached blond bangs (Clairol, not Clorox), a tattoo of a scorpion (her astrological sign, on her chestbone), and six piercings in her left ear (at a time when even the most rebellious among us wore only three earrings and the only acceptable girl tattoos were the Led Zeppelin IV Zofo symbols, butterflies, and roses—on your shoulder blade). Every time she got stoned, she would walk around saying she was a tree, and once she'd chanted the names of every species on the eastern seaboard. Plus, she wouldn't listen to Pink Floyd, Led Zeppelin, Black Sabbath, or even the Who anymore, and she was always trying to get us to go with her downtown, to Manhattan, to hang out.

None of my friends went to Manhattan to go out in those days unless it was to Madison Square Garden, a Dr Pepper concert, or Laserium, the rock-and-laser light show at the Hayden Planetarium. The closest most of us had ever been to a real rock club were the blood bars on Valentine Avenue where Twisted Sister used to play. And they sucked. Or Detroit, up in Portchester, to see Rat Race Choir. And they sucked too.

"C'mon guys, we have to go to Heat," May-ree said. "The club is so hot. The bands are so hot. The guys are so hot. And Johnny Thunders is playing tonight. He is so hot. C'mon, don't be faggots. Who's coming with me?"

All I heard was the name: Heat. I didn't know who or what Johnny Thunders was and didn't care. The frozen core of my brain pictured a Hawaiian-themed palace with bikinis, thatched umbrellas, and flaming drinks. It didn't matter that I wouldn't be legal for another five months; all I needed was my high heels and my fake ID, and I could be warm.

"I'll go," I said.

"Wicked," May-ree said. "Meet me at seven o'clock."

Nikki and Dawn couldn't believe it. "Are you crazy? You don't know what they do in Manhattan." I didn't care if they tattooed and pierced their *totos*. All I thought was after two-and-a-half months of freezing, I was finally going to be warm. I didn't dare tell May-ree this would be the first time I'd go into Manhattan with just one other girl.

I met May-ree at seven o'clock that night. We smoked a bone and hopped on the number 6 train. The entire ride downtown she talked about seeing bands I had never heard of with people I didn't know and about how the second she turned eighteen she was going to go live in the Village.

"Good for you," I thought. "I just want to get some heat and go home."

Finally, we got off the train at Bleecker Street, and I had no idea where we were. The neighborhood wasn't the Twenty-first-Century So-Hopeless shopping mall East SoHo is today; it was dark, scary, and dirty. Of course it was—only artists and drug dealers dared live there.

After slipping along slushy cobblestone side streets in my open-toe Candies, the only high heels I had (May-ree had changed direction, cursing, several times), she suddenly grabbed my hand and steered me into a club.

The club was narrow and it stank. It was dark and it was freezing. A slightly chubby older girl with bleached blond hair and hairy armpits who was making a big show of not checking IDs at the door asked where I got my gloves. "My dad made 'em," I said as I staggered past her and along a long, black, crowded bar toward a dim yellow light at the end of the room, toward salvation—warmth. You don't understand. I had been continuously cold for almost three months, and my Caribbean DNA leaves me predisposed to lying naked and indolent under palm trees, not wearing my entire winter wardrobe in a cold bar that smelled like hot piss.

As I got to the stage, I got a glimpse of the singer. He was short, he was skinny, and he was nodding out against the mike stand. His mouth and fly were both wide open and his entire penis was just hanging out. And I mean hanging—basically, in front of my face. I had never seen a naked adult penis that close before. It looked much bigger than what I had ever felt through my clothes the few times I had actually made out.

At first it was kind of scary . . . but then again I had to admit May-ree had been right. If this was Johnny Whoever-he-was, he was kind of hot. As I leaned in for a closer look, I heard a yell. I reluctantly turned away to see May-ree fighting with the biggest, ugliest woman I had ever seen before in my life.

"Aw, c'mon baby," the woman said. "I wouldn't have worn a dress if I knew I was gonna see you tonight. Look what mama got for you."

Then she lifted her pink and black, satin-and-lace, Laverne-and-Shirley-looking prom dress to reveal . . . the second naked adult penis I had ever set my eyes on. May-ree yelled, "Get away from me faggot!" Then the whatever-it-was ripped off a long tangled blond wig and took off the biggest pair of Candies I had also ever seen.

"Who you calling faggot, faggot!" it yelled and then threw the shoes at us.

I didn't have time to be shocked. All I could process was that I had gone all the way to Manhattan just to have another person throw footwear at me. I tried to turn back to the stage where the still-exposed singer had now fallen over, but May-ree grabbed me by the hand and pulled me through the club back out into the street.

"Wait, my gloves. I lost my gloves!" I said.

"Fuck your gloves, you *wanta* get killed?" May-ree yelled from two steps ahead.

That's when I saw there were three of them chasing us now; three of the biggest, ugliest creatures I had ever seen, wearing ripped-up 1950s prom dresses and moth-eaten fur things, cursing and throwing their shoes. Luckily, one of them fell over a garbage can, and they gave up the chase to help their friend, still screaming, "Who you calling faggot, faggot!"

I took one last look behind me and saw the white awning above the door said CBGB OMFUG.

When we got back to the Bleecker Street station, I asked May-ree, "CeeBeeGeeBees? I thought the place we were going was Heat?"

"Yeah, well, I forgot where it was, so we went to CB's instead."

"Who was that?" I asked, meaning the passed-out-with-his-cock-out guy on the stage.

"What, you never saw a tranny before?"

"Huh?"

"You know, transvestites, he-shes, TVs. Fucking bunch of man-*huas*." She paused, then said, "You gotta get out of The Bronx more."

Actually, I never wanted to leave The Bronx ever again. When I got home, my mother was in the building lobby waiting for me. The train had been slow and I was over an hour late. She pushed me up the stairs.

"Do you know what time it is? Where have you been?"

"Hanging out with May-ree and a TV."

She took off her *chancleta* and swatted it at me. I didn't care. It was the truth. And the slipper at least was warm.

Years later, I was at a video club called The Cat Club with May-ree, who had become one of the few people from the park I was still friends with. She pointed to the screen and said, "Hey, Shell, doesn't that look like that girl in that club that night?"

I looked up expecting to see a tranny—they were no big deal to me anymore—hey, I had been to art school. Instead there was a much thinner, much blonder, much less hairy version of that non-ID-checking girl writhing on a boat in a canal wearing a wedding dress and fingerless gloves.

Perhaps it was the same girl who had complimented my home-made gloves (thanks Dad), at that club door years before. Maybe I unwittingly gave away the hottest trend of the 1980s on a cold winter night in 1978 in a club I thought was called Heat. I'll never really know for sure.

What I do know is that my mother would later find out she had been suffering that winter from the side effects of one of her latest meds and would not go through actual menopause for another five years. And maybe coincidentally and maybe not, but also after that winter, she now speeched only a few times a year.

In any case, I know she has saved the orange T-shirt with the lightning bolt for me for when my time of heat comes. I know that time is soon. . . . And sometimes, on a really chilly night . . . I can almost feel it.

28

THE POLITICS OF PANTIES

Dear Michele,

I just heard the news from your mother; finally, you have your first novio. Well mija. I have to tell you it is about time—seeing as you are almost eighteen. To be honest, I am surprised that you were even able to get a boyfriend in the first place, but then again I heard he was Irish. Pobrecita. I guess that was all you could get.

If you ask me, it is all your mother's fault. She is the one who left El Barrio. She is the one who brought you up with white people. She is the one who lets you listen to those Peter Floyds, Lead Zeppelins, and Black—coño mija–that is NOT musica. I just hope she is teaching you how to . . . please the boy; otherwise this novio . . . might be your last.

But I know your mother, and so I know she has taught you nada about nada. So if you don't want your toto to grow cobwebs and you die una jamona virgeña, listen to your Titi Ofelia. I know all about men—after all, I'm about to marry my fourth husband.

Now back in my day, a mujer was smart. She was selective. And she always followed these rules. First: Siempre vaya a bailar primero. (Always go dancing on the first date.) Hanging out in a schoolyard talking and drinking cerveza is no way to get to know a man. To find out if you are truly compatible with someone, you must get him to take you dancing so you can see how comfortable he is with his cuerpo. Because if a man is self-conscious, stepping all over you and apologizing when he is standing up . . . that is exactly how he is going to be when he is lying down.

Second: Nunca tenga sexo con alguien que no le gusta la comida. (Never have sex with anyone who doesn't like food.) After a man has passed the dance test, it's time to get him to buy you some dinners. And you make sure to watch him while he is eating. Because if he eats like un puerco, he'll most likely treat you the same way. If he eats the same thing all the time, your other activities will also lack variety . . . If you know what I mean. But if he eats with manners and pleasure and, better yet, offers to share his food with you—save the bizcocho for when you get home!

And last, but not least: Lavar sus panties cada noche. (Wash your panties every night.) You might be only fifteen, but it is nunca too early to learn that the way to get a ring on your finger is to put one through the man's nose. And mija, your panties are the exact weapon to do this. Men want to get in them. Women need to make them think they can. First, you let them see, pero no tocar. Breathe, but not taste. Touch, but not, well, you know. And you ALWAYS make sure your panties are clean, clean, clean because one day mija, and no mujer knows the hour, one day they WILL come off.

And you can tell your mother this from me, she who siempre goes on and on about how she married the only man who ever touched her—which by the way does explica a lot—but never mind. You tell your mother I said a mujer can be the Grand Canyon, the Holland Tunnel, and the Cross Bronx Expressway, but as long as you wash your panties in the shower every night, no one can ever call you a slut.

Well, I have to go now. Gilberto is calling me for some Sabado

Muy Gigante if you know what I mean. Oh, I forgot, you are just twelve. Never mind. The way you are going, you'll be lucky if you get "it" when you are twenty-five!

Con mucho amor,
Titi Ofelia

29

THE CLAM

Titi Ofelia, of course, didn't actually write me that letter. But she might as well have. She could never remember how old I was. She never could forget that my mother had only married once—to her first and only boyfriend. And she could not handle the truth, my truth: sex and the Puerto Rican? Not as hot as you might think.

According to all I had ever seen, read, and heard in movies, on TV, and in magazines, I was part of a culture that was naturally better at doing "it" than anyone else. My white girlfriends had Charlie's Angels as unattainable role models to make them feel inadequate. I had Charo. Every time I saw her work her coochie-coochie routine, it was clear that I, too, was expected to flounce around in Qiana lingerie cooing "*Ay mami, Ay papi*" to everyone I met. (Wonder Woman and Daisy Duke, the only other Latin or part Latin women on prime-time TV, would hide behind Anglicized last names for years.)

The message? As a Latin female, my role was to be the world's eternally hot-to-trot sex-machine stereotype. Always ready. Always available. Always thirty seconds from inducing or achieving a universe-destroying orgasm.

However, my family (with the notable exception of Titi Ofelia) from the very first day of my very first period had trained me to:

- Walk as if a dime were clenched between my butt cheeks— so my hips wouldn't betray me and get me pregnant.

- Never be alone in a car with a boy—or I would get pregnant.

- Never even tongue kiss—not even once—because that would most certainly get me pregnant.

And that . . . well, . . . that was a lot of mixed messages for a seventeen-year-old who was, actually, the last virgin in her crowd.

Maybe it was because you can't really flounce in the rock concert T-shirts, jeans, and Lil' Abner work boots I usually wore as opposed to dresses that were short, red, and tight. Or maybe it was because I spent more time drawing cartoons than putting on makeup. Or maybe it was because what goes on between consenting adults stays behind closed doors and what does or doesn't go on among teenagers gets displayed for all to see.

One sharp autumn evening I walked into the park and saw spray painted on the handball court wall in blue letters two feet high: "Shell Is The Clam." I could not deny the cutting brilliance of the play on words with my nickname. I also could not deny the humiliation that went from the catch in my throat, traveling deep down to the place where no man had gone before. I had actually expected and dreaded seeing this public confirmation of my carnal inexperience. What I did not expect was that the truth would hurt so much.

It was true. I was St. Peter's Park's one and only Clam. Everyone else I knew over the age of fifteen had done "it," except me. In the immortal words of my friend Janey-the-Waste, "Yeah, so, I got down with Jackie—what the fuck."

In my crowd you skipped second and third bases and went straight from making out to the Eastern Women's Center in Queens Plaza for your abortion. How many times had I cut school to be there with a girlfriend and held her hair while she puked outside afterward? How many times did I help someone come up with the lie we were going to tell her mother this time? I never saw

anyone's boyfriend at the clinic. Ever. That, more than any admoni-
tion I had received, made me decide I was not going to be pregnant.
Ever. So . . . that meant that after years of random make outs I had
never had a real boyfriend. Because to have a real boyfriend, you had
to "get down." You had to do "it."

Proof of Titi Ofelia's womanhood could be found on the fourth
finger of her left hand. Proof in my neighborhood was found around
a girl's neck. Not hickeys—even I occasionally had those—but by
an ankle bracelet worn as a necklace, a symbol as irrefutable as the
wedding-night sheets paraded through the villages of my friends'
Irish and Italian ancestors. Yellow gold with a single heart was good.
White gold with double hearts was better. Diamond chips, pearls,
and engraving was the best and most expensive of them all, which
meant the boy definitely loved not only you but also the way you got
down—a lot. Like the single earring a lot of boys now wore in their
left ears, an ankle bracelet was evidence you had left childhood behind
forever. But around my neck I wore a small silver cross shaped like two
nails, to bear witness that I was *una jamona virgeña*, a virgin spinster.

One spring morning, I met Brendan "the Burnout" Reilly. Brendan was not from my park, but from 192 Schoolyard up in Throgs
Neck. I knew him from school, or rather from outside of school where
he hung out every morning, from seven-thirty till homeroom, next to
the phone booths in front of the diner across the street, occasionally
selling the loose joints we called "bones" and the mild, peach-col-
ored, triangle-shaped amphetamines we called "peaches."

Brendan was the kind of boy that everyone liked but also the
kind everyone made fun of because he was a little goofy. Rumor
had it that he had done acid every day for an entire month—orange,
double-barrel sunshine no less. Plus, he'd do things like sing the entire *Yessongs* album from start to finish for no reason—hence, Brendan the Burnout. I had copped weed from him from time to time, but
never paid him much attention until the day he asked if I could draw
him something.

That morning before first period, I had bought a bone and started
to cross the street when I heard him call out, "Hey Shell! You're the

one who draws, right? Can you make me a Zofo? I saw the tattoo
you made for Gizmo and the jacket you painted for Tommy. They're
out-fucking-rageous."

I had drawn a naked girl with a top hat and a rose in her teeth
for Gizmo and painted a space fish from Yes's *Tales from Topographic
Oceans* album for Tommy. Both were my crowning achievements at
the time, and I had gotten five dollars each for them. I turned around.
The Burner was actually pretty cute: tall, six feet three inches or so,
and slim, with long blond bangs that hid his eyes. His bangs had
gotten messed up from him running after me, which revealed round
blue eyes made even rounder by extremely dilated pupils.

"Okay. When?"

"Uh, today is good. You wanna cut out and go to my house? No
one's home . . . I have windowpane."

We went to his house on Hollywood Avenue and took the acid,
and I drew the Zofo symbols from *Led Zeppelin IV* on looseleaf paper
for hours until I got them right. When I was done he kissed me. A half
hour later, when I nervously asked him to stop, he did the unimagi-
nable. "Okay," he said. "Do you wanna go to Louie's and get pizza?"
I couldn't believe he just—stopped.

With every other boy, my chastity was what caused our immediate and complete breakup, but Brendan didn't try to seduce me the
next day or the next or even the next. Finally, I got the courage to tell
him I was *una jamona virgeña*. I was sure that he'd tell me to get bent
and that would be the end of us, but he just said, "That's cool. I can
wait."

I was shocked, . . . even though Brendan came from 192, everyone knew he had done "it" with Laura Borelli, one of the strange
girls who wore too much black eyeliner and hung out by the monu-
ment shop, across from St. Raymond's Cemetery. People said those
kids climbed the fences at night and tripped (ingested psychedel-
ics, not stumbled, although they may have done that as well) among
the tombstones. And not even I, who'd spent my childhood catching
bugs in St. Peter's Church's small graveyard and who was known for
saying "I'll try anything twice," would dare to do that. Those same

people told me the "it" had even been done in the cemetery . . . at midnight. But Brendan had to be home by 1:00 A.M. on the weekends, 10:00 P.M. on a school night, so I wasn't sure if that was true. I mean sex took a long time, didn't it?

Yeah, Brendan was definitely not like any other boy I had ever been with before. But I liked hanging out with him. And I was relieved the pressure was off, . . . but for how long?

From that day of Zofo on, the Burner and Shell were ham and eggs, peanut butter and chocolate, Acapulco Gold and Strawberry E-Z Wider. School nights we'd drink beer, hang out, talk, talk, talk (which would have made Titi Ofelia toss her panties in despair), and then go home and talk on the phone some more. Weekends, we'd ride around in his van singing every eighteen minute prog rock tune you can think of (plus some you have mercifully blocked out), or we'd split a tab of blotter and draw (which not even my mother could claim would get you pregnant).

One long Saturday, we did chocolate mescaline and lay in his bed fully clothed for hours, kissing, stroking each other's hair, and sucking on each other's necks while listening to *Led Zeppelin III* over and over till our mouths were dry and our necks were bruised meat. Instead of a prom that June, kids from every hangout from St. Peter's Park to Zappa's Corner to Edgewater celebrated Lehman High School's graduating class of 1978 by going to Orchard Beach for an antiprom tripping party (only straight kids and the disco-loving, platform-wearing Hollywoods from Loreto and Waterbury Parks went to the actual prom). Brendan and I did purple mescaline and ran singing through the woods behind the parking lots until people started pouring beer on us to make us stop. A week later I wore a black and blue flowered satin cowl-neck dress my mother had gotten me from Bonwit Teller, and I stepped into Lehman High School for what I thought would be the last time.

In July, Brendan and I had our three-month anniversary and I turned eighteen. I'd never been with a boy so long before. We were so inseparable that I was almost convinced we didn't need to have actual sex. But more often than not, it was Brendan who was the one to make us stop, and I'd lie there in silence while he finished. Sometimes I watched. Most times I didn't. He never made me feel guilty about it. Our clothes never came off. We never crossed the make-out line.

I knew what Brendan and I were or weren't doing, but once the summer was over, I noticed the boys in my park throwing Brendan slimy looks of approval whenever he drove down to pick me up. They who had never gotten any more than tongue from me were now giving the Burner respect for the first time in his life. They'd punch his shoulder or clap him on his back, and Brendan would just smile and duck his head, happy for the attention.

And why not? We had been going together since May, and they all naturally assumed *the Burner had opened the Clam.* All that was missing was the proof.

My girlfriends knew better. When I finally confessed to Nikki, Janey, and Dawn we hadn't yet done it, they looked at my neck with the same look of disgust my mother had that morning when she saw I had a fresh hickey. "You don't have an ankle bracelet? You've been together six months, and you haven't gotten down yet? What are you waiting for Shell—you're eighteen, you gotta do it before it dries out. Besides, you're Spanish. Aren't you *supposed* to do it?"

The night came when I walked into the park and saw the writing on the handball court wall. Brendan and I were supposed to go see *Halloween,* but I turned around and ran straight home. It was bad enough when a girl was called a whore, or as the linguistically challenged wrote, *hua, hoe,* or *whoa.* But for the world to know that after having a boyfriend all this time and not having done it was almost worse. I was afraid of what would happen when Brendan found out.

That next evening Brendan and I did go to see *Halloween.* He picked me up at my house instead of at the park, where we usually always met. He doubled around the block and drove past there on the way to the movie, which was kind of out of the way, and as we passed it I saw the bottom half of the handball court wall had been painted over in black. I looked at Brendan, but he stared straight ahead. It was the first time we had ever driven anywhere in silence.

At the movie, I cringed every time Jamie Lee Curtis so obviously didn't get killed because she was the movie's one and only *jamona virgeña,* and I wouldn't let Brendan make out with me at all, not even after we went to sit in the very back row and opened a bottle of Yago. On the way home he popped in an eight-track, but I still didn't feel like singing. He rolled down the window and tried anyway.

"Long distance . . . runaround . . ."

I rolled the window back up. It wasn't summer anymore; it was October. It was starting to get cold.

When we got to my house, he spoke.

"I saw what they wrote. That sucked."

"Yeah."

"It's gone now."

Then he handed me a box.

"Uh . . . I know it's not Christmas yet but . . . uh . . . here." He ducked his head, his long blond bangs, as always, covering his face.

I opened the box. Inside was a silver wishbone on a silver chain. I drew a breath. It wasn't what I wanted. What I wanted was a white gold ankle bracelet with double hearts, diamond chips, and black-and-white pearls. It was the ultimate, *Sabado Muy Gigante,* crotch-less-panty motherlode of all ankle bracelets—the ankle bracelet that said you got down forward, backwards, and sideways, even though I hardly deserved one. I hadn't earned it.

He fiddled with the cross hanging from his left ear. "It's a wish-bone. It's for us. A wish. And you don't have to get down with me right now if you don't want to. I just wanted to give you some-thing."

I really liked Brendan. More than I had ever liked any other boy. Being with him made me feel like I belonged to someone in a way that for the first time was completely mine and mine alone. If I was going to get down with anyone, it would be him.

For my actual Christmas present, he got us tickets to see Aero-smith at Madison Square Garden. We did some purple THC, and he also bought us matching T-shirts. It was a great concert.

It was now a new year. And Brendan was still waiting.

30

EZ EDDIE

February 1979. The Bronx had burned. Now it was my turn.

By now I knew that Latin men were most women's fantasies. I had also lived with Latin men my entire life. I heard them yell. I saw them eat. I watched them scratch. I wanted something different. And I got it: a tall, blond Irish boy named Brendan "the Burnout" Reilly. We had been going out for almost a year and even Titi Ofelia had to admit, "Well, at least she got something." As Brendan's girlfriend, I knew who I was, better than I ever had before, and that was almost enough. I was almost happy . . . until I met EZ Eddie Torres.

One warmish mid-winter night I had gone to hang out with Brendan at 192 Schoolyard and saw a boy I hadn't seen before talking with our friends Billy and Renée. He was leaning against the chain-link fence, smoking a bone, and drinking a Champale. I dropped Brendan's hand and stared. For the first time in my life I felt a quickening, a twinge of liquid heat between my thighs, a signal I had not yet felt with Brendan or ever before.

He was Brendan's exact physical opposite: short, maybe five feet six inches, and solid in build, with honey-colored skin just like Titi Ofelia and almond-shaped dark brown eyes.

There were only the five of us hanging out that night, and we all sat in a circle and talked. A six-pack and a couple of bones later, I found out the new boy's name was EZ Eddie, and his family had moved up from Miramar, Florida, that January. I knew where Miramar was. It was close to the South Florida towns where most of my father's family lived.

I had a vision of the two of us making out naked on a white sand beach and staring into each other's eyes, but I just told him that I had been to Miramar.

He laughed and asked, "Why?"

Something in his voice made me think that maybe, just maybe, he might be Latin like I was, but I who would usually say anything to anyone at any time was somehow hesitant to ask him directly. I was afraid to know the truth.

Brendan and Billy went to get more beer and Renée asked what I couldn't: where he was from. Eddie laughed and said his real name was Eddie Torres and he was half Irish . . . and half Cuban . . . and he had been out of the sun for so long, he was definitely looking more Irish. I just stared.

Someone that fine had to have a girlfriend, and I was sure someone would come in any minute and claim her territory. The only people to come back to the schoolyard though were Brendan and Billy, and by the time we finished the second six-pack, I learned he wasn't seeing anyone. As far as I was concerned, that was it.

Brendan drove me home that night and we both sang out the window, but for totally different reasons. He sang because, well, that's what the Burner did. I sang because for the first time in my life I had looked at a Latin male and wanted to see him naked. It didn't matter that he wore a Members Only jacket and five scraggly hairs on his chin. For the first time in my life, I was in lust, I was in love—with Eddie. It was perfect except for one thing: my boyfriend.

A boyfriend whom, after almost a year together, I still had not had sex with. A boyfriend who stopped our marathon make-out sessions only when he could take it no longer—and then took care of himself and never ever made me feel stupid about it. Sweet, goofy Brendan who I drew cartoons with, got stoned with, listened to music with, had fun with, and felt as comfortable with as my own skin.

Suddenly, I who always had preferred my park and friends to his now made excuses to hang out at 192 Schoolyard. I even started go-ing there when I knew Brendan wasn't, walking forty minutes from my house each way on the chance Eddie would be there.

I heard Eddie liked Led Zeppelin, so I did what I did best: I took a couple of Brendan's peaches and stayed up all night painting the cover of *Zeppelin IV* on the back of my dungaree jacket, including all the runes. I wore it out even though it was thirty-eight degrees and raining, only to hear Eddie say that Zeppelin now sucked and the Clash ruled. The Clash? Who the hell were they? I went to the Westchester Square headshop/record store looking for their album, but they didn't have it. I even tried drinking Champale, but it just made me puke. You don't understand. I was getting desperate. Be-cause everywhere I looked, I saw EZ Eddie.

I saw EZ Eddie when I was making out with Brendan every day. I saw EZ Eddie when I lay with my legs spread under the bathtub faucet every night and when my bearded Titi Carmen dragged me to church because in my crazed teenage lust I forgot to lock the bath-room door the night I stayed over at her house. I looked up at Pastor Ramirez and saw EZ Eddie. But EZ Eddie didn't notice me. And then one day, he did.

It was at Nikki Boom-Boom's and my very belated graduation/ St. Patrick's Day party at Nikki's house. We both had to repeat half our senior years at Lehman High School and didn't receive our "of-ficial" diplomas until that January. Her boyfriend Tommy Piss Clam had just given her a redone ankle bracelet, adding a row of black dia-monds, when Eddie walked over to me and asked me for a light.

A light! My hand trembled as I lit the match, and he said, "I heard you're Puerto Rican. That true?"

"Si. Uh, yeah, my mom is from Corozal and my dad is from Cabo Rojo. But I was born here."

"I can tell. Me too. My old man's from Havana though. We just moved here."

"Yeah, I know, from Miramar."

"Yeah. How'd you know?"

"You said, that first night we met."

"Really? When was that?"

Before I could answer with the exact day, hour, and minute, he said, "Hey, you like Salsa dancing?"

"Uh . . . sure. Yeah. Of course."

"I go to this little place down in Spanish Harlem every Monday. Wanna meet me there? We should go. You and me, we're the only blood around. And hey, you don't have to be nervous; it's just me, EZ Eddie."

That's when I noticed my hand was still shaking. Oh my God! He asked me to go dancing. On a Monday night! Never mind that I had met him just a couple of weeks before and had barely spoken to him. Never mind that I had never danced Salsa before in my life. Never mind . . . that I already had a boyfriend.

I spent the week trying on everything in my closet, but rock concert T-shirts and Lil' Abner work boots were for hanging out in schoolyards drinking *cerveza,* not going dancing with *un hombre,* a man. Titi Ofelia would have been proud of me . . . if I had told her. But not just yet. I closed my eyes and imagined the look on her face, on all my family's faces when I told them I was EZ Eddie Torres's girlfriend. Going out with him would at long last make up for every bad thing that had ever happened to me. Every time I had been called spic or Speck, spit on, beaten up or stabbed, yelled at, and dismissed or ignored would then be erased forever.

None of my girlfriends had anything appropriate for a night of Salsa dancing. And could I trust them? Really trust them? I wasn't afraid that Nikki, Dawn, or May-ree would betray me. I was afraid they would talk me out of it. They all had grown to love Brendan. Nikki and May-ree would even mock fight over which one of them would eventually be my maid of honor. I would have to do this all alone, like a mature, grown-up woman: a *mujer.*

In desperation I tried on the black and blue dress I wore to what I thought had been my high school graduation that past June. After nearly a year of every night munchies, I had gotten a little chunky again and had to rig safety pins to the dress's back zipper in an effort to close the inch-wide gap along it and my back. Maybe Eddie wouldn't notice. In the middle of all this, Brendan called and I was immediately struck by a sneezing fit. He said I sounded like I was getting sick.

Sick? Here I was being transformed by true love for the first time in my life, and my boyfriend thought I was sick? It was a sign. After all, weren't EZ Eddie and I the only Latin kids in our part of The Bronx? I knew, with all the conviction of my eighteen years on the planet, that if only I could make EZ Eddie my boyfriend, everyone would know that at last I was a true Latina and my life would have peace.

We met at a storefront club on 106th Street in Spanish Harlem; I didn't want him to pick me up, just in case anyone from the neighborhood saw us. As I got off the subway at 103rd Street, I realized that I had never been in my parents' old neighborhood as an adult by myself before. It was only fitting that I was returning to claim my one and only True Latin Love.

Instead of walking into an illegal social club that night I saw a starlit realm that I imagined to be the Rainbow Room, *Saturday Night Fever*, and CBGB all rolled into one. Eddie saw me right away, took my arm, and steered me right to the bar where he bought me an Amaretto Sour, a love nectar. Another sign. When that sign had been drained dry, he bought me another and another and still another. Finally, Eddie took me by the hand and led me to the dance floor. "Sure you can handle this?" he asked. "This ain't no punk rock, you know."

The sight of EZ Eddie in his Le Tigre shirt drove me wild, and I couldn't wait to show him all my moves, which after four drinks on an empty stomach were the kick to the shins, the elbow to the neck, and the ass on the floor. But I didn't care, I was with EZ Eddie. And when he finally gave up and led me to a sofa, all I could think was that he was going to kiss me and I was going to die!

I had a flashback of Brendan's and my six-month anniversary. It was a chilly November afternoon where he led me into his room, and I found a rose on the bed, a bottle of Mateus on the nightstand, and Led Zeppelin's "Since I've Been Loving You" playing on the stereo. Speaking of flashbacks, there was the time I took a hit of acid that was just plain bad—way too speedy—and I had my one and only really bad trip, but Brendan didn't let me freak out. Even though he'd taken twice as much as I did, he talked to me and made me drink water until I came down.

I shook all that off. That was puppy love. This, now, was real. And when Eddie kissed me, all thoughts of Brendan vaporized, just like the TVs, VCRs, and boom boxes from the stores on Fordham Road had during the 1977 blackout.

After the kiss, I felt a gush of heat like the night in the schoolyard, only now in a more urgent way. It felt like my insides were going to melt, the way it did when I touched myself. Brendan never kissed me like that. Brendan didn't make me feel like that. Who was Brendan anyway? I made up for my shortcomings as a dancer with what I knew was my superior make-out ability.

Even when one of the safety pins I had rigged my dress with broke open and stabbed Eddie in the hand, I took his squeal of pain as another sign. A sign that EZ Eddie and I were destined to be 192 Schoolyard's power couple, its one and only Latin King and Queen. It was destiny. It was Kismet. It would be forever.

A half hour later when we got to the point where Brendan would always stop, Eddie stopped too.

"Come on. I'll drive you home."

Eddie had a car too? Life was just too perfect.

Instead of driving me home, he drove to the parking lot at Orchard Beach. Oh, he wants to make out some more, I thought. Cool.

We got into the backseat, shared a bone, and started making out again. This time was different. He pulled up my dress and put his hand down the waistband of my pantyhose, something Brendan had never done before. I pushed him away.

"What's the matter? You don't have to be nervous. It's just me, EZ Eddie."

We started making out again, and I let his hand move around down there. I really didn't like it. It didn't feel like my fingers did. This felt scratchy and burny and . . . just plain wrong. The rising volcano that had been inside me sputtered and went out. I dismissed it.

No, this is it. I thought, "I'm finally going to get down with someone and it's going to be Eddie and we're going to go out and he's gonna buy me an ankle bracelet and I'm gonna wear it and then he'll come to all my Titi's houses with me and then . . ."

"*Mami, dime. Dime que me quieres. Tocarme bicho.*"

"What?"

"Tell me you want me. Touch my dick. . . . Ow! Not like that!"

"Umm . . . Okay . . . yeah, Papi. Oh Papi. Si Papi. *Que . . . Que . . .*"

Eddie took his hand out of my underwear. I could smell myself, which both frightened and aroused me. I couldn't wait for what I was sure was going to happen next. Instead, it was Eddie who sat up.

"*Que* nothing. You don't even speak Spanish right. Oh, what the hell."

Eddie straddled me and in one motion tried to take my panty-hose and panties—the weapon by which I was supposed to control men—off. I froze. I think I said, "No!"

Eddie sat up again.

"Are you a fucking virgin? You are a fucking virgin aren't you? You know something? You're full of shit. You're worse than these white girls—you're a fake. Forget it."

He pulled up his pants, climbed into the front seat, and pulled out of the parking lot.

"And you're lucky I'm a nice guy, because otherwise, I'd make you blow me. And then I'd make you walk home."

On that horrible ride home. I stayed in the backseat trying to put myself back together and realized the truth. Eddie didn't like me because I could draw or because we liked the same music or because we got high and had fun together—or even because I was Latin like he was. He didn't like me at all. Eddie never liked me. He just wanted to fuck. And what was now churning my stomach and threatening to explode from my eyes was that I had to admit I had wanted to fuck too. Except I had wanted to fuck my boyfriend.

We drove back to my building without another word. He stopped barely long enough to let me out . . . and then he burned rubber up Westchester Avenue. I don't remember walking up the five flights to the apartment, going inside, or getting into bed. Kevin tapped on the false wall.

"Michele, what's wrong?"

"Eat shit and die!"

The next morning I skipped work, and my mother reminded me yet again how I was out of high school now, and if I wasn't going to go to college, I had to work. I didn't tell her what I'd told my brother. I just stayed in bed and cried.

The next day, Renée, my girlfriend from 192, called to tell me Eddie had been going around saying I had given him a blow job. A blow job! That was a "blow" from which your reputation could never recover. It was fine to get down—with every boy you went out with too. That was normal. But to have it known you sucked a boy's dick? In the immortal words of Janey-the-Waste, "That's not necessary. Any girl who does that is a filthy *hua*."

There was no way that lie could make it down to my park. If they'd written that I was "The Clam" on the handball court, what wouldn't they write now? Big Lisa couldn't hang out anymore because someone had written on the handball court that she and Joanie Burns from 119 Park were the Grand Canyon and the Holland Tunnel.

I would never be able to show my face anywhere ever again. What was I supposed to do? It wasn't as if I could just go and make new friends. I was out of high school now. I forced myself to get out of bed, get dressed, and go to 192—for what, I was not yet sure. I just knew I had to.

I walked into the schoolyard, and there was EZ Eddie drinking that fucking awful pisswater Champale, talking with a group of kids, smirking. On the other side, was Brendan, sitting against the fence alone, his bangs in his eyes, drinking a big bottle of that equally fucking awful too-sweet-and-nasty Mateus. I walked up to Eddie, shaking, just like the night I had lit a cigarette for him at Nikki's house two weeks and a lifetime ago.

"I didn't blow you and you know it. Did I? DID I?"

Eddie was surprisingly speechless. Everyone stared. Even though it was that last cold night before the spring really kicked in—about thirty degrees—I could feel my entire body flame on but now in an entirely different way. Somehow, my shame had given me power. Instead of using my panties as a weapon, I used words.

"Why don't you tell them the truth? You couldn't even get it up. And you know why? Because it's . . . SMALL! Get BENT!"

I threw my lit cigarette at him. Eddie yelled something at me, but I didn't care. That was the easy part and it was done. Now I had to make it right somehow with Brendan.

I looked over where he was sitting and saw he had heard the whole thing. He smashed the Mateus bottle against the concrete where it shattered into a thousand glittering pieces. He rose slowly, wobbling just a little, and stood among the cold shards of glass for a moment. He turned and walked out of the schoolyard and I followed.

"Don't follow me, I'm going home," he said.

"No, wait," I pleaded.

"What, Shell?" He turned and whispered, "What?"

I stood there with the wind howling down Hollywood Avenue and told Brendan everything about that awful night. How Eddie and I didn't get down, even though, yes, I had wanted to, and how I now knew it was a horrible mistake. I told him everything, . . . everything except my delusion that having sex with Eddie would have somehow made up for the way I was to my family, the way I was to myself. That final humiliation had to remain mine and mine alone. At last, I begged him to go back with me.

"I don't know. I have to think about it."

I cried. But I understood. I had publicly disrespected him. He had been with me for almost a year and never cheated (which by the unspoken schoolyard rule was the boy's right while he was waiting for the girl to make up her mind), only to have me get down with someone else. And even though I didn't, I might as well have.

Three days went by. Three days in which I threw up, had diarrhea, listened to *Led Zeppelin III* over and over, and screamed at my family every time they tried to find out what was the matter . . . until they finally gave up and let me alone.

Each day I locked myself in the bathroom, smoked cigarettes

out of the window, and cried for hours. I looked in the mirror. Even though my face hadn't changed, I had. I had been innocent. And even though I was still technically a virgin, I wasn't innocent anymore. Finally, Brendan called me from the pay phone on the corner and told me to come downstairs.

"We can go back, but on one condition. We have to do it."

We went to Orchard Beach that night—to the same woods where the Great Tripping Antiprom had been the summer before. He spread out a quilt, rolled out a sleeping bag, and twisted the cap off a bottle of Little Rhine Bear, the cheap Leibfraumilch that was one step above Mateus—and my favorite. And The Burner and The Clam Finally Did It.

It hurt. A lot. But I have to give Brendan credit. Even after everything that happened, he was patient and gentle for the two hours I cried and clenched until it finally happened. Three minutes later, after it was done, he kissed me.

"I love ya, Shell. Didn't you know?" He stroked my hair for a minute or two and fell asleep.

I lay there in his arms, and despite the sleeping bag and the quilt, Orchard Beach was itching me. Except for the sand, I had felt nothing; but soon that would change. Brendan, being Brendan, was just as patient and gentle as he had always been for the entire month it took for me finally to realize, "Ah-ha! So this is Why People Do It." It would be another month before I understood that what people said about boys with big hands and big feet—like Brendan—was all too true, and that the not-so-sad truth was, Eddie *was* small.

Life went back to the way it had been before, . . . kind of. Titi Ofelia had been right after all: Brendan was all I could get. Maybe I wasn't good enough, hot enough, Latin enough to get the boy who made me melt, who drove me mad, and who made me almost throw everything away for just one night, but I did get my best friend back. My sweet Burner, who sang to me, knew what I liked to drink, stroked my hair, and told me he loved me.

That night on Orchard Beach, before I, too, fell asleep I thought, "Maybe it is going to be okay. Maybe this will be enough."

31

ESCAPE FROM 192 SCHOOLYARD
To Be Good Is Not Enough When You Dream of Being Great

"You have to do it, Shell," Renée said. "You have to find a way."

She glanced over to where her new ex-boyfriend, Billy, was talking to my still-boyfriend, Brendan—both of whom, incidentally, were pretending not to look at the two of us. Renée continued, "I might even have stayed with Billy, except . . . well, . . . you know why. See ya." And she walked out of the schoolyard. She wouldn't be back. She'd be going to SVA, the School of Visual Arts, soon.

I, too, had wanted to be an artist more than anything. I, too, had once dreamed of going to art school. I was afraid that for me, it was too late.

Ever since I could remember, the way I coped—with uncertainty, with frustration, with disappointment, with fear, and with shame—was to draw. Even now that getting high had become my other escape, I still drew. If something wasn't going right with a drawing, I could always just erase it and start over. If after a couple of tries it still wasn't working, I'd just rip the whole thing up and be done with it.

How many times had I put all my fury into rending, tearing, destroying, and obliterating a botched drawing and then calmly started over. How many times had I wished I could do that with my life? For the last year or two I had seen the posters Paul Davis drew for SVA. They were up and down the entire number 6 line. There was one with a Pagliacci-type clown, which said, "To Be Good Is Not Enough

When You Dream of Being Great." And there was another one of a man stuck behind an iron grating that said, "Paul Gauguin Worked for a Bank Until He Was 35. It's Never Too Late." They were beautiful posters, but seeing them always made me feel worse than sad, more like I had forever missed out on my one chance in life.

I hadn't been able to go to A&D because I had the mumps the day of the test, and I didn't go to college right after high school. In fact, I had barely gotten out of high school at all, although it wasn't entirely Brendan's fault I spent the last half of my senior year tripping, listening to music, making out, and just not going to school.

At what I thought was my graduation that June, I wasn't allowed to get my diploma, even though I'd taken all my Regents (New York State exams) over the years and qualified for a Regents Diploma. I had somehow passed five tests: Algebra, Science, English, Social Studies, and Spanish (yes, I took Spanish all through high school and finally—or mostly—understood it, although I still had trouble speaking the language). I hadn't taken the SATs though and had no guidance from any guidance counselors. Their efforts of course went to the kids who showed up for their appointments—straight.

My mother and father both had to go in and talk with the deans, but I had missed too many days. I had to go back for an extra six months and make up six credits, getting my diploma for real the following January. Brendan, who was in a similar situation, just dropped out.

That January I had also found a job . . . at a brokerage company at the end of Wall Street, where Dawn worked, and where you could see, hear, and smell the endless construction of what would soon be the nearby South Street Seaport. Nikki would soon join us there also. Janey's mode of employment was still drugs.

It was a repetitious, mind-numbing, soul-crushing, back-office, clerical job that paid $83.79 a week. My life was at a standstill. All I did was go to work, hang out with Brendan at either St. Peter's Park or 192 Schoolyard, and get high.

And all I was drawing now were tattoos for people who'd pay me $5 or $10 for one, depending on the size. Tattoos were still illegal in New York City, so everyone went to Big Joe's in Mount Vernon. Big Joe liked my work and sent word I could come and get a free tattoo from his flash wall (a predesigned tattoo as opposed to an original design) anytime I wanted. I went up there one Saturday with Nikki, with the idea of getting the *Led Zeppelin IV* Zofo symbols on my stomach. Nikki went first, and as she was getting a purple butterfly (on her shoulder blade), she screeched in pain, which made me decide to forget it. I never did get a tattoo.

Every time Brendan and I would come home from yet another concert or a Laserium, I'd see those posters on the train and just cry and cry—on the inside. The longing and the frustration was even worse than my misguided crush on EZ Eddie—who thankfully no longer was at 192—after our little scene, he had gone "Hollywood" with the disco-loving Waterbury Park crowd whose idea of a good time was to go dancing at the Stereo Lounge in Westchester Square or Frankie & Johnny's in New Rochelle. Barf. But my life was really no better.

Brendan and I had been spending a lot of time with Billy Devlin and his girlfriend Renée, who had been my friend throughout the entire EZ Eddie scandal. We hung out together a lot, but I had never thought of Renée as a close friend, just the girlfriend of Brendan's friend, if you know what I mean.

Renée liked taking pictures and carried a Canon camera with her everywhere. We had often all gone camping together, and she would take pictures of spiders in their webs, the insides of broken trees, and dead animals we found run over on the highway.

One day in the midst of my EZ Eddie mania, she took all those photographs to SVA—and she got in. When she told me, I told her my secret that I wanted to go there too but had no idea how. She said I had to try for it. Just knowing she was going there had changed her life.

A month later Renée took me aside again and told me she had broken up with Billy. She said she might have tried to stay with him, except he told her he had been punching holes in the condoms so she would get pregnant and not go to SVA. The messed-up thing was, she *had* gotten pregnant, but she did not say a word. She just went to the Eastern Women's Center by herself because "Nothing is going to stop me from being an artist. NOTHING." The way her voice changed when she said Billy's name just froze me. It was a venom I chillingly recognized but had never heard before from someone who was not my mother. Like the hand that rose from the swamp at the beginning of every Saturday afternoon *Chiller Theater* episode, that conversation sparked something in me that had been dormant for too long.

But that summer, my father had suddenly and unexpectedly lost his job when the construction company where he worked closed shop overnight, and my family had to go on welfare (we would remain on it for the next two-and-a-half years). And when I found out how much going to SVA would cost—$75 a credit, or $1,000 a semester—I panicked. My $83.79 a week didn't go far even if I was still living at home. I had to give up my dream.

I did look up another two art schools I thought I could get into. They were Cooper Union, which was free and F.I.T., the Fashion Institute of Technology, which was cheap. City colleges, which had been free for years had started charging tuition a couple of years before, but they were still much much cheaper than $1,000 a semester.

I told Brendan of my new life plan on the way upstate camping. He said, "Whatever you want to do, Shell. I can't stop you, can I?"

It sucked not to have support from my boyfriend, but it was worse not to have it from my family. When I told them I was going to quit my job to go to art school, my father said that no daughter of his was going to be a Dirty Bohemian. I kind of expected he'd say that since he hadn't wanted me to go to A&D either. But that had been six years ago, and what happened then? I ended up at Lehman where I basically got beat up and took drugs. I was nineteen now. Things were going to be different this time.

In September Renée took me to Pearl Paint, which I remembered from my graffiti days as heaven on earth. Still, $25 or even $15 for a real artist's portfolio was way over my budget. I couldn't ask my parents for money. There wasn't any. I couldn't ask any of the *titis* either, that would have shamed my parents and I knew not to open that door.

But by the beginning of the new year, I had put together what I thought were my best drawings, cartoons, tattoos, and fashion designs and applied to both Cooper Union and F.I.T. for the Fall 1980 term.

Both attempts were a disaster. I totally failed the test for Cooper Union. My literal little brain just could not grasp the concept of drawing an empty room—among other tasks—so I walked out halfway through, cursing them and myself.

At F.I.T. I thought I had aced the interview, but when I brought my manila envelope out, the interviewer gave me such a condescending look that had she done so in my neighborhood she would have gotten the hell beaten out of her. She told me I would never be an artist, but if I "felt the need to continue my education," had I heard about the Katharine Gibbs School for secretarial training?

I was crushed. When I told Brendan, he hugged me, said he was sorry, got us some mescaline, and took us for a wild weekend at Hunter Mountain with our new hangout couple. Now that Billy and Renée had broken up, we went places with Brendan's dealer Petey "Rat" Basile and his girlfriend. When we got back, I decided I had to try just one more time.

I finally did what I probably should have from the beginning: I called the SVA admissions office and asked them what I had to do to go there. They were very patient and nice. They told me that since I had not taken the SATs, I had to get into another college with an art program for a year and then they could consider me as a transfer student. They recommended New York City Community College, in Brooklyn, which had a two-year art program. Their application deadline was very soon.

I was thrilled to have a second chance. When I told my family, my father just said I was nineteen and was not a kid anymore and had better shape up.

I listened to him. I shaped up by staying home and drawing every night after work instead of hanging out. I applied to New York City Community College right under the wire for the fall semester and got in. That September I started a new routine of getting up at seven each morning for the hour-and-a-half subway ride to Brooklyn, getting home twelve to fourteen hours later.

The teachers were very understanding when I told them of my dream and did everything they could to help me with my SVA application and interview, which, they told me could happen the next February if I wanted. If I wanted? Finally, someone else saw what I thought I had, and it gave me hope. When I told Brendan, he asked if we were going to be like Billy and Renée. I had to tell the truth. I didn't know.

We started going camping a lot more that fall—almost every weekend—and then one night Rat Basile told me that Brendan had been trying to sabotage me the same way Billy had done with Renée. That he had heard Billy tell Brendan, "If you let her go to that school, you'll lose her." Rat felt he had to tell me. He liked my drawings and thought it wasn't right for Brendan to do that, although if it had been his girlfriend, he said, he probably would have done the same. I don't think I'd ever met anyone with a more fitting nickname.

And then—I was late. I'm sure you know, or can guess why.

I thought about what it would be like to have an abortion. I'd have to go to the Eastern Women's Center by myself, just like Renée had. If I told my mother, she'd either throw me out of the house or start speeching back up again. I couldn't take that. I didn't want any of my girlfriends to know. They all thought Brendan and I were perfect together, and they wouldn't have understood. And there are some things a girl just doesn't share with her father. I thought about what it would be like if I married Brendan. And I realized if I didn't go to hell for having an abortion, I would certainly be in hell on earth if we got married.

But before I could make any final decision, I woke up suddenly, in the middle of the night, with the worst cramps and bleeding I had ever had. I made my way to the bathroom, where I stayed for most of the night, then went back to bed, afraid if I went to sleep, I would die. The next morning I skipped work and went to Planned Parenthood. I wasn't pregnant. It was just a late, bad period, but they examined me to make sure. After the exam, I asked them to put me on the Pill, which I would stay on, with very few breaks, for the next twenty-five years.

On New Year's Eve I decided to break up with Brendan. I waited until his twenty-first birthday had passed, because I didn't want to ruin it. I think he knew it was coming. Soon afterward was my SVA interview. At the interview I ran into Pasha, a boy from New York City Community College who was in the same art program as I was. We were school friends—and I had always been attracted to him.

Pasha was from Jackson Heights in Queens, had been born in Russia, and had come to the United States as a child. He was tall, though not as tall as Brendan, with sandy brown hair and olive skin from his Tartar Muslim father and large round blue eyes from his Ukrainian mother. He was smart and funny, plus he didn't just get high, he did stuff. He went to see old movies, roller-skated, and played the guitar. In his sketchbook were intricate multilayered drawings that were part M.C. Escher, part Hieronymous Bosch. He went to see bands that weren't Pink Floyd, Led Zeppelin, or Black Sabbath, plus he hated Laserium and loved *Star Trek*. He asked me that day if I still had a boyfriend. When I said no, he cocked one eyebrow like Mr. Spock and said, "Cool." Pasha and I would both be accepted to SVA. He would become my next boyfriend, and we would stay together almost seven years.

Later that spring, I was coming home early from Brooklyn when I heard a voice say, "Shell?" I turned and had to look twice to see it was EZ Eddie. I almost didn't recognize him. He had gained weight and didn't have the swagger I remembered . . . He seemed . . . subdued somehow. I asked him what he was doing. He said he worked at a bank and he hated it. He asked me what I was doing. I said I was in one art school and was going to another one in September. He then looked at me as if he had never seen me before, which made me so uncomfortable I said, "This is my stop, I gotta go. See ya," and I took my portfolio and got off the train. I had gotten off three stops early. I knew he knew it too.

Sometimes—for some things—no matter how old or young you are, . . . it is too late.

32

UNCLE JUNIOR

Dear Michele,

You didn't know him. He didn't want to know you. He doesn't care about you. He doesn't care about anyone. If he did, he wouldn't of done what he did or be what he was.

Don't play dumb. You know I'm talking about Uncle Junior. You think I'm dumb? You don't think I saw you talking to him at Grandma's funeral and after at the house? Did you know he took the marijuana the doctors gave her for the chemo? She wouldn't even smoke it because she was afraid to be high. She was afraid she'd end up like Junior.

He is no good. Do you understand? Oh, you think he is misunderstood. You think he is an artist? Well let me tell you, I saw you showing him your drawings when you were little, and if he put that idea in your head, it is one more reason for me to tell you he has brought nothing but shame and suffering to this family. Why do you think Grandpa had so many heart attacks? Why do you think Grandma had the diabetes for so long? Because the truth about their son made them sick. So sick they had no energy left for me, your Uncle Freddy, Papo, or Frankie, or anyone else.

You think because he lives in that apartment in the Village and draws pictures and writes things, he's an artist? He's a fake. Uncle Junior isn't an artist; he's on drugs. A doper. A junkie. He takes heroin and has since he was a teenager. I don't care what he says about being "clean" for the last ten years. I don't care if he's a counselor helping other drug addicts now. Good for them. It doesn't change what he did to Grandma and Grandpa and all of us.

Did you know he also has a wife and two children back in Puerto Rico that he hasn't seen since you were a baby? Of course you don't. Did you know that the woman he lives with isn't his wife? She's a junkie just like him and so is the son. Of course you don't.

Don't you understand? I don't care if they say they're clean now. You just see the apartment in the Village and the books and the paintings and the records, and you want to live there. I heard him say he'd give you the lease to the apartment when they move. I don't want you to live there. I don't want that kind of life for you.

Michele I love you and I don't want you to be that way. I can't stop you from going to art school; you are of age now. But I won't help you pay for it. I won't help you end up like him. Please don't be like him. You are not an artist.

I am your father and I love you.

Your father,
Rudy

33

SHOWTIME

Uncle Junior did ask Cousin Isabel and me if we knew where Grandma Izzy's medical pot was. We didn't know. We didn't tell him we had been looking for it too. My father and I didn't stay in Florida for very long this time though; we stayed just long enough to see Grandma Izzy home from the hospital. I had to get back to New York. I was about to start my new school.

I loved New York City Community College and soon found I was getting almost straight As. My fellow students in the art program were really nice, and I soon had a new group of friends. Most of the other students were really nice too. Well, almost all . . .

One early December afternoon, I was in the cafeteria yelling at some boy who was trying to hit on me. He was ugly, but I was polite and used the time-honored, face-saving letdown, "Sorry, I have a boyfriend," which was the truth. He was either partially deaf or wholly delusional because he persisted, at one point grabbing at my arm. This is when I yelled, "I told you I had a fucking boyfriend you fucking moron, now leave me the fuck alone!" That's when the teacher came up to me.

I shut up right away, scared that I was going to be in trouble and embarrassed because I realized I was a little too old to be in this kind of trouble. But instead of reprimanding me or reporting me, she asked, "Can you sing?"

I didn't know what to say, so I said, "Uh, yeah. . . . Kinda."

"Well, my name is Dr. Emilie Weber and I'm the chairman of Theatreworks USA here at New York City Community College. We're casting for our spring show. It's *Guys and Dolls*. Have you heard of it? Can you come today at four P.M. for an audition?"

I was so happy I wasn't going to be in trouble, I said yes. Luckily for me, my last class on that day was done by then, so I went. An hour later, I was Miss Adelaide.

I knew what *Guys and Dolls* was because I'd seen it on Channel 9's *The Late Show* and on Channel 7's *The 4:30 Movie*, but I'd no idea what it was like to be in a play. I'd never been in one, unless you counted being an angel once in Sunday school—and I didn't think it did.

When I told my family, strangely, my mother seemed the most excited. She said she had seen both the movie and the Broadway show back when they had come out. Then she went into her closet and brought out some of her outfits from the 1950s and said, "In case you can use them." The perfectly preserved chiffon sundress, wool crepe sheath, and satin cocktail suit, of course, didn't fit (as I was four inches taller and twenty pounds heavier than she had been at my age). After she zipped her clothes back into their protective plastic bag, she said, "Well, maybe I can show you what it was like back then."

She went up into a closet and took out a photo album I hadn't seen before. In it were pictures of my mother and father when they were young. One was of my father with some other teenage boys on a street corner. Behind them was a fading poster advertising War Bonds. There was another one of him on a rooftop among rows of cages and pigeons. There were pictures of my mother too: one standing on a stoop with her friend Daisy, another posing in front of Cleopatra's Needle in Central Park, and another park photo, this one of my mother and father holding hands in front of Belvedere Castle.

"Your father and I used to go there a lot," she said and looked almost wistful. There were other photos of family members she quickly went through. On the last page was a picture of me holding Kevin, taken soon after he was born. She looked at it intently for a moment or two, then abruptly slammed the album shut, got up, and put it away. She then went back to her housework without saying another word, leaving me to think.

This was the first time I really saw, really understood that my parents had a life before me. I thought about the picture of them in front of Belvedere Castle and remembered my mother saying they had gone there a lot. "What for?" I wondered. I thought about what Pasha and I did on the few and far-between times we could be alone and shut my thoughts down entirely. Thankfully, the photo album didn't reappear.

My father's reaction to me being in a play was, "Are you going to come home even later?" He didn't like it that I rode an hour and a half each way from our apartment to Brooklyn to go to school. Sometimes I didn't get home at night till eight or nine. Now it would be even later.

I loved being in the play. Maybe I didn't know any real acting techniques or have the real-life experience of a 1950s Hot Box Girl to bring to it—but I knew what it was like to pretend to be someone you weren't and to want something you couldn't have, so in that sense, it came easily to me.

We rehearsed until 10 or 11 P.M. after a full school day. Sometimes I got a ride from the stage manager, who lived in Co-op City, but most nights I was on the number 6 train alone at midnight. I used the rides to practice my lines and my singing. I figured if people saw me talking to myself, they would think I was nuts and leave me alone: art imitating life.

I also practiced at home. I bought the cast sound track and also *Jesus Christ Superstar* (because I heard that was going to be their next production) and recruited Kevin to help. We acted and sang out both plays in their entirety in our living room at least once a week. Kevin made me promise not to tell his friends, but I know he had almost as much fun as I did.

As for my after-school life, I didn't have time to hang out at the park much (of course, I never set foot anywhere near 192 Schoolyard again), but on the couple of nights I did go to St. Peter's I found out that Dawn had a new thirty-year-old boyfriend and didn't come around much anymore, and that Janey, whose nickname had playfully always been Janey-the-Waste, had really become one.

Nikki told me Janey's parents were about to kick her out of the house for doing drugs, and sometimes she slept in the park. Nikki was still working at the job on Wall Street. They had promoted her to assistant something or other, and she was thinking about marrying Tommy. "It's what I got, Shell," she had said.

I didn't know what to say about any of it. Since I had broken up with Brendan, my life totally changed. I was back in school. I was in a play. Maybe now my life would be good.

Things were looking up; so as luck would have it, both Grandpa Ezekiel and Grandma Izzy died early that spring. As often happens when a couple has been together for over fifty years, one goes and the other soon follows.

Grandpa Ezekiel suffered a fifth heart attack loading his car on the way to go fishing. Grandma Izzy had been fighting diabetes for more than twenty years, and it had turned into pancreatic cancer, which she fought until Grandpa died. She joined him a month later. They would both never know I had made SVA.

Out of all the brothers, my father seemed to grieve the most. He stayed by himself a lot at both funerals, and I heard him fighting with Uncle Junior more than once. Cousin Isabel was inconsolable too. She had been very close to Grandma Izzy. She too seemed different somehow. She had just gotten married and had a baby, so I figured that was why.

Of course I was sad too, but not like them. I wouldn't understand what it was like to lose a parent till much, much later. Besides, I hadn't been around Grandpa Ezekiel and Grandma Izzy all that often really—just for a week or two in the summers mostly—so I didn't know the secrets, subtleties, and conflicts in my father's family as I did my mother's.

If I close my eyes, though, I can still see Grandma Izzy in her backyard in Hollywood, surrounded by us cousins. She's eating a mango and laughing. The sun shines through her hair and her ancient toothless tuxedo cat, Puchito, dozes at her feet. That is how I remember her.

When I got back to New York from the Florida funerals, I didn't have time to think about anything besides the play. I really liked the routine of school and rehearsal and loved the friends I had made among the cast. It was almost like a family, though not like any family I was used to. Here, everyone looked out for each other and took each other's back when someone forgot a cue or flubbed a line or missed an entrance.

I asked the boy who played the gambler Nathan Detroit, my boyfriend in the play, if it was always like this when you acted, and he said, "No. Sometimes it sucks. But this is a good play and a good cast. Welcome to the theater." At twenty-one, he was the veteran, having been in the company since he was nineteen.

So this was what it was like to be an actor? It was like the graffiti days except so much better. This was something I was good at, so everyone liked me. I wondered if I should give up trying to go to SVA and try to be an actor instead. But what would I have to do? Maybe I could ask the director, Dr. Weber, who had treated me with patience and respect, teaching me how to be a believable performer and how to sing with a vocal coach, and never made me feel like an outsider even though they had all been working together for two years. Life was perfect again until my little acting family fantasy bubble burst.

It was three weeks before our opening night, and I had neglected to put together my portfolio for the SVA interview and had missed a couple of rehearsals to do so. Dr. Weber had been furious. She said my responsibility was to her production and anything else had to be secondary.

I said I had my SVA interview coming up, and she said she didn't care; she had found me and she could replace me. I was in shock. She had yelled at other kids during rehearsal, but never at me.

Later, when we were going through the Hot Box scene where the Dolls sing "Take Back Your Mink," I kept forgetting the lines. She yelled at me again, I don't remember exactly what, but it made me sing back to her, "Take Back Your Mink, Take Back Your Play, Go

Find Yourself Another Adelaide," and run from the stage into the dressing room.

If the rest of the cast had been friendly before, they were overwhelmingly so now. They had all come to stroke my back while I cried, telling me she didn't mean it and everything would be all right. I didn't understand. I didn't realize that this type of behind-the-scenes drama was part of every production. I had been so starstruck that I was blinded to it. Dr. Weber came into the dressing room. She told me to get the hell back onstage like a professional and act, damn it. I told her I quit.

She looked at me calmly, and instead of yelling, she softly said she was disappointed because she thought I was tougher than this. That was why she had picked me that day in the cafeteria, and now she saw she was wrong. But she understood. I could go.

That Dr. Weber was smart like a fleet of foxes. She knew exactly what to say to get me out of feeling sorry for myself into thinking "Oh yeah, I'll show her!" I stood up and said, "Oh no, you have to fire me to get me to leave," and went back onstage. We resumed rehearsal.

Somehow I made it to my SVA interview. I went there with my two new girlfriends from my art classes, Aimee (with two e's) and Tahnya (with an h). Walking down 23rd Street, I wondered what SVA students looked like. Then I walked through the doors and saw I didn't look the part at all. Both boys and girls were wearing coats and jackets that looked like they came from the Salvation Army with tight skinny jeans and some of the girls wore really short skirts and lace-up boots with gum soles I would later learn were called Doc Martens or flat white shoes I would learn were Capezios. I looked down at my turquoise carpenter pants and pink thermal shirt and felt like a clown.

But everyone I met and spoke to couldn't have been more welcoming. Two people asked me questions, went through my portfolio, and thanked me. On my way out, I ran into another fellow New York City Community College student, the cute guy I had kind of a crush on, Pasha—and we talked! I left SVA floating on cloud feet. A month later, our dysfunctional little acting family made it to opening night. That night and that performance was just amazing—perfect. We all were.

I remember looking at Dr. Weber at one point. She was sitting in the front row, and she had the same look on her face that Titi Carmen did when she saw Jesus. I understood why. I felt it too.

After everything that happened all year, it had all been worth it. As we took our bows, I stood onstage for an extra second and let the applause wash over me. I felt like I had finally found the thing that I wanted to do with my life. It was a rush of energy and lightning that was almost like being high. In fact, I couldn't remember the last time I had gotten stoned. I had just been too busy.

I quickly changed and ran back into the auditorium. My family was there: my father, Kevin, *abuelita*, Titi Dulce with Ray-Ray and Evie, and Titi Ofelia with Benny. Titi Carmen would have come too, but she was in the hospital. I didn't know. So much had happened in the last few months, it was hard to keep track of it all.

My mother hadn't come either. She had said she was going to, but when I asked my father, he just shrugged and said, "She couldn't make it. We're here."

He and Kevin hugged me and told me they were proud. Benny, Ray-Ray, and Evie kissed me, and Titi Dulce was right behind them. *Abuelita* hugged me and said, "Play very good, very nice," even though I knew she probably had barely understood half of it. Titi Ofelia looked at me with something approximating respect for the first time in my life.

My new boyfriend Pasha was also there, with Tahnya, Aimee, and her boyfriend Cevyn (pronounced Kevin, he too preferring the "artistic" spelling of his name). I had invited my park girlfriends also, but only Crazy May-ree came. She wasn't afraid of going to Brooklyn. I introduced them all. But it didn't register with me. Under my natural high was a current of deep disappointment.

I had wanted my mother to come. I remembered when she had told me a little about what it was like in New York in the 1940s and 1950s when she was growing up. I had never talked with her like that before and didn't know why we hadn't again after that one day. I didn't understand that she had always been a bit agoraphobic and that something in that photo album had been a trigger for her, and she just couldn't do it. I tried telling myself I was twenty years old now—and I didn't need her anymore—only that made me want to run away, scream, and throw things, . . . but I couldn't because a man had come up to us. He congratulated me and said he wanted to speak with my father.

When my father came back, I asked him who the man was and what he had said. He said the man was an acting agent and had given him his card. He wanted my father's permission to talk to me; he had thought I was under eighteen, which I thought was weird since this was a college show.

"What should I do?" I asked my father. My disappointment over my mother evaporated. This was exactly what I had been thinking about for months: how to become an actor, but now that it was right here in front of me, I was afraid.

"It's your choice," my father said. "I'm not going to tell you what to do. You won't listen anyway." He smiled and went to talk to Titi Dulce.

I remembered when I had gotten my acceptance letter to New York City Community College almost exactly a year before. My father told me that I would be the first one in the family to go to college, and whatever I did would now set an example for the younger kids. I looked at Kevin and my cousin Benny, who were in high school and Ray-Ray and Evie, not far behind. I looked at my new boyfriend and friends and remembered all I had gone through that year to get into SVA, and I thought, well, I could always be an actor later, right? I decided to know what it was like to be an artist first. I wanted my brother and cousins to see me do it. I never talked to that man. I don't know what agency he was from. My father never even showed me the card.

If you have ever worked on a play or a film, you know the immediate closeness and connection that develops from working so intensely together. You also know that those friendships generally only last for the duration of the production. I, along with Pasha, Tahnya, and Aimee, had gotten into SVA. Cevyn would be going to the Parsons School of Design. I wouldn't be joining Dr. Weber and her theater group for *Jesus Christ Superstar* that fall, so at the end of *Guys and Dolls'* three-week run when I said good-bye to everyone at the cast party, that was it. And that was okay. I was going where I had dreamed of being good enough to be. I would, at last, be at SVA.

34

ATTACK OF THE REPUBLI-RICANS

I almost had to drop out of SVA before I even began. From tuition to books to the endless amount of overpriced art supplies that needed to be bought, I was on my own.

Even though my father had said he wouldn't help me go to art school, the reality was, he couldn't. He still hadn't found work and we were still on welfare. I remember the big orange blocks of cheese that were impossible to cut or melt, which were better used as doorstops, and the cans, yes the cans of peanut butter that tasted as if it had been made from the shells.

It made me feel guilty I'd ever complained about my mother's Libby's corned beef *piccadillo*. Worse, though, were the endless, demeaning "intake" interviews my parents had to go on. On one of them, the welfare people told them our family couldn't continue to get benefits if I was in college because now that I was twenty-one, I was too old to be in school anymore.

My father wasn't a violent man, not at all—ever. But as he told it, he upended the table saying, "Godamnsonuvabitch, my daughter stays in school!" and they never mentioned it again. I've asked my mother about this (it took a lot for her to leave the house to be there), and she never said it did happen that way—but she never said it didn't either.

Even with my two jobs (at the art supply department at Gimbels on 86th Street and The Bronx Council on the Arts, where I had once worked on the Summer Youth Employment Program while I was a teenager) and my Tuition Assistance Program (TAP) grant, I didn't have enough money to buy what I needed.

I hadn't applied for any other financial aid. I just didn't want to answer the race or ethnicity questions on the many forms I'd had to fill out. I was so disgusted by anything having to do with what I was or wasn't, I'd put Redhead for ethnicity and for race, Human. Luckily, SVA guidance counselors (especially the beautiful, capable, and compassionate Pam Miller) were nothing like the ones at Lehman High School.

Pam tracked me down and asked me to bring in my birth certificate, which, of course, said "Mother's Place of Birth: Puerto Rico." In Pam's office I learned that somewhere between the 1960s and 1980s, I had become a separate race: Hispanic. She handed me a stack of forms. I refilled them out and got some more money.

Pam also said that I'd been doubly stupid for evading those questions because there was so much other help I qualified for that other students couldn't (it didn't register with me at the time, but almost everyone at SVA was, you guessed it, white).

So when I applied for financial aid for the following year, I also applied for something called The Minority Student Internship Program that happened over the summers. Out of nearly a thousand applicants, only twelve people were accepted each year and I got in. I was going to have a paid summer job at an advertising agency and make professional contacts that could help me when I graduated. Pam Miller said, "See, I knew you could do it."

That next June, as I walked to the Internship Orientation on the 42nd floor of a big advertising agency on Sixth Avenue, I was more than a few minutes late. (Like many others of the Latin persuasion, I occasionally suffer from an affliction called Latin People Time, or LPT. LPT is a subcategory of Colored People Time, or CPT, a misapplication of the space/time continuum that causes the afflicted to leave their house at the time they are supposed to be wherever it is they are going. I fight against it daily.

I was afraid to open the door. What would I find in there? But I figured we're all minorities. I bet I'm not the only one who's late. In fact, I might even be the first to arrive. I opened the door.

Was I wrong. Not only had everyone inside been waiting for me for fifteen minutes, the orientation had already begun. I ran into the conference room and joined the group. I could tell who they were because they were young, brown, and beige, and everyone else was older and paler.

As I tried to worm my way into the middle where I hoped I would blend in, I overheard someone behind me say, "Who is this white girl and what is she doing here?"

I was surrounded by little Yuppie wannabees wearing sport jackets with pink and green polo shirts and boat shoes or little bow blouses under Benetton vests and low-heeled pumps. I was wearing a violet zebra-print off-the-shoulder T-shirt, skinny black jeans, and white Capezios (yes, I admit it, but before you laugh, what were you wearing that summer of 1982?).

We sat at the conference table, and I noticed how my fellow internees all spoke in what seemed to me to be business speak. I suppose they were trying to transcend their neighborhoods and correctly so. I was the only idiot asking—no, not asking but *axing*—could I get a *cawfee* and drawing cartoons on my writing pad instead of listening to the speakers.

I also noticed that none of my fellow interns had spoken to me at all. And after we had received our assignments and were leaving, I was called back. The leaders asked me please not to be late in the future, and by the way, where were my parents from again?

I said my mother was born in Puerto Rico. If that hadn't been true, I think I might have been thrown out. As it turned out, my internship was at that same agency.

The first morning there was a welcome breakfast for the other intern who had been assigned there and me. I remember standing at the window just staring at Central Park. I had never seen anything like that view before. I had never been that high up in a building before. And then they brought in the breakfast. I had never seen a croissant before either, and that first morning I ate three of them with about a half stick of butter spread on top and was nauseous the entire afternoon.

We interns also had weekly lunch meetings in that conference room at which we would talk about our experiences. At our first one, none of the other internees would talk to me again, but I didn't care because we had food that I hadn't seen since Nikki and Tommy's wedding at the Marina Del Rey: more croissants, fat boiled shrimp, little crackers with smoked salmon, little red potato slices topped with creamy stuff and crunchy, squooshy orange fish dots I would learn were salmon caviar, and delicious little jam-filled cakes I learned were called petit fours.

Since what I had been eating at home for the past two years was basically hot dogs, brick cheese, and peanut shells, I just ate and ate until I realized everyone was looking at me. I stopped and I was embarrassed because I noticed no one else was eating much at all. And I thought why do you have all this food if no one is supposed to eat any of it? Welcome to advertising.

The reality was, I was afraid. I was afraid that I had gotten this internship not because of merit but because of an oversight, a mistake. In the back of my mind, I was thinking I might never see food like this again, so I better eat it now before they threw me out. Then I would have to go back to that four-room fifth-floor tenement walk-up and ROT because I wouldn't be able to afford to go back to school as I was a fraud. And that would be exactly what I deserved because I did not know how fit in. Luckily, that positive train of thought ended up being interrupted because we were all going on a tour of the agency, and the first place we were going to visit was my cubicle.

Did I say lucky? When I realized where we were going, I wanted to go break one of those hermetically sealed windows and jump out. I'd decorated my cubicle like the full teenage bedroom I'd never really had and suddenly realized that maybe that wasn't such a good idea.

Almost every spare inch of wall was filled with flyers stolen from the Ritz, Irving Plaza, and Peppermint Lounge, and almost every inch of my desk was crammed with little knickknacks I had no room for in my half room at home, like a foot-wide rubber spider and a tall can full of peacock feathers, along with a small collection of beer glasses I had appropriated from the just mentioned clubs. And did I mention the one wall covered in tinfoil and Christmas tree lights? And to top it off, instead of agency work on my drawing board was a light box with a sheet of tracing paper and a T-shirt taped to it.

That summer was one of the New York City Dr Pepper concert summers. They had once been held at the old Wollman skating rink in Central Park that had been broken for as long as anyone could remember. In the past two summers, Pasha and I had seen Devo, the Pretenders, the Talking Heads, the B52s, the Go-Gos, the Ramones, Blondie, and more. You didn't even need to buy a ticket; you could just climb up on a rock and watch.

This year the concerts were going to be at Pier 84 on the West Side, and Pasha and I had a plan. He was working in a silkscreen studio that summer, and after hours we would sneak in and print T-shirts we designed. We were going to sell them at the concerts for $10 each. The T-shirt on my desk was a design Pasha had drawn from King Crimson's *Indiscipline* album. I was trying to make it go around a barcode, because 1984 was only a couple of years away, and we all knew what that meant—we'd all be imprinted with barcodes, of course.

I had tried to stand in front of the drawing board, but one of the most Yuppie-looking male interns (he wore a different weird-patterned sweater every week and the Cosby Show was still two years away) looked at the T-shirt and said, "You like Robert Fripp?" And out of my mouth came, "Like him? He asked us to make these shirts *for* him." Which was, of course, a lie, but I started talking about the Dr Pepper concerts and about my boyfriend and I making T-shirts for them, which was technically true, if not yet.

The intern said, "Wow," and asked me questions about where we bought our T-shirts and what kind of ink we used.

A couple of the other interns began a discussion about overhead, licensing and profit margins, and suggested it would be better if Pasha and I set up a booth, but then the Internship leader came back to get us and finish the tour. But when everyone left, the interns who had been in my cube said, "See you next week." And then I got an idea.

Every week I was asked how my "T-shirt business" was going, and every week my stories became more embellished. I would talk about what concert we had seen (true, except I didn't say that we usually sold only two or three shirts), how Robert Fripp himself had one of our T-shirts (half true—Pasha had thrown one onstage while they were playing), and how I met Blondie in the bathroom and gave her toilet paper under the stall and didn't even ask for an autograph (a total lie). But at least they were listening to me.

At our weekly lunch meetings, I was now part of the group, and one of the girls also confessed to me how she had wanted to eat all the food that first day too because her family had been on welfare also and how she thought I had guts to do that. "Yeah, but I gotta watch it or I'm gonna get a gut," I said, and everyone laughed.

I had never met people like this before—most of them had voted for Ronald Reagan, which I thought was crazy. I had grown up listening to people talk about the Movement and the Establishment and the Man, whose apartments had John F. Kennedy and Martin Luther King's pictures on the walls.

When I mentioned this at home one night, my father said, "Those kids are smart. I voted for Reagan. What did I get from Carter? Welfare." And Kevin, who wouldn't be able to vote for president until 1984 (and who would vote for . . . Ronald Reagan) said, "Yep, we're Republi-Ricans now, Michele, get with the program."

That September, Kevin's new favorite show would be *Family Ties*. He would also enter Baruch College as a finance major, start wearing Le Tigre shirts, and call himself "the White Anglo-Saxon Puerto Rican."

I did get with the program. I learned a lot at the internship besides how not to make a glutton of myself at a catered lunch, and what was not appropriate for office décor. I learned I had a good design eye and was told I should consider majoring in advertising design and become an art director instead of the cartoonist or illustrator I had originally thought I would be.

In September I had to declare my final major and took their advice. I also learned that the most surprising people could surprise you. The most Alex Keatonish intern knew who King Crimson was, and my own father had denounced the traditional political party of his demographic and became a Republi-Rican.

On the last day of the internship, I was struck with LPT again and was late for our closing lunch. I paused in front of the door to the conference room. Had I missed it? Maybe they took it without me because I really wasn't like them. I took a breath and opened the door, and when I did, eleven smiling faces waved at me and told me to hurry in, they were going to take a picture and had saved a spot for me.

They told me they'd told the photographer to wait because the picture wouldn't have been the same without me. The Dr Pepper concerts wouldn't be the same either. A man named Donald Trump announced he would renovate the skating rink where the old concerts had been held, and Miller Beer would sponsor the next summer's program. It was the eighties. Progress.

35

REDEMPTION BIRTHDAY

When the eighties started, my father lost his job. The construction company he worked for closed down overnight and moved to North Carolina. He didn't work for two-and-a-half years—and it turned him from a lifelong Democrat into a "Republi-Rican." We endured welfare surplus food: peanut butter that tasted like the can it came in, cheese that tasted like mutant Velveeta combined with spackle, and various powdered food products that none of us dared talk about. My mother's now occasional forays into speeching centered on prosperity and blessings, as opposed to venom and condemnation.

Then one afternoon, a middle-aged custodian hit the new, legal number (a.k.a. Lotto), took his million-plus dollars, and retired. Somehow, my dad ended up with his job at the courthouse on 100 Centre Street, where *Law & Order* would be filmed years later. But this was 1982, and my father's days were spent screwing in lightbulbs and following the cops and detectives around all day picking up the trash they left behind. My father would bag it up and put it out back, on Baxter Street, to be picked up.

One day after work, he was leaving the courthouse from the back, Baxter Street way and saw the neighborhood homeless guys picking through the trash bags. "Hey Rudy!" they called out to him. They all knew who my father was because he would buy them coffee every morning. There was Flaco, who was fat; Lucky, because he obviously wasn't; and Ching who was, well, Ching: the Drunken Kung Fu Master of Columbus Park.

"Hey Rudy, can you do us a solid? If you separate the deposit bottles and cans from the rest of the garbage, we'll cut you in, 10 percent."

"What do you do with them?" my father asked.

"We take 'em to the Pathmark on Cherry Street; can make $20 a bag. C'mon man, do us a solid!" I can only imagine the ring of lightbulbs appearing around my father's head as he did the math: Up to 10 bags a day at $2 a bag, every day.

"Deal."

In the wake of the first wave of Reaganomics, a new economy was born. My father was making up to an extra $100 a week. Until one day Flaco disappeared, and Lucky and Ching, being small, skinny, and quite likely in the final ravages of alcoholism, couldn't handle the load by themselves. It was fully summer when he finally saw the two of them together in Columbus Park again and said, "Where you guys been? You gotta get those cans out!"

"Yeah man, we do it, we do it. Give us time, man," they said.

But my father had run out of time. Later that afternoon, his boss opened up the storeroom, saw all the bags, and told my father he had to get them out of there or else. That evening, my father went back to Columbus Park, found Lucky, and told him he'd pay him to get the bags out of there.

"Yeah, man, no problem, I meet you ten o'clock tomorrow morning."

"Tomorrow? Tomorrow's Saturday. Oh . . . well . . . okay."

Well that Saturday morning happened to be my twenty-second birthday, and my father was going to take the family to Carmine's Seafood restaurant at the new South Street Seaport for lunch. Early that morning, as we were having breakfast, he said, "Uh . . . we need to leave now. You and your brother have to come to work with me first, I need help with something."

We got to the courthouse, went to my father's storeroom, and found it filled top to bottom with huge black industrial garbage bags bursting with cans. "Just help me load this up outside," he said. "Someone is going to come and get it." We carried the bags outside and we waited and we waited, and Lucky never showed up.

After a while, Ching passed by and asked my dad for a quarter. My father brushed him off. "Where's Lucky? You guys gotta take these bags, I can't keep them inside anymore."

Ching said, "Hey, man, not my problem."

My father turned and said to us, "Okay, the hell with this, we'll just leave the bags, let's go."

As we were dragging the bags to the curb, a cop, who obviously had been watching us the entire time, came over and told my father he couldn't leave the bags there. My father said, "Well, I can't bring them back inside."

"Hey, man, that's not my problem," the cop answered.

My father turned around to offer Ching $20 to take the bags, but Ching was long gone. We'd no choice but to take the bags ourselves. We loaded them into a wheeled canvas dumpster that looked like the biggest shopping cart you ever saw, and my father said, "Look, we'll just bring the cans to Pathmark and someone will take them. It'll be fine."

It took all three of us to wheel that huge canvas dumpster chock-full of garbage bags the fifteen or so blocks from Centre Street to Cherry Street and the FDR. All along the way people were looking at us funny, my brother was almost crying from humiliation, and my father was quite visibly pissed. But I was okay with it. I thought it was kind of punk actually. When we finally made it to Pathmark, my father saw Lucky, grabbed him, and said he had to take the cans, but Lucky told my dad to fuck off. Of course he did. He was homeless, he was happily drunk at 11:30 A.M., and he had already done his cans and gotten his $50, so why should he do any more work?

My father was so angry he himself used the F-word, something he almost never did. "Fuck it! We're leaving them here. Let's go!"

But as we started unloading the canvas dumpster, the same cop, who must've followed us all the way from the courthouse, came over and said, "You can't leave them here."

My father said, "Well, what am I supposed to do with them?"

The cop pointed across the parking lot to the row of redemption machines and the lines of homeless people in front of them. My brother couldn't take it anymore and really started crying. With the cop watching us, though, we had no choice. We took our bags and took our place among the homeless.

It wouldn't have been so bad if it hadn't been July and the cans hadn't been so sticky, with so many yellow jackets buzzing around. After doing a bag or two, my brother refused to do any more and walked over to the side of the parking lot to sulk.

I went to him and said, "Why are you being such a pussy? I'm the one spending my birthday with homeless people."

He threw a can at me. I went back to the redemption machines. My dad was kind of slow at it, but for some reason I got the hang of it right away. You just tossed a can into the slot and pressed a button. For every five cans, you got a quarter. It got to where I was doing two machines at a time, right-and left-handed, and I was so quick, some of the men on the line offered me a cut if I'd do their bags.

I looked over at my father, who I knew was keeping an eye on me the entire time. It never crossed my mind that I might have been the only female under fifty ever to grace the Pathmark Redemption Center. Even at twenty-two, I still looked about fifteen, and with my black jeans, Doc Martens, and Devo T-shirt, not to mention my new "Flock of Seagulls" haircut, they all probably thought I was a boy anyway.

I said okay, and on top of the bags we brought, I must have done an extra five bags. As promised, the homeless men came back and gave me my cut. Some of them looked at my father and nodded. I guessed they thought he had brought me up right.

By the time we finished all the cans, it was three o'clock, and we had made nearly $200 dollars—in quarters. We still had to split up the change and stand on yet another line to redeem the quarters. By then, it was after four. My father finally said, "Okay, let's eat."

We took the dumpster back to Centre Street, which went a lot quicker being it was empty, and walked back to the Seaport. Only now we were all filthy. Our hands were black and sticky, my brother's new, white, New Balance sneakers were new and white no longer, and all our shirts were disgusting. People were looking at us. We looked homeless.

My father said he'd buy us some new clothes, so we went to the new Pier 17 shopping mall where he took us to the Gap. My brother smiled for the first time all day. Now I wanted to cry. The Gap? No! The shame! But I had no choice.

My father bought us all new T-shirts and jeans (lucky for me they had black), and we had to go to the public bathrooms to clean up and change. In the ladies' room, a couple of people looked at me with averted eyes. I resisted the temptation to ask them for a quarter.

When we finally got to Carmine's, we had the Lobster Fra Diablo, the Veal Marsala, the Eggplant Parmigiana, and the Zabaglione with Ricotta Cheesecake. After all, it was my birthday. My mother never made it. Between Lucky and Ching and the cop and the cans, my father had forgotten all about her. When he finally remembered and called from a pay phone—from outside the restaurant—she was so angry we could hear her where we were standing. My father joked that between the dinner and the new clothes, we really wouldn't have a lot of money left over for her to eat anyway.

We walked up Fulton Street back to the subway. My father and Kevin were going to go back up to The Bronx, I was going to go to the Prince Street Bar in SoHo to meet Pasha. And standing on a corner, who did we see but the same cop who had been the catalyst to all the events that day. He unwrapped a piece of gum and tossed the wrapper into the street. My father walked right up to him and said, "Hey, you can't leave that there."

The cop looked at my father for a long moment, bent down and picked up the wrapper, stuck it in his pocket, and said, "Even."

As we walked away, my brother asked, "Daddy, you *know* that cop?"

"Who?" he asked. "Officer Colletti? He works at the courthouse. I used to pick up his cans all the time. Not anymore."

I saw my father in a different light that day. Like I'd soon learn with my brother Kevin's conversion to Yuppiehood, sometimes the people you think you know the best, you don't know at all. My father whistled all the way back to the subway.

36

SHE LOOKS LIKE MANHATTAN

One of the things I loved the most out of all the things I loved at SVA was the Cave. The Cave was the locker room in SVA's main building on East 23rd Street. It was in the basement and it was a piece of history in itself. All over it was graffiti, some by famous artists who had been at SVA before us: Jean-Michel Basquiat who tagged "Samo," Keith Haring's lightbulbs and outline babies, and even Kenny Scharf, although I don't remember what he wrote. Shell dug out her old miniwide and took a tag or two for old time's sake. I wonder if it's still there. I wonder if the Cave still exists.

My life had changed completely again. Maybe I hadn't become a famous Broadway actor, but I was studying art with famous people. I took cartooning with Harvey Kurtzman, who founded *Mad Magazine* and drew "Little Annie Fannie" in *Playboy*. I took illustration with Marshall Arisman and advertising with Ron Travisano of Della Femina Travisano & Partners, one of the best-known ad agencies at the time. Richard Hell, from the punk bands Television and the Voidoids, came in to speak to one of my English classes . . . and nodded out in a chair.

Every day I'd learn something else about art or the world. Every night there was another art opening to crash at galleries and clubs in the East Village such as New Math or The Pyramid Club, Club 57, the Fun Gallery, and Gracie Mansion.

Sometimes I'd see people from the 1970s graffiti days who were now painting canvases. And sometimes we'd go into SoHo and Tribeca. The Tony Shafrazi and Clocktower openings were the friendliest (easiest to crash). But more often than not we'd call those nights "So-Hopeless" as we'd end up wandering around all night and getting nowhere.

It was fun though. We didn't care if we weren't part of *Bright Lights, Big City*, or *Slaves of New York*, the soon-to-come books that supposedly personified "our" generation. For us skinny little new-wave dance nerds, it was enough to go to the Ritz and watch videos or go gallery hopping with Victor, a guy who'd have two baggies in the pockets of his jacket: one for the crudités and one for the dip. Or we'd hang with Gina and Carrie, the Roller-Skate Twins, best friends and graphic design majors from Oceanside, Long Island, who wore their skates to school every day.

When Pasha and I weren't in class, we'd go to drink beer at the International Bar, go to eat mushroom soup and challah toast at Kiev, or go to see old movies at the St. Marks Theater or Theater 80, which were right around the corner from each other on St. Marks Place. One weekend we went to visit a friend of his who went to S.U.N.Y. Albany and saw the bands Squeeze, UB40, and Depêche Mode. Another, we went from seeing *Un Chien Andalou* in one theater, to *Eraserhead* in another, bought matching World War I gas mask bags at Unique Clothing Warehouse then went to the Ritz to see Romeo Void. We just thought we were "radical" and "excellent," my two new favorite words.

But sometimes, when we'd walk down that block on Second Avenue between Nightingale's and Dan Lynch and pass the Chinese restaurant Jade Garden, I'd think about Uncle Junior and wonder if he still lived in that apartment. I hadn't seen or heard anything about him since Grandma Izzy's funeral. I wondered if he knew I had finally made it into SVA. A couple of times I was tempted to ring his buzzer, but I never did.

Every once in a while I'd still check in at St. Peter's Park. Nikki Cleary, who was once Nikki Boom-Boom and was now Mrs. Nikki

Della Rossa, would sometimes be there with or without Tommy. May-ree would sometimes be there too. She had a boyfriend called Weezer (née Ronnie) from Zappa's Corner and had made good on half her boast from years ago. Maybe she wasn't living in the East Village, but she hung out there almost every night. Dawn never came around at all anymore, even though her now thirty-three-year-old boyfriend had left her for an eighteen-year-old. Janey would always be there, she was basically homeless now and living under the pool. She'd usually ask me if I had any spare change, but I would say I didn't have any and give her cigarettes instead.

I had learned that from my father. Whenever he was approached by panhandlers he would offer to buy them a meal to see if they were really hungry, "Because most of the time they *really* just want booze or dope." If the bums did decline the egg on a roll and coffee, then my father would give them a cigarette, so at least they had gotten something and would then leave him alone.

The other person who was always still at the park was Pat Baleena. Now twenty-three, he still ruled St. Peter's Park the way he had over a dozen years before. Or at least he thought he did.

The neighborhood had changed. Once my family had been the one and only Latin family around. Now there were dozens, and a Spanish bodega had taken over where Artie's, the Italian deli, had closed. And what was once Pat's childish if annoying penchant for teasing and bullying had grown up and become serious. Pat may have left me alone after getting me stabbed during one of our high school's yearly race riots, but Nikki and May-ree told me that he and some other boys—young men, really—beat up "faggots" at the Huntington (the stoner crew that Janey once hung out with there were long gone). Or they'd get into cars and cruise around the Throgs Neck projects to shoot BBs at black and Latin kids. And where once Pat had something to say because I was different, he now would have something else to say because I was different again.

I ran into May-ree at the Ritz one night, and she told me Pat told her "I thought I knew who I was" now that I was going to "Fart School." And if I was going to come to the park "looking like Manhattan," I could just stay there. When I heard that, I did what was one of either the bravest or the stupidest things I had yet done in a long career of stupid things. I decided to bring some of my SVA friends to the park.

I don't know why I was still hanging on by the thinnest of threads to a place I no longer, if ever, really belonged. But something in me told me I had to try, so I did. And Cevyn, Aimee, Victor, and Tahnya rode up to The Bronx with me after school one day.

The plan was to go to the park, have a beer, and then go back downtown to the Pyramid and see who wanted to come with us. I thought for sure May-ree would, maybe even Nikki if Tommy was working. Neither Nikki or May-ree were there. Pasha hadn't come either; he had to work that night and told me he thought this was a bad idea, but I didn't listen. Later on, I'd be glad he hadn't come because basically as soon as we walked into the park and sat on a bench, we heard Pat yell, "Get those niggers and faggots out of my park, Speck!"

I froze. He hadn't used that voice or called me that name in years.

"It's not your park," I yelled back. "It's a free country and we can hang out anywhere we want."

Pat jumped down from the top of the sliding pond, where he had been sitting. A couple of guys followed him. I didn't recognize either one of them.

"Go back to Manhattan, " Pat said. "That's where you and your faggot friends belong."

"Let's go Michele," Aimee said. "Come on, these people are assholes," Cevyn said, and he took Aimee's arm and walked out. Victor and Tahnya had already gone.

I was furious. It was one thing to call me names; I was used to that. But I had brought my friends all the way up from 23rd Street to hang out where I came from, and no way was this fucking stupid, stupid fuck going to ruin another day for me.

I remembered Pat when he was fat and crying with his naked butt glued on a chair. Maybe he needed to be reminded of that.

I didn't even register that he had two friends with him, and perhaps I should have remembered the small scar on my right shoulder. Before I could open my mouth and make an already bad situation worse, Janey-the-Waste saved me.

She had appeared out of nowhere, or perhaps from under the pool. "Sh-e-l-l-l-l," she croaked. "Hey man, you got any spare change?" I hardly recognized her. She was bone thin and dirty, and I couldn't even see her face between the now twilight and her tangled, dirty hair. She used to have the prettiest hazel eyes too. I don't know why I remembered that.

Pat whirled around to her, "Get the fuck outa here, you stupid junkie slut." I had heard and seen enough. I shut my mouth and walked out of the park. A full beer can thudded a foot or two behind me. I didn't look back. I remember thinking he must really hate me to waste a full beer.

"Those were your friends?" Tahnya asked as we walked back toward the train.

"No," I answered. "My friends weren't there." That was as close to the truth as I wanted to get.

1983 began. May-ree and Ronnie would break up six months later. She would have a nervous breakdown and would never be the same, although we'd still keep in touch for a few more years until I moved to Brooklyn. Dawn supposedly moved to Brooklyn too, but I've never seen her. But then again, there are many different Brooklyns. For all I know Nikki and Tommy are still married. I hope so. They always made a nice couple. Janey died the next summer. One night she nodded out on a bench, fell over face first into a puddle, and drowned in two inches of water. I didn't think that could be true, but it was. And Pat, well, he hated Puerto Ricans so much, he married one, or a half one—a half Irish, half Puerto Rican girl named Lisa Lopez from, of all places, 192 Schoolyard. And the last I heard, he got fat again.

As for me, I did see Uncle Junior one last time too. Cousin Isabel had gotten into some trouble and had come to New York to get out of it. She was staying at Uncle Junior's, and when my father, Kevin, and I went to see her there, I almost didn't recognize her either. She looked thin and drawn like Janey had the last time I saw her. Uncle Junior looked better—filled out, smooth, and placid. They seemed to have changed places with each other over the last ten years.

We sat in the brick-walled kitchen and had an awkward conversation over *café con leche*, which Uncle Junior made with a *colador*, just like Grandma Izzy used to do. I mentioned that I had been going to SVA, and Uncle Junior's eyes went huge but he said nothing.

My father said, "I couldn't stop her, but it seems she's turning out all right." But he kept his eyes on me the entire time we were there.

Uncle Junior was moving. He and his wife and her still-fat, still-pimply, still too quiet son had bought a house and were moving to, of all places, Long Beach, Long Island. (What was it with my family and the ocean?) And Uncle Junior said he could arrange for my name to be put on the lease. He would tell them I was his daughter from his first wife, and that when he moved, I could take over the apartment. I would be a lot closer to school and to the art world.

I couldn't believe it. I was beyond thrilled! I could have a four-room garden apartment on Second Avenue between 11th and 12th Streets in the East Village that cost $300 a month? (He'd been living there since the 1960s.) Even I could almost afford that, I thought. I started calculating. Maybe I could get Aimee to move in with me, or maybe Tahnya . . .

"No." my father said, interrupting my dreams. "Absolutely not."

"But . . ." I began.

"But nothing. I'll know when it's right time for you to be on your own, and now is not it."

We left. Kevin said to me, "Why would you want to live there? That place is a rat hole."

That was when I realized how different Kevin and I had really become. I saw brick walls and a fireplace and a garden with ivy. I could see how I would fill it with artwork and friends and plants and parties. Kevin saw a four-room railroad apartment where you had to have the lights on during the day and a backyard that was really a brick-walled alley between two buildings that had one trash tree and a kitchen-table-sized patch of dirt.

But I knew what Kevin wanted. He wanted to be a Wall Street trader and live on the Upper East Side in a doormanned elevator building—the absolute last place I'd want to live. I realized how I didn't really know my brother anymore at all. How could two people who came from the same womb and grew up in the same place be so completely different?

I would never live in Uncle Junior's or anyone else's apartment in the East Village. Just before Thanksgiving and right in the middle of packing, Uncle Junior would leave St. Vincent's after work, turn the corner, and drop down to the sidewalk dead. They said his liver just exploded. Even after being clean for over ten years, the decades of doing heroin had just been too much for it. They said he probably never felt a thing. I hope not.

When my SVA graduation came around, some of my friends talked about moving into a squat on Avenue C and asked if I wanted to join them. I said no. I had seen that squat. For almost twenty years I had lived in a five-story walk-up that had "occasional" heat and hot water troubles and I occasionally had to walk over, dodge, or otherwise watch out for drunks or junkies and quite frankly I wanted something different. So I declined. My father had been almost right. When it would be time for me to leave home, I'd know.

37

CONTRABAND

In some ways, my father was the Ralph Kramden of St. Peter's Avenue. He always had some plot, some scheme to try to make extra money.

When we first moved to St. Peter's Avenue, he used to play the numbers. No, not Lotto, but the real, old-school number "played" to scary old men in the back rooms of candy stores that sold wormy Chunky bars and pretzel sticks so stale you'd break off a baby tooth just looking at them.

My mother hated it, and whenever she found one of those scribbled little slips of paper in his pockets, she'd stick in another with a Bible verse about the evils of gambling. But that never stopped him from trying to hit "the big one." Usually, he only won enough to keep playing. But once as if by some quasi-divine intervention, he hit the big one just after our ancient black-and-white TV fizzled out. He bought a huge console with color TV, turntable, AM/FM radio, and an 8-track that sat in my parents' apartment for the next fifteen years.

My mother looked up from watching *Star Trek* (she liked Captain Kirk) in color for the first time and told him he had gotten lucky and now should stop. But he didn't listen.

Then the day came when he missed the light, and in the minute he waited to cross Westchester Avenue, the cops swarmed in on the candy store, arresting everyone inside. That was the end of his gambling days.

Before that and before I had gone to live with my *abuelita*, my father had been Hunts Point Avenue's self-proclaimed Animal Cop. He had always loved animals and had tended pigeons on many rooftops in Spanish Harlem as a child and teenager.

I dimly remember a makeshift animal ward on the fire escape just before Kevin was born. A shoebox that first held a broken-winged pigeon (that disappeared), then a baby squirrel (that died), and then a couple of poor, mangy, flea-ridden kittens, one of which my mother actually let me keep (sadly, it died too).

One day on his way home from work, he saw a puppy get hit by a car and thought if he saved it and found its owner, he'd get a reward. My father brought it upstairs and shaved its bloody leg, then cleaned up the gashes with hydrogen peroxide and sewed up the biggest one with my mother's crochet thread. He made a splint for the broken paw, with sticks from the popsicles he bought after dinner. He gave the puppy a bath, fed and brushed it, and petted it until it fell asleep. It was the best treatment that poor dog probably ever had, and as I recall, my father didn't get bitten once.

When my father tracked down the owner—who happened to live in our building—the owner said he had thrown the dog out on purpose; he wanted him to die.

My father said, "What? How about I take you outside and throw you in front of a car, see how you like it!"

He started to walk away. He really wouldn't have done anything more than talk, but the man replied, "Oh yeah, how about I punch you in the nose!"

My father walked back, and a nose-to-nose face-off of words ensued until someone finally went downstairs and got my mother. I don't remember what happened to the dog, but that was the end of my father's veterinary hobby.

Years later, when I was in junior high, my father got the idea he could rewire lamps people had thrown out and sell them back to the junk shop (this was before "junk" became "vintage").

My mother said, "What do you think you're doing? You know nothing about electricity."

But since, or maybe in spite of her not being able to find any Bible verses about lamp wiring in either the Old or New Testaments, our living room was soon filled with a collection of lamps that had probably been "the cat's pajamas" when they were new.

One day I came home from school and plugged one of them in. The next thing I knew, Kevin was crying, and when my mother said, "I told you not to bring junk into the house!" my father yelled back, "Well, who told her to plug the lamp in!"

Meanwhile, I was sprawled on the living room floor with overcooked spaghetti for limbs and brain and little black marks on my right thumb and left toe. The trip to the emergency room ended up costing my father more that he would have made on ten lamps. That was the end of his electrical career. Then there was his last venture, a short-lived stint as a deposit can middleman. That had been almost two years before this already-humid early June evening began.

My father had been sitting in front of the TV, watching the Mets and drinking his nightly quart of fresh iced tea, when Ralph Kiner and Bob Murphy started talking about this certain issue of *Playboy* magazine. It was the one with Marilyn Monroe as the "Sweetheart"— they hadn't even been called "centerfolds" yet—that had just sold at an auction for $10,000. When my father heard that, he leapt off the couch, ran to his closet, and tore it apart.

"Ten thousand dollars! Ten thousand dollars," he moaned as he tore the bottom of the closet apart. "Where is she? Where's my Marilyn? Goddamnsonuvabitch! Ten thousand dollars! Lucy! . . ."

Up until that point, everything in my childhood had always been a secret: the Spanish language, certain whereabouts of certain relatives, and the bottom of my father's closet. Even when Kevin had been sure our Woolworth's turtles Charlie Brown and Snoopy, the only pets we had been allowed to have in that apartment, had crawled out of their tank to commit suicide in there ten years before, we didn't even so much as stoop down to look.

"A man needs his privacy," my father said. "You'll understand when you're older," he said to my brother. "You're old enough to understand that now," he said to me.

My mother just rolled her eyes and said nothing. He didn't dare say anything to her. "Grrrrrrr!" my father growled as he accused my mother of throwing the magazine out.

"Grrrrr yourself!" my mother hissed back. "You have *Playboys* in my house around my children?" As if she hadn't been married to him for almost thirty years and never suspected, and as if there were any actual minors still living in the house—Kevin and I were now a ripe old twenty and twenty-three, respectively.

My father looked at me and in one second dismissed me as the traitor. Next, he looked at my brother who immediately paled and looked at the floor. Kevin then slowly walked into his half bedroom, and we all followed him as he went to his bed, pulled up the mattress, and saw Marilyn jammed in there.

My father picked, or rather scraped and peeled, the magazine off the box spring, held it up by one corner, and looked as if he were going to start bawling.

Marilyn was definitely showing her age. Obviously soaking wet when she was stashed away, all her Technicolors had run together into a streaked psychedelic mud. She was peppered with dried mildew spots and her edges were starting to crumble, much as if she might have looked had she allowed herself to live. My father's eyes went from Marilyn to my brother, and you could see they were both shaking—but for totally different reasons.

My father put one of his hands on my brother's shoulder—he had to reach up, Kevin was now six feet one inch tall. He asked, "When?"

Kevin's face had now turned completely red. I could tell he had forgotten about this a long time ago and was not only embarrassed but a little frightened.

He squeaked, "Suh . . . suh . . . seventy-six."

It took my father a few seconds to do the math. "You were . . . thirteen?"

"Not yet, Daddy, it was March."

"Hmmmph," my father said and gave Kevin a little head nod and smile. He put his arm around Kevin, and they went back to the living room to watch the Mets. If I remember correctly, they won. Again. Pat Zachry, Hubie Brooks, and Joel Youngblood had given way to Ron Darling, Dwight Gooden, and Darryl Strawberry. They were starting to be good now. Really good.

I wasn't staying to watch the game though, I was going out to meet Pasha at the Ritz. I think we were going to see Oingo Boingo. But when I went to say good-night to my mother, she was still standing there in front of the closet, staring.

The next June I walked into Lincoln Center wearing a green and black-checked miniskirt suit with flanged padded shoulders. I was finally graduating from SVA. Not only did I graduate with honors, I had one of the top three portfolios in the advertising design department. It was a proud, happy occasion for my family—after all, I was the first one on both sides to finish, never mind graduate, college.

At our celebration lunch at the Lobster Box in City Island, Titi Ofelia—who I later found out not only arranged the lunch but paid for it—told me after a couple of piña coladas that I had ruined my life because I could have been "something" but that she wished me luck anyway. To her it meant someone who worked at doing something she could understand. I wondered what it would be like to work every day at a real advertising agency. I had already lined up a job that was to begin in September. For some reason this terrified me, and I suddenly wished I was a kid in seventh grade again, my only "responsibility" trying to figure out how to hit up a subway train.

Later that night, I smoked a cigarette out of the bathroom window. I could smoke in the apartment, but I always liked looking out this window. I saw a group of boys hitting up the layups. I thought about what my father told me the opening night of *Guys and Dolls* back at New York City Community College five years before. And how I did set an example for Kevin and my cousins by graduating college. I thought about how far I'd come. How far would I still have to go?

Years later I found out my future husband had been tagging those layups all the time that year . . . and swore he was there that June. He would show me the pictures to prove it.

When my father died, I was the one who cleaned out his closet, and besides the mummified remains of two Woolworth's turtles, I found his entire stash of old *Playboys*, all with their centerfolds ripped out: Bette Page, Jayne Mansfield, Bebe Buell, Barbi Benton. All worth something then. All gone now. And there was something else. A box with a Marilyn Monroe doll in that famous pose from *The Seven Year Itch* still sealed in its box.

I don't know why he had it. Maybe it reminded him of his and my mother's first date, when they had walked down Lexington Avenue, stumbled into the film shoot for *The Seven Year Itch*, and watched her being filmed standing on the subway grating in that famous white dress. That date had been over thirty years ago. Before my mother got sick. Before she went into the hospital. Before things happened.

The doll was pristine and untouched in its box. It had never been opened. There was a piece of paper taped to it that said in my father's scrawl, "I can still dream, can't I?"

I don't know if that note was for my mother's benefit, or for his. I'll never find out, but I can guess. The doll is out of the closet—she sits in my writing studio now—still in her box, and I know exactly what she's worth. Doll: $25.00. EBay bid from memorabilia collector: $750.00. Revealing memory of your father: Priceless.

38

SPANISH ON SUNDAY (part 5)
Papa de Sofa

Titi Carmen was sick. She had diabetes and had been in and out of hospitals for years. She had just been in again, but had gotten out in time for Thanksgiving, and we were all at *abuelita*'s apartment on Amsterdam Avenue.

It was a small apartment, and it was crammed when Cousin Evie let me in at two in the afternoon. The women had all been in the kitchen getting the meal ready to serve and everyone else: Titi Carmen, my father, Kevin, and Cousin Ray-Ray were in the living room. A football game was on, and as usual, everyone was talking over it.

Abuelita was standing on a ladder, half on the top where you're not supposed to stand, with a curtain panel in her hands and a bunch of hooks sticking out of her mouth. Typically for her, she had decided that she needed to hang some new curtains at that exact minute, and no one and nothing was going to stop her. The toes of one foot were curled around the edge of the top step while the other foot was poised to join it, and the men lounged unaware on the couch eight and a half feet below.

Now *abuelita* was a multitasker long before it became a catchphrase. For her to be supervising Thanksgiving dinner, making pot after pot of coffee (the old-fashioned way, with a *colador*), making sure Titi Carmen was comfortable, getting together the meal she would later bring to Papa Julio in the nursing home, and hanging a new curtain, all at the same time, was normal to her. I understood it. I did it myself. But she was seventy-five—and on the top step of a ladder.

"*Abuelita*, what are you doing?" I asked, even though it was obvious.

The hooks didn't prevent her from cheerfully answering, "Hello Mee-chele. *Nadie ayudarme.* Nobody's helping me."

"We'll do it Grandma," Kevin said.

"Yeah, we'll do it," Ray-Ray added.

But they both had their eyes glued to the TV screen. I could see my father had dozed off. He always fell asleep on that couch. I put down my shopping bag with the box of pastries from Veniero's and my famous fresh cranberry-orange relish, and Evie and I walked toward the window. As I passed the couch, I playfully nudged Kevin and Ray-Ray.

"Come on, stop being *papa de sofas* and get up," I said.

Titi Ofelia came into the room. A large carving fork was in one hand, a cigarette in the other. No one else was allowed to smoke at *abuelita*'s anymore. I knew why she was getting away with it, but I still didn't think it was right. She had been caught in mid-drag and expelled a stream of Virginia Slim 100 as she said, "What did you say?"

Titi Dulce followed carrying a large *caldero* full of *arroz con gandules* and put it on the kitchen table, which as always, had been moved into the living room. Kevin and Ray-Ray had gotten up and were helping *abuelita* climb down as she, of course, simultaneously shooed them both away. Looking at the three of them made me laugh, and I was still chuckling as I said, "*Papa de sofa*, you know, couch potato. No one was helping Grandma."

My mother and Cousin Evie brought in the plates of turkey and *pernil*. My father smelled the food and opened one eye.

"You can't say that," Ofelia said. "There's no such word. You have to say *bago* or *perezoso*."

"Or *lento*," Titi Carmen added, helpfully.

"But that just means lazy," I said. *Papa de sofa* is a couch potato. You know . . . when someone just sits on the couch and gets planted there . . . like a vegetable . . ." I didn't like where this was going. I had been in the apartment for only ten minutes, and it looked like something bad was about to happen.

"Ofelia," *abuelita* said. "Mee-chele is making *chistes. Dejala. Vamos a comer!*"

Evie went to push Titi Carmen's wheelchair to the table. My mother had gone back into the kitchen. My father got up to stretch before dinner. But once you gave Titi Ofelia a bone, she couldn't let it go until there was no meat left.

"There's no such word. You can't just make up Spanish."

"Well, there should be . . ." I said in an attempt to pacify her.

My mother came back into the living room. A marshmallow-and-sweet potato casserole was in her hands.

Ofelia moved to block her way. "You know what the problem is, Lucy?"

My mother calmly put the dish on the table and turned to Ofelia with a look I hadn't seen on her face in years. All of a sudden I felt cold.

"What, Ofelia?" my mother said. "Tell me. What is my problem? I don't have a problem. Last year my daughter graduated college. Next year, my son. Where is your son?"

All at once this had become something totally different. No one had talked about Cousin Benny in almost a year.

"He's . . . away," Ofelia started.

"You don't know where he is," my mother said. "No one knows. He's gone."

It was true, that past February, Cousin Benny had left his job at Trinity Cemetery one evening and vanished. No one knew if he was dead or alive. The police had said if he was alive, he had made sure he would not be found. He had only just turned twenty-one.

My mother and Titi Ofelia both started talking at the same time, ignoring *abuelita's,* Dulce's, and Evie's "Please stop." "It's a holiday." "Titi Carmen just got out of the hospital." "Can't we just forget it. . . ."

Kevin and Ray-Ray were still standing by the ladder, I could tell they didn't know what to do, and I could see Carmen praying silently in her wheelchair not two feet away. I could also hear my mother's breathing quicken and knew she was about to say the one thing that could never be taken back. I was afraid of what would happen when she did. But before my mother told Ofelia—what if not she, at least certainly I was thinking—that if Ofelia had been my mother I would have disappeared too, my father stepped in.

"Lucy. We're leaving. Now." He didn't say it loud, but it snapped both my mother and Ofelia out of it even if for just a moment. My father put his hands on my mother's shoulders. Her face was bright red. I thought she was going to start speaking again, but instead she went into *abuelita*'s bedroom, got her coat and pocketbook, and left without saying another word.

My father looked at Ofelia, but said nothing and followed my mother out. Kevin went to get his coat and I just stood there. I hadn't even taken mine off yet.

Abuelita and Ofelia went into the kitchen where, of course, a heated discussion in Spanish had begun. Shards of phrases leapt out at me: *"Por qué hágale siempre . . ."* Why do you always . . . *"Tu no puedes . . ."* Can't you ever . . . *"Soy tan cansada."* I am so tired . . .

Titi Dulce and Cousin Evie came up to me. "Please stay," Evie said. "It wasn't you," Dulce said, "She was looking for any excuse. It's hard for her, you know."

"It's hard for everyone," I thought. But I didn't say that. I just said I was sorry and left.

On the elevator I almost wished my mother had said the unforgivable. Why not? Everyone else could. If she had, I wouldn't have to go to *abuelita*'s anymore and make excuses about why I never went to visit Papa Julio. At least I'd been spared that today. They were my family and I loved them, but sometimes I couldn't stand any of them. It was like Kirk had told Spock, "Sometimes the needs of the one outweighed the needs of the many."

My parents and Kevin were still in front of the building. My mother and father walked to the curb. Kevin pulled me aside and said he hoped our mother wouldn't speech for the rest of the weekend because he had to study for finals and he was so, so tired of this. He couldn't wait to graduate, get a job, and move out, just like I had. Meanwhile, my father hailed a cab.

"Are you coming?" he asked.

"I'm going to Pasha's," I said.

They all got into the taxi. I didn't say good-bye to my mother. I knew she wouldn't have heard.

When I got back to Astoria, the apartment was empty. Pasha had gone to his parents' house. We'd always gone to see both our families and had double Thanksgiving dinners since we'd been going out, but this year we both decided just to go to our own families. I was glad that today he hadn't been with mine.

But I'd left my shopping bag of pastries and relish on the floor of *abuelita's* house, and because it was Thanksgiving and we had anticipated a week's worth of family leftovers, there was almost nothing in the apartment to eat. I could have gone to Jackson Heights to Pasha's parents, but I didn't want human company.

I made a cup of tea and walked into the bedroom. Max, our brown tiger kitten, was curled up sleeping in the middle of the bed. When I walked into the room, he picked up his head. I put down the mug, lay down on the bed, and curled up next to him. It was only four o'clock in the afternoon, but I was exhausted. And I didn't care if I ever spoke Spanish again.

Max purred. The last thought I had before I fell asleep was that Kevin was wrong. I wasn't really "out" yet. Not at all. In my own way, I was still as trapped as he was. When, when, when was it ever going to be all right?

There weren't many more chances left. In the next couple of years, Titi Carmen, *abuelita*, and Papa Julio would all be gone. And Cousin Benny would never be found.

39

"MATTE KUDESAI"

I was in a room with Pasha, Aimee, and Tahnya, and we knew it was the end of the world. The lights in the fixture above us started to dim and we tried to say good-bye, but none of us could speak. The room fell away, and we floated up through the ceiling and could see crowds of people in panic below. As we rose, a flock of white birds, albatrosses, I seemed to remember they were called, came to escort us on our way. I was separated from the others, but I wasn't afraid, my escort was with me. I could see what looked like the ocean in the distance and things that looked like points of light floating toward it. I looked down at my body, but couldn't see it. I wondered if light was what I had become.

But just before we got to the ocean, we passed over one last neighborhood that looked like a huge oil refinery with pipes and tanks and valves, and it was aflame. Among the fires were people suffering and maimed, with disfigured melting faces, who were also inflamed with hatred, and they were trying to pull us down with ropes. A few of the points of light became ensnared and were pulled down to the mob below, but the birds pushed us to fly higher and we escaped. I could smell the ocean now, but it didn't smell like any ocean I could remember. Its fragrance was sweeter than any perfume, more nutritious than any Thanksgiving dinner, more comforting than sleeping in your own . . .

I woke up. Pasha was next to me sleeping. Our kitten, Max, was curled up on his chest. I had been so happy when Pasha brought him home. I had forgotten how much I loved cats, and since we never really had any pets when I was growing up (except two suicidal Woolworth's turtles), Max was the kitten I had always wanted but was never allowed to have. I fed him, played with him, brushed him, and loved it when he curled up next to us to sleep.

Later that afternoon, I took what I called a "kitty nap." I climbed into bed with a cup of Earl Grey tea and looked at the ailanthus tree and the Long Island Rail Road trestle outside the window for a while, then I lay down next to Max and listened to him purr. It soothed me. It made me feel safe. It made me feel like I was at home. Even though I really wasn't.

Pasha and I were living together. Kind of. He had gotten an apartment in Astoria after we both graduated SVA and gotten jobs, but I never moved in completely. I would stay there four or five days and then go back home for a day or two and start over again. It was not an ideal situation and I don't remember why or how it evolved in that way, but we had become used to it. We had been together now over six years. It was a habit.

As I stroked the cat, I thought about what had happened barely a month before. I had gone into the bedroom to get Max when Pasha and everyone else in the apartment screamed. I ran back into the living room carrying Max, and everyone screamed again. Max, who didn't like loud noises, squirmed out of my arms and ran back into the bedroom. I sat down wondering what I'd missed in the two seconds the announcers had been talking and hoped there'd be an instant replay.

We were watching the Mets. They were great that year. In fact they had been great for the last couple of years, but this year they were in the World Series. They had come a long way from the years Darlinda and I would climb up a fence onto the top of a phone booth and then up another fence to sneak into Shea Stadium.

Pasha's and my entire social life centered around baseball that year. At the beginning of the season, we and our friends Aimee and Cevyn had put our money together and bought tickets to twenty-five home games. That's a lot of baseball, about a game a week and it wasn't cheap, even though most of seats were in the red nosebleed section where you could yell all you wanted, smoke undisturbed, and drink the six-packs of Heineken cans we had frozen and sneaked in along with the bags of chips, buckets of Kentucky Fried Chicken, or foot-long heros we also sometimes brought.

It was easy to do that back then. No one cared what was in your bag. Shea Stadium was one big party that spring and summer with the "Curly Shuffle" and "We Will Rock You" as the sound track. Pasha and I had even entered Banner Day that year along with Darlinda, who was now back from the Army. The three of us were Met maniacs.

But baseball was the only thing we had between us now—besides Max. Slowly, almost imperceptibly, since graduation our lives had become routine in every way. We had become one of those couples I swore not ever to become. You've seen them. They sit at brunch or dinner reading or not looking at each other. It didn't help that Aimee and Cevyn kept talking about how they were thinking of getting engaged or that Pasha's parents had said they would buy us a co-op on Junction Boulevard if we got married. We could walk to Shea Stadium from there. But that wasn't a reason to get married, was it?

I was lucky. I hadn't missed the instant replay. It was the famous Game 6 of the 1986 World Series between the Mets and Boston Red Sox, where in the tenth inning the Mets had rallied after being one out away from losing the series. The game had been tied and Ray Knight was on second base when on a full count and after several foul balls Mookie Wilson hit a dribbler up the first base side that went through Bill Buckner's legs. The Mets won and would go on to win the World Series that following Monday. The moment after Jesse Orosco threw his glove into the air, Astoria exploded as if it was the Fourth of July plus New Year's Eve.

It was better than Greek Easter, when there had been a candle-light promenade throughout the neighborhood. Fireworks were shot off, horns were honked, people yelled out windows, and spontane-ous parties erupted in Astoria Park, even though the next day was a workday. It had been an amazing end to what had been an amazing summer, I thought, as Max and I fell asleep.

A few weeks later, Pasha woke me up from another kitty nap. Aimee and Cevyn were at the door with snowflakes clinging to their hair and two bottles of champagne: one for them, for they had finally gotten engaged, and one for us, for we were going to be next. We drank them both and went out for more.

The next morning I asked Pasha when we were going to get married. He looked at me with sad eyes and said we weren't. I didn't argue. I knew. I don't even remember crying at the time. I just got out of bed, got dressed, packed up my clothes, said good-bye to him and Max, and went back to The Bronx. I had nowhere else to go. And I had never really left anyway.

Don't get me wrong. Pasha and I had loved each other. We had been together for almost seven years. But every relationship eventually gets to the point where either you get married or you break up. We broke up. After their wedding, Aimee and Cevyn moved to San Diego. I wonder if they're still together.

When I told my mother what had happened to Pasha and me, she said the reason why we didn't get married was that I gave him sex. I knew better. Pasha had been a very good boyfriend. The reason we broke up was that sex wasn't enough.

40

AFTER DARK

"Nothing good ever happens after 2:00 A.M." That's what my mother told me whenever I tried to get my curfew raised.

When I was twenty, I thought I'd made the right choice by choosing to go to SVA and live at home. I could get home cooking and do my laundry anytime. I could do my homework on the subway and have more time to go dancing. I didn't think my choice would have its price and that the price would be my freedom.

"But Mom, I'm in college now. I'm an adult," I would say.

Now my mother had not been known as the Jackie O of East 103rd Street for nothing. Her regular voice was a soft, well-modulated stage whisper (just like the real Jackie) with no Spanish accent whatsoever. But when she pissed me off, as she was doing now, she sounded just like Rosie Perez—and I mean that in the kindest, most respectful way.

"*Mira. Adulto? Como* you are *un adulto*, you will live in your own house. *Pero*, as long as you live under my roof, you will be home by 2:00 A.M!"

So for the next five years I obeyed her. I came home drunk. I came home tripping. Once or twice I even came home without my underwear, but by God, I was home by 2:00 A.M.

Finally I graduated, landed a job, and kind of moved in with my boyfriend. But now that Pasha and I had broken up, instead of going back to a 2 A.M. curfew (which, believe you me, would have been enforced regardless of how old I was—twenty-six and change in case anyone's counting), I decided to be *un adulto* and get my own apartment.

Do you remember what it was like to look for an apartment in the pre-Internet late eighties? Yuppies had the *New York Times*. Neighborhood people had The *Post* and *New York Daily News*. I, however, was no longer a neighborhood person.

My only hope was the *Village Voice*, and I knew that to get the best listings, I would have to be at the newsstand across Lafayette Street from the Astor Place cube at . . . 2:00 A.M. on Wednesday morning when the truck came with the delivery. I would have to scramble for a paper along with the other couple of dozen apartment and job seekers, find a spot on the curb to scan the listings, and then run to the pay phone on the corner to leave messages because there were not any cell phones yet. And God help you if you did not have enough quarters.

I did leave a message that night for one of the two apartments I thought I could afford. One called the next day and said I could come see it that Saturday. I had already hung up before I realized the apartment was in Brooklyn. I asked my father if he would come with me. But when I told him it was in Brooklyn, he said forget it. For some reason, he just hated Brooklyn.

Alone on my way to the apartment, I looked at a subway map. The neighborhood was right near Prospect Park, wherever that was. "Perfect," I thought, "just about as far away from my family as I could get and still be in the same city."

Now my father had taught Kevin and me how to rent a safe apartment. He said, "First you go in and check the outlets to see if they spark. You go into the bathroom to see if the toilet flushes. Then you go to the kitchen and make sure there are no holes under the sink. Then you ask to go to the roof. If they say no, you say okay—and then when they leave, you sneak up there anyway. You walk to the four corners of the roof, and if you see any projects—you don't take the apartment." This was from a man who had grown up in Spanish Harlem.

The apartment only passed the project test, but I took it anyway. Oh, excuse me, did I call it an apartment? Ever hear of the film *This Property Is Condemned*? I lived there. The bathroom ceiling dripped, every outlet sparked like a Tesla coil, and the hole under the kitchen sink was large enough for a German shepherd to crawl through. All this for just $550 a month.

But it did have a backyard that could have made a pretty nice garden—if it was cleaned up. I was sure it would only take a week. After two months, a change of employment, and several bouts of boredom, loneliness, and self-pity, I dug up a half century of fossilized pets (I kept some of the more interesting bones), a foot-high pile of rusted nails, and a dollar in Indian-head nickels, and was only half done. Every time I cut myself on yet another piece of beer bottle made before my parents were born; I saw it as one more manifestation of my rotten, miserable, new adult life.

And then, just when I thought things couldn't get any worse, I lost my job. My new job. The job where I hadn't yet worked nearly long enough to qualify for unemployment.

I had a little over $2,000 dollars in my savings account, enough for about three months rent and about $66.66 a month for everything else, including feeding myself and the two kittens I had gotten to keep me company: a tiny Russian Blue I named Boris and a brown tabby female who reminded me of Max, who I named Kimchi.

One morning I looked out of the window at the finally clean, tilled garden. Whenever I looked at it before, I had pictured a soothing floral oasis for my tortured soul. Now I looked at it and saw dinner.

I ran from the apartment and went straight to the Grand Army Plaza library where I took out every book I could find on organic gardening (no Internet yet, remember?). In the afternoon, I went to the Caton Avenue stables and pushed home a creaking shopping cart filled with plastic Key Food bags overflowing with horse manure.

The kittens would spend the night rubbing themselves crazy over my sneakers.

Before the next week was out, I had planted my miniature farm with plum and beefsteak tomatoes, green beans, zucchini, eggplant, and thirty-six stalks of evenly spaced Silver Queen white corn. All under the watchful eyes of my next-door neighbors, a family of indeterminate Eastern European origin consisting of a fat mother with an eye patch, an even fatter drunken husband, and their skinny teenage son who liked to sunbathe in his rotting yellowed underwear.

They all had something to say while I planted garlic, scallions, marigolds, and nasturtium in between each row. *"Vy* you is *plantink* flower *mit* food?" my neighbor asked me in her indeterminate Eastern European accent. "You are knowing nothing of garden. All plant *vill* be *diet*. You *vill* see . . . ugly girl."

I thought I knew what I was doing. According to the organic gardening books, planting the herbs and flowers would guard my vegetables against mold, infestation, and rot. But not, unfortunately, against theft.

By the middle of August, my garden was like a Henri Rosseau painting bursting with life and color; my neighbor's, a soggy heap of mold and rot. *"Vat* you do my plants, ugly girl?" my neighbor asked as she shook her fat fist at me.

What could I tell her? That all the bugs and germs that were repelled from my garden were feasting on hers? Besides, I had other things to worry about: I had not been successful finding a new job and was now living off the bottom of a ten-pound bag of rice. But the first veggie to be ripe, a fat purple eggplant, was just a day away.

Have you ever been hungry? Really hungry? The kind that wakes you up at night and keeps you on edge all day. I know I was always just a phone call away from my parents, but I was stubborn. I intentionally had moved as far away from them as I could, and I was determined to be *un adulto* and deal with this on my own.

That morning, I went into my garden and my perfect eggplant was gone. The next day, the next eggplant was gone. Then the zucchini. Then, half my tomatoes. I couldn't understand. And then one morning, a message in the dirt: a fat bare footprint next to the chain-link fence and on the other side, a stepladder. How could I have been so stupid? I looked into my neighbor's yard and she smirked at me. "*Vy* your plant is *livit* and mines is die. Not correct . . . ugly girl," and she put out her unfiltered cigarette with her fat, bare foot.

I had never been so furious in my life. I wanted to climb that fence, break off her fat fingers and her fat foot, and stick them into the fat hole where her right eye used to be. But I knew if I even so much as touched her, I would be the one to go to jail. I went into my apartment and cried and screamed until I collapsed onto the floor. I was a total and complete failure as an adult and would now have to call home and beg to come back.

As I resigned myself to a lifetime of 2:00 A.M. curfews, Boris, the tiny Russian Blue kitten, who I caught eating a water bug the night before, went into the litter box and took the worst-smelling cat crap I ever smelled in my life. And through the miasma, the hunger, and the tears came an idea.

I went into my backyard at 2:00 A.M. It was cool and peaceful under a full moon. I waited until all the lights on the block went dark, then I crept into the garden. I compared the last two eggplants, only the plumpest, ripest one would do.

Lying on my back, I took out my sharpest X-Acto knife, and slowly, carefully, sawed a circular plug out of the bottom of the egg-plant and hollowed it out, all the time comparing it to the circumfer-ence of the cat turd in the baggie at my side. The sky began to grow light. I was sweating. I saw a light go on in my neighbors' kitchen, slipped the turd up into the eggplant, and replaced the plug just as I heard their screen door open.

I crawled back into my apartment, just in time. Later that day, I saw my neighbors on their front stoop. They wouldn't look at me. "How is garden?" I asked. They banged into their house and locked the door. I thought I was going to break in half laughing because what I was dying to know was how and when did they find out about the booby, or should I say "poopy," trap? Did it slide out into her hand as she picked it? Or did it liquefy inside as she steamed it for her family whole? I would never know.

What I did know was that nothing ever disappeared from my garden that summer or any other summer for the five years I lived there. Funny thing is, now, for some reason, there's one vegetable I really don't eat much anymore. So nothing good ever happens after 2:00 A.M.? Sorry Mom, this time, you were wrong.

41

GOOD-BYE '80S!
(Escape from CBGB's, part 2)

"Hear ye, hear ye," I yelled above the music at a rock bar called the Continental Divide. "Tonight is March first, 1990—and I will never go out with Adam Gold!" And then I fell off the table I had been straddling. I think I might have had five beers. I also vaguely remember hearing people cheer.

In the two years since Pasha and I had broken up, I had the usual romantic experiences a woman in her late twenties should have, the fling, the transitional boyfriend—and the mistake. But in September 1989, my friend Eddy's band was playing at CBGB's Gallery, and he asked if I was going. He said there was someone he wanted me to meet.

Eddy Melendez and I knew each other from Gimbels on 86th Street where we had both worked in the art supply department. We had become friends, but were never romantically involved. I was still with Pasha when we met, and by the time we split, he was taken. I maintain to this day that Eddy Melendez is the only Latin man I could ever see myself with.

Eddy was a musician, a guitarist, and a great one. On certain club bathroom walls in the East Village in the late 1980s and early 1990s, you might have seen scrawled, "Eddy Melendez is God." This was that Eddy. His latest band consisted of him on lead guitar, his brother Willie on drums, a gorgeous West Indian–looking man with waist-length dreadlocks on bass named André, and a Gothic Southern blonde with a voice of silken steel named Plain Jane. They called themselves Laguna Morée, and why they did not become rock superstars is a mystery to me. I absolutely think they should have been, and I want to think they could have been. Bands that would later become famous, like the Spin Doctors, used to open for them. But this story is about Adam and me.

It was over ten years since I had been chased by rabid, ripped-fishnet wearing crossdressers from CBGB's main club, and I had been back there a few times since. The night I met Adam Gold, we were next door to CBGB's main club at their space called CBGB's Gallery. I was wearing a brand-new pair of ankle-zippered Guess jeans and being my normal, ladylike self (dancing on top of a stack of Marshalls with my girlfriend Tahnya).

Tahnya and I went to every gig of Eddy's we could. We, along with a group of people who followed the band, called ourselves Goonies. Our signature was that when the band played a song called "Slash," we'd all rush in front of the stage and start dancing like crazy, and I do mean crazy. Really crazy.

But this night Tahnya and I were dancing on top of the amps when I heard Eddy say, "Hey! Come down!" When we did, Eddy introduced us to Adam Gold.

Adam was tall, with a slim, wiry build. He had a full head of thick, wavy, dark brown hair, a wide smile, and what looked like green eyes under a pair of wire-framed glasses. He also looked very, very, *very* young. Eddy finished his introductions, and the four of us hung out intermittently throughout the night. As I was leaving, Adam ran up to me and asked if he was going to see me again. "Sure, see you at the next gig," I answered.

I did, in fact, see Adam at the next Laguna Morée gig and the next, and the next, when I finally asked him his age. He had just turned twenty-one—I was twenty-nine. I told him as far as dating was concerned, forget it. He was eight years younger than I was, and I wasn't interested in cradle robbing (the term "Cougar" wouldn't be coined for another fifteen years).

Eddy had confessed to me at CBGB's Gallery that Adam had been in a funk. Adam and Eddy worked together, and for the previous two weeks, Adam had done nothing but mope because he had just broken up with his girlfriend. Eddy comped him for the gig that night, saying he would meet two hot, single women: Tahnya and me (thanks Eddy!). When Adam saw the two of us dancing on top of the amps, he told Eddy we were both hot and asked which one he should talk to. Eddy pointed to me and said, "That one. She's sweeter." Not that Tahnya would have gone out with Adam either.

Tahnya was twenty-eight, and in her words, she "didn't look at anyone under thirty-five." She liked men, not boys. I was in the market for a man myself. My last encounter, the "mistake," had been with someone three years younger than I was, and I had decided I wasn't going to look at anyone under . . . thirty. Why Eddy would think either Tahnya or I would be attracted to a guy so much younger than us was puzzling. But Eddy always liked "older women." At twenty-seven, his girlfriend, Jeannie, was thirty-four years old.

That wasn't for me. I need a mature man, not a googly-eyed boy who would hang around me at every gig, which is what Adam did. But . . . I liked Adam. I enjoyed talking to him. He was different from anyone I had ever known.

One midwinter night, as I was leaving a gig, Adam asked me for about the twentieth time when was I going to go out with him. I patted him on the cheek and said he was a nice boy and good-night. He grabbed my wrist and said he was a *man*—and had been around the world.

"Really?"

"Really," he said.

His father was an astrophysicist who had taught at universities around the world and from the ages of seven to fourteen Adam had lived in England, France, Germany, Denmark, Japan, and India, with stops in Greece, Italy, and Egypt. I was floored. We sat and talked until the bar closed. But I still wouldn't go out with him.

A couple of weeks after learning of Adam's "worldy man" status came my infamous announcement (okay, plunge) at the Continental Divide.

Even after that, Adam and I continued to fall deeper into our nonrelationship relationship. We would see each other a few times a month at gigs. He would ask me out. I would say no. But before the no, we'd have hours-long conversations about music, the primacy of art, *Star Trek*, . . . and the 1970s graffiti days.

I wasn't surprised that besides Laguna Morée Adam listened to the Clash, UB40, . . . and Black Sabbath, wanted to be a famous painter, and loved *Star Trek*—both the original series reruns and *Next Generation*. What was crazy to me was that we had graffiti in common. When Adam told me he used to hit the Zerega Avenue layups, I asked what year. When he told me from 1984 to 1986, I stared at him in disbelief. I told him I grew up on St. Peter's Avenue and used to stand at my bathroom window smoking and watching kids tag. At the next gig, he brought in a photograph of himself on the layups in front of a train. He was sure that on one of those nights I was looking at him.

Slowly, it dawned on me that I had at last met my male equivalent: a New York City born-and-raised, ex-graffiti writer and artist who was the black sheep of his academic family, as I was the red sheep in mine. But I still wouldn't go out with him.

He would write his phone number on a napkin and stick it in my coat pocket. I would rip it up in front of him. He would do it more sneakily the next time. I would find it a week afterward—and then rip it up.

On one night we both went to a Goonie gig separately—with dates—and spent so much time talking to each other that our respective dates left . . . together. But I still wouldn't go out with him. And then came the intervention.

Tahnya and I also hung out with a pair of sisters, Diana and Chloé, who had both also gone to SVA. They lived together on East 3rd Street with Diana's young son, and Tahnya and I would meet them at their apartment every week to drink wine, munch on cheese, and watch *Twin Peaks*.

This week, I had caught a case of LPT and was a little late. When I arrived, the TV was on, and there were seven women in the room all looking at me. It really was an intervention.

Each one of them stood up and spoke her reason why she thought I should go out with Adam. They all knew the two of us. They had all seen the two of us at Goonie gigs. And they all thought they knew better than I did. The top three reasons they gave (all Tahnya's) were, and I quote:

"You don't have to fuck him. You don't have to marry him. You just have to go out with him. For God's sake, you are the only two who still listen to Black Sabbath—how bored can you be for three hours!"

Tahnya was right. About the Black Sabbath, and as it turned out, about everything. And so in November 1990, I finally agreed to go out with Adam Gold.

Our first "official" date was at a Goonie gig on Staten Island that nearly turned into a race riot worthy of Lehman High School, 1975. The Neanderthal, way outer-borough rednecks there could not grok that a punk-rock-gothic funk band could have "spics and niggers" in it, and we basically barely got out of there with our lives—or without the wrath of the police who unsuccessfully tried to break it up.

On our second date, we went to Phebe's on the Bowery and ate Black Jack burgers, played pool, and drank beer all night, and I went home in a cab alone.

I don't remember what we did on our third date. But that's the night Adam came home with me and never left. The Red Sheep and the Black Sheep would be together for nearly fourteen years.

42

LATINOS IN THE WORKPLACE

When I finally got the courage to tell my family I had been accepted first to New York City Community College and then to SVA, it was just two more drops in my bottomless lifetime bucket of failure.

"Artist? *Ay, no,* how can you do this to us? We didn't raise you to be *una bohemian.* What are we going to tell Pastor Acevedo? Why can't you be a teacher like your cousin Evie wants to be? That's a nice job. Why can't you get a *nice* job?"

This is what I heard—through all five years of art school. I felt so guilty for being such a *decepcionado,* or as Titi Ofelia put it, *doble decepcionado.* So instead of moving into an East Village squat right after my SVA graduation with most of my class, I decided to make my family happy. I got a job—a *nice* job—as an assistant art director at a big, famous advertising agency. That job didn't work out.

I then got one at a smaller agency, this time as a junior copywriter. That job didn't work out either. Nor did any of the others: as paste-up artist, illustrator, or assistant fashion stylist. I eventually found work as a freelance copy editor/proofreader at a fashion/catalog advertising agency. It was perfect. Since I was in production, I'd have no creative responsibility—which meant no pressure or long hours. I wouldn't have a good salary or benefits either, but because the job was finite: stack of work to edit and stack of work done; I would have time to pursue my artistic dreams.

At last, here was something that would make everyone proud of me. I was fully grown up now and could leave all the drama and mistakes of my youth behind. From now on, everyone I came in contact with would be mature, rational, and sophisticated.

Monday morning, twelve noon. I opened my boss's door. "Idiot!" he yelled at me. "No, stupid idiot! I said *diet* RC Cola!"

So, my glamorous new fashion job wasn't exactly what I imagined. My boss greeted me thusly when I couldn't find him a Diet RC Cola at the corner deli, when RC Cola hardly existed anymore. Or when I couldn't tell him what was on MTV's *House of Style* the night before because I didn't have cable. Or when it was raining and his hair frizzed up and his editorial didn't get picked, again. I heard this all day, every day. It was kind of like being with certain family members. Except now I was being paid to be insulted.

Three months into the job, my boss called me into his office and said, "Is it true you're Spanish?" Someone had heard me speaking "Hispanic" in the elevator and recommended I work on the agency's new account: a huge hair care company famous for its exotic shampoos and conditioners. They wanted me to translate their U.S. ads into Spanish for the Caribbean market. "I, uh, I can't do that," I said. "I'm not fluent. I only speak Kitchen Spanish. You know, "*Sus chuletas siempre son sabroso, abuelita.* You need someone who speaks Spanish all the time, someone who is really bilingual, you need . . ."

"What *you* need Missy," my boss interrupted, "is your job."

I barricaded myself in my cubicle with an English/Spanish dictionary and translated the ads as best I could. "I always knew you'd be good for something someday," my boss said. My family's response was, "You're translating Spanish? *Oyé,* they better get a lawyer."

I was furious. I was so tired of feeling like the pariah, the outsider, the *decepcionado.* So what if I listened to Blur and Sublime instead of Marc Anthony and Menudo? So what if I couldn't dance salsa? So what if my Spanish sounded like I learned it in high school Spanish classes, which, yes, I basically had. I washed my panties in the shower (almost) every night. I wore *chancletas* in the house (sometimes), and I knew how to make killer *coquito*—always. "I can speak

Spanish," I said. "And I'm getting paid for it!" The getting paid part
shut them up for a while.

A month later my boss called me into his office again. "Idiot!" he
yelled. "No, stupid idiot! You just cost this company a million-dollar
account! You put a bad word into the shampoo ads!"

"Bad word?" I said. "What are you talking about?"

"*Pelo!* See? *Pelo! Pelo! Pelo!* What the hell does that mean?" and he
threw a highlighted copy of the ad at me.

"But *p-p-pelo* isn't a bad word," I stammered. "It just means hair.
I swear. I'll prove it to you."

So we walked downstairs from the creative department, with
its windowed offices, leather designer chairs, and fresh flower ar-
rangements, to the back offices, where the other Latin employees of
the company worked. We went to see Hector, a *Chicano* who worked
in the bullpen; Edwige, the Argentinean American production manager; Yvette, a *Dominicana* from human resources; and Marci, the re-
ceptionist, a Brooklyn *Boricua*. All of them said *pelo* just meant hair.

"See," I said, feeling vindicated.

And then I saw Soledad, the intern from accounting and originally *Calle Ocho*, Little Havana, Miami. Flushed with victory, I did my
best Stray Cat Strut over to her and called out, "*Solie, ven aqui!* Is there
anything wrong with the word *pelo*?"

She grabbed me and whispered, "Shush, don't say that in front
of a man. It's bad!"

"I knew it!" my boss yelled. "I always knew you were good for
nothing." And he told everyone that the ad I had translated for the
Caribbean said, "Try our Exotic Conditioner for lustrous, manageable, brilliant *pubic* hair."

It didn't matter that Soledad was only seventeen and a member
of a Pentecostal sect so extreme the women weren't allowed to wear
lipstick, shave their legs, or even tweeze their abundant chin hairs.
And it didn't matter that *pelo* just meant *pelo*! I was fired. Or being
that I was a freelancer, I was "unbooked"—indefinitely.

The next day I had to come back to the office and finish picking up some stuff. Strangely, though, all the offices, cubicles and bull

pens were empty, and I could hear a commotion in the conference room. For some reason, I decided to check it out. I walked in to find the entire company crowded around the TV used for presentations, awaiting the verdict in the O. J. Simspon trial.

On one side of the room, Caucasians; on the other, African Americans and Latinos. Me? I saw I was standing smack in the middle, right beside the company's lone Asian employee.

The verdict was given and the reactions were as expected. Brown and beige hooted and hollered; pink and peach stood bewildered. I saw my ex-boss looking at me, which made me uncomfortable because I realized I didn't work there anymore. I headed back to my former cubicle.

As I packed my backpack, rumors of riots—and worse—had already begun. "They" were in Grand Central Station. "They" were running through Penn Station. "They" had cordoned off Port Authority Bus Terminal.

The decision was made to close the office early. Many of the young, blond female account managers who had to go through Grand Central, Penn Station, or Port Authority Bus Terminal to get home were terrified that "They" would get them. And whom do you think escorted these women to their destinations, ensuring their safe exodus from Manhattan? You got it. "They" did.

As for me, I was supposed to meet Adam at the Art Students' League, so I said my good-byes and started to leave. A couple of people asked me if I was going to be okay. I took it to mean okay "out there," not okay "without a job." I wasn't afraid of walking alone, so I said, "Yes, take care and see you . . . around."

My ex-boss was in the elevator with me on my way out. There was nothing I could say, so I just stared straight ahead.

It was an interesting walk up Madison Avenue. Stores were closing early, and on every block you could hear the clanging of gates being pulled down. The streets were crowded, and you could feel a collective sense of anxiety. People who usually took the subway at Grand Central were so nervous about what *could* be happening, they lined up five and six deep waiting for express buses. The sidewalks became so packed, I had to walk in the street. A taxi backfired and people were startled so badly, they bumped into each other and tempers flared.

It was a bad situation. One idiot and there could be a stampede, like the Who in Cincinnati. I cut across to 9th Avenue, where there were empty sidewalks and some peace.

When I finally reached 57th Street where Adam was waiting for me, he asked, "What kept you?"

"Fucking O. J.," I answered.

"Assholes," he said.

That was a cool thing about Adam. We were always on the same wavelength. We went for a walk in Central Park and it was a beautiful day.

The next morning at 10:30, the phone rang. It was my ex-boss wondering why I wasn't at work.

"Um . . . because you fired me," I said.

"You can't be fired," he said. "You're freelance. Are you coming in or do I have to book someone else?"

So I went in to work. And when I got home, I found a box on my doorstep. It was from the hair care company. Inside was a letter belatedly thanking me for "my invaluable contribution to its Caribbean campaign" and six bottles of its exotic shampoo and conditioner.

I never found out what caused my boss to change his mind, and I would work at that company for another seven years—outliving his tenure. Maybe it was because we didn't really lose the account. I just know that for the next year, I had the most lustrous, manageable, . . . and brilliant *pelo* in all of Brooklyn. All over.

43

THE FALCON AND THE HANGMAN

"Make me a coffee," my father said. "No, not with that," he said when I picked up my brand-new French press coffeemaker. "The real way, with a *colador*! I can't get your mother to make it that way anymore."

A year after I moved to Brooklyn, my father visited for the first time. He saw Prospect Park and the neighborhood and loved it. Not enough for him and my mother to move there, which I tried to convince them to do, but enough to come back once a month, usually with Kevin. My mother didn't come over much. I only saw her on my infrequent visits to The Bronx now that *abuelita* had died. But I did call every week.

It was a warm magnolia trees-in-full-bloom spring Saturday, and my father, Kevin, Adam, and I had gone to the P.S. 321 Flea Market on Seventh Avenue in Park Slope. My father loved that flea market. He could spend hours looking at all kinds of stuff—and then he'd flirt with an older female vendor named Helen. He'd call her Toots or Sweetheart and I'd cringe. She seemed to like it though and always smiled back. I've never met anyone who didn't like my father.

My father liked Adam. A lot. More than anyone else I had ever been with. He had a "test" he gave to the three boys I had dared to bring home. He poured out two shots from an ancient bottle of Fundador Brandy he kept on a top shelf in the kitchen and watched for their reaction as they drank it. My father was not a big drinker, just a beer or two at a barbecue or a ball game and some *coquito* on the holidays, but he and his brothers used to do these shots at Ruby Clubs when I was little (for all I knew it was the same bottle from the 1970s), and he could down it like water.

Brendan had almost thrown up, even though he was Irish. Pasha, who was Russian, did a little better. Tears welled up in his eyes and he coughed. Adam, on the other hand, threw back the shot and banged the glass on the kitchen counter saying, "Thank you sir, may I please have another." My father loved it.

"You finally brought home a real man," he said, conveniently forgetting the fact that Adam was eight years my junior.

As I was making coffee, the *real* way, Adam told my father and Kevin about an adventure we had a month before.

While checking out Battery Park City's brand-new scenic walkway, on the other side of the World Financial Center, we strolled by an area still under construction. Adam stopped suddenly and asked, "What's that?"

"What's what?" I asked.

"Shush," he said, pointing. "That. Look!" And he bent down, taking me with him.

On the other side of a fence in what looked like a construction yard was a cat stalking. But Adam was talking about a bird, a large chick standing in the grass. It was quiet. Defiant really. You could swear its chin was pointed straight up and its mouth was pointing slightly down—if it had a chin and a mouth.

"I know what it is," I whispered excitedly. "It's a falcon!"

"A peregrine," Adam said. "And it looks like your brother."

That was another very cool thing about Adam. Not only was he a nerd about certain things, such as knowing about bird species, like me, but he was right; Kevin did have a bit of a protruding chin, and the bird's posture did resemble Kevin's usual picture-taking pose. I cracked up.

When I finished laughing, I said, "We have to do something. We have to save it. Maybe we can get a reward or something." Adam was out of work and my copyediting was our only income; money was supertight.

"Yeah." Adam said. "Maybe I can ask that guard if we can get in and save it."

We went to ask the guard. We told him it was an endangered species. "How do you know it's a falcon?" he asked me.

"Because I know," I said.

"I think it's a pigeon," the guard said. "Let the cat get it. Now get out of here before I call the cops." And he went back into his booth and his little television.

"That guard is a dick," I said.

"Yeah, fuck him," Adam said. "I'm getting that bird. Give me your bandanna. Cover me."

Adam hopped the fence, shooed off the cat, which had come back for another try, and hopped back over with the bird as the guard came over brandishing his walkie-talkie. "I seen *youse*," he said. "And *youse* are trespassing. I called the cops."

"Good." Adam said. "We'll wait for them with you." The guard made a face at us as if he had sucked an entire lemon. When the cops came and we showed them the chick, they told the guard that we had saved an endangered species. And if the guard had let the cat get it, he could have been prosecuted and fined or gone to jail.

As the guard stood there with his mouth hanging open, the cops asked us to get in the car with them. They took us to their station to find out what to do with our rescued endangered species.

The officers were Port Authority police officers, and their station was in the World Trade Center. We talked to one of them while the other made some phone calls, and we found out that they had both been there in the bombing in 1993, four years before. We know now what happened a little over four years after that day. I hope they lived. I wish I remembered their names.

When the other officer came back, he was excited. "It's a kestrel!" he said, and he had found a woman who fostered abandoned or injured kestrels and falcons before reintroducing them into the wild. The officers let us ride there with them.

The foster woman lived near Bellevue Hospital, and when she answered the door, we almost burst out laughing. She looked like a bird and was about as friendly as one. But she took our phone number and let Adam and me know when she was about to release the chick. We went a month later, and saw the bird hesitate, then soar into the sky above the Cloisters. It was amazing.

The officers drove us back to Brooklyn after dropping the chick off at the Bird Lady's apartment. I said that the last time I rode in the back of a police car I was thirteen and had been picked up for writing graffiti. Adam said, "Me too, when I was sixteen." We all laughed. Those officers were really, really nice.

When Adam finished telling the story, Kevin said, "Wow! That was freaking cool!" and made the kestrel face. My father hadn't really been listening. He had been wandering around the apartment, poking in the fridge, and opening all the kitchen cabinets.

He went into the tiny bedroom and came out with our cat, Kimchi, who immediately jumped out of his arms. He went back to the kitchen and picked up Boris, who obligingly purred. He looked at all the plants on the window shelves, then walked through the middle room, our living room, to the front of the apartment, where we had converted the front room into an artist's studio for Adam. He looked at all the paintings on the walls and on the easel.

When he came back into the kitchen he said, "This is not the life I would have chosen for you, little girl."

That totally seemed to come out of nowhere, and all I could say was, "What do you mean?"

My father said, "This is not the life I saw for you. I always saw you with an older, professional man. With kids and a house on Long Island with a white fence and a lawn. Not like this . . . artist . . . stuff . . ." and his voice trailed away.

Adam got up and said he was going to the store. He made Kevin go with him.

When we were alone, I said to my father, "Why did you say that? That's not the kind of life I want. If you wanted that kind of life . . . why didn't you give it to Mommy?"

My father's face dropped. He looked as if I had punched him in the stomach. He looked as if he was going to cry, though he didn't.

I felt really bad, but what he said *really* hurt. I thought Adam and I had a good life. Maybe we didn't live in a fancy house and maybe we didn't have a lot of money, but we were both doing what we wanted to do and for the most part, we were happy.

I thought I had to do something right away before this got worse, so I said, "Look at me, Daddy. Do I look hurt? Do I look sick? Do I look sad? Is there food in the refrigerator? Is the house clean? Are the plants alive? Are the cats healthy?"

"Yes," my father said. "But you and Adam are . . ."

"Artists," I said. "Yes, Daddy. We're artists."

He was silent for about a minute. I was scared to hear what he was going to say next.

"I miss you," he said. "With you gone, it's never even anymore. It's always your mother and Kevin against me."

"I can't be home anymore, Daddy. I have to have my life."

"I know, little girl. But I can still miss you, can't I?"

When Adam and my brother came back to the apartment, my father and I had made up and were sitting at the table having another coffee. "What took you so long?" I said. When Kevin and my father left, my father did something he never had before. He hugged Adam.

"You're a good painter," he said.

When they left, Adam asked, "What was that about?"

"I'm not sure," I replied.

Later on, I figured it out. My father never did much of anything in his life besides work. That was his way of making it as stable as he could for Kevin and me. He didn't drink except for special occasions. He didn't gamble except for his daily number. He didn't fool around as Titi Ofelia's husbands always seemed to have. He could've left us when my mother became ill or afterward. I believe he stayed because he loved us. And I believe he at last accepted my life because he saw Adam and I loved each other.

A couple of weeks later, I was offered a really big face-painting job. It was the only art I did anymore: painting tigers, dragons, pea-cocks, and butterflies on kids at The Bronx Zoo or wherever the face-painting group was hired. We were in demand as our style was not just to make little pictures on your cheek; each face was a true work of art. I was lucky to be working with this group of artists.

But this job would take place on Father's Day, and my family had made plans to go to Tito Puente's new restaurant out in City Island to celebrate. I struggled deciding whether to take the job for over a week. On one hand, the job would pay $500 for the day, and Adam and I needed the money. On the other, after the talk my father and I had, I didn't want to wait until his birthday in July to see him again.

In the end, I blew off the job and went to Tito Puente's. The agent was pissed. Adam and I were still broke. The food there was horrible. But I'm forever grateful my father and I were together that day.

44

THE ACCIDENT

They say that when one door closes another one opens. It just doesn't feel like that while the door is closing on your foot.

I was lying on a gurney in the emergency room of Brooklyn Hospital. A livery cab making an illegal turn while running a red light had broadsided the livery cab Adam and I were riding in. It was 8:00 A.M. on Saturday, July 19, 1997. It was my father's birthday. We were on our way to his funeral.

One minute I was going over the eulogy I had written; the next I was flying, first into the metal partition separating us from the driver and then up against the window. Adam, who had been sitting on the side that was hit, screamed, "Are you okay?" In our seven years together, I had never heard him scream like that before.

I tried to say, "I think so," but couldn't form the words—a fountain of blood was spraying from my mouth. Instinctively, I leaned forward so it wouldn't get onto my funeral clothes. A lifetime of up-bringing by women who can spot an unplucked eyebrow at thirty paces sometimes had its advantages.

Two pairs of hands opened the cab door, lifted me out, and carried me to lean against a parked car. "Put me down," I tried to say, "I can walk," but I just swallowed more blood. I couldn't seem to put my lips together at all.

The women who had carried me out of the cab stood over me.

Somehow, I sensed from their complementary looks of concern that they were a couple. I remember thinking, "Wow, I've been saved by lesbians. That is so Brooklyn!" I looked past them and saw our driver crying and clutching his neck; Adam getting his head wrapped by someone; and a man shouting at two cops. I guessed he was the one who had hit us.

This made me really angry because this was not just any old car crash. This was the morning of my father's funeral, and now I was going to be late. I rose from the car bumper and lurched over to the man. When he saw me, he flinched. I tried to yell at him, but still could not put my lips together and could only croak, "Look at me! LOOK at me! You did this to me. My father is dead, and you did this to me on the way to his funeral!"

The man mumbled something and tried to back away. The cops he had been yelling at sprang forward and led me back to where an ambulance had now appeared. "Where's Adam?" I tried to say. "Shush," answered one of the cops, with that false reassurance medics in war movies use to soothe the about-to-die-horribly. "It's going to be all right."

As I climbed into the ambulance, I saw my reflection in a chrome paper-towel dispenser. The left side of my face had been butterflied open from halfway under my left nostril straight through my upper lip. Two flaps of torn skin framed shredded gums, exposing the roots of my front teeth. I reached my hand to where my lip should have been and my fingers went right inside. It was not going to be all right.

It had taken almost twenty years, but I had come full circle: once again I was an actress. I had my first taste of the acting bug doing *Guys and Dolls* at New York City Community College, dropping that pursuit when I decided to continue my original plan of transferring to SVA instead. But at the age of thirty-four—the age where most people quit—I decided once again to try acting. In three years I had gone from taking classes to answering ads in *Back Stage* magazine to auditions with casting directors who were starting to remember me. Maybe I only had small roles in independent films and glorified extra parts in mainstream ones (including the last two minutes of *Living in Oblivion*), but I didn't care. I was proud that I was achieving more with each passing month.

Just two days before, I had shot a Johnnie Walker Red UK print ad where I stood smiling in the setting sun as its rays reflected off my red hair. I was booked for the U.S. version scheduled to shoot that Monday. This was the only thing I had done with my life so far that seemed as if it could finally be something. This was the dream that I had postponed for so long and was finally coming true. Now my mouth was ruined.

I tried to explain to the doctor examining me that I had to be fixed up quickly. I was expected at a funeral in less than an hour, and I was an actress in the middle of a photo shoot who needed to keep her job. The doctor looked at me with uncertainty, excused himself, and ran from our curtained-off area.

A few minutes later a different doctor appeared, who smelled like cigarettes. Mmmm, cigarettes. I thought of the delicious Nat Sherman Phantoms I had in my pocketbook—not that I could have actually put one in my bloody mouth. I would later find out this doctor was the hospital's plastic surgeon. It was supposed to have been his day off. He had just finished a graveyard shift and was standing outside the hospital waiting for a lift to Jones Beach when the ER doctor, who did not think he had the skill to fix me, ran outside and begged him to come back in.

The surgeon bent down and gently closed the gap in my face with his fingers. I say "gently" because I'm sure he was gentle. It just felt as if he were searing me with a blowtorch. "I can fix this," he said. "But we're going to have to put you to sleep for a little while first."

"No! No sleep! You don't understand. My father is dead and everyone is waiting for me. . . . I have to give the eulogy." I sprayed him with blood and spittle, and just when I needed him most, Adam walked in and explained everything. The surgeon said, "If you need to be functional, I can give you locals. It's going to take some time to stitch everything back together and it will hurt—but we'll get you there."

I motioned for a pen and paper. "Go ahead," I wrote. "What can possibly hurt more than this?"

It took eleven needles to numb me properly. I felt the first four. It was the worst pain I'd ever endured. Imagine a swarm of a thousand bees stinging as one, first in unison and then separately, overcoming you so completely that you can no longer remember feeling any differently. I couldn't tell if the pain was coming from the needles, from the stitches, or from a place where tears were no longer of any use.

Three hours later, I careened down a path at Trinity Cemetery in Washington Heights, flush with pain medicine and the memory of the night before my father died. It was on Tuesday. I had called and he wasn't feeling well. My parents' air conditioner had broken and my father was uncomfortable. Adam and I had bought my parents a new air conditioner that we were planning to surprise my father with for his birthday, so I said, "Drink some iced tea and hang in there Daddy, I'll see you Saturday." He said he was going to go lie down. I remember it was a little after seven in the evening. He was dead at seven o'clock the next morning.

My entire family had been waiting at the foot of a hill since 9 A.M. They had come from Washington Heights, The Bronx, upstate New York, Long Island, and Florida, and there were two ancient creatures I didn't recognize, who had come all the way from Cabo Rojo, Puerto Rico. They all barely recognized me.

My left shoulder was in a sling; my right knee looked as if it had been replaced by a watery red softball. Amid the Goth-perfect, deep-purple bruises on my face, a web of over fifty stitches held my mouth together. I knew upon stepping out of the taxi (yes, we had to take another car service), I would be overwhelmed with sympathy, compassion, and pity, but I was already beyond overwhelmed and only wanted this horrible day to be over. "Let's do this," I whispered and went into the chapel.

I started the eulogy by saying I'd never met anyone who

didn't like Rudolph Carlo. I ended by saying that he may not have been wealthy in most people's opinions, but he was the richest man I knew. Everyone had to strain to hear me because I could barely open my mouth—as it was practically sewn shut—or speak louder than a whisper. My mother and brother couldn't look at me. Everyone else cried. Afterward we went to a restaurant where, of course, I could eat nothing. When Adam and I finally got home, I collapsed onto the living room couch, where I would spend the next three weeks.

I didn't cry at the funeral. I physically couldn't. But I was devastated. Not only did I lose my father, but, with the accident, I also lost my purpose. All my life I had tried to be an artist, an art director, a copywriter, an artist again, and I had failed at all of it. Imagine a surgeon going blind or a lawyer losing his vocal cords or a teacher in a world without children. If I could no longer be an actor, I didn't know what to do.

I tried to distract myself by reading, to no avail. I tried daytime television, but one week of Richard Bey and Ricki Lake was enough for me to break down and finally order cable. I remember thinking that my father would have rolled over in his grave if he could see me; he didn't believe in paying to watch television. But I was desperate.

"Hello . . . 1-800-CABLE . . . I want MTV. I said . . . I want MTV! No, I can't speak any louder. . . . I have wires in my mouth. Can you come tomorrow? Next TUESDAY!" In my frustration I popped ten stitches and had to have them redone, but I got my MTV. I spent the time between doctor appointments alternating between watching an endless loop of videos, *Criminal*, *Don't Speak*, and *Beautiful Freak*; hugging Adam, Boris, and Kimchi; and looking in the mirror.

When the stitches were finally removed, it took three days for my repressed grief to exhaust itself. I mourned and howled and then howled again, for the loss of my father and the loss of my hope. The Johnnie Walker people never rescheduled. When I walked into my first casting appointment sporting my new braces and a fresh pink scar over my left lip, which, due to residual nerve damage left me with a slightly crooked smile, I was not called back. By that agency or any other, except for one commercial where I was supposed to be . . . a nerd with braces.

My fledgling career as a "legit" indie film actress was over. There was only one creative outlet left open to me. One I had been resisting for over a year because it wasn't really acting. It was performance art.

Somewhere in the beginning of 1996, I ran into a woman I'd met while taking classes at Gotham City Improv a couple of years before. She invited me to a performance open mic in a space on the Lower East Side called Surf Reality. I didn't want to go. I told her one of my other acting teachers had suggested I try to do stand-up comedy, so I'd done a *New Talent Night* at a well-known comedy club where I begged five friends to pay $10 plus a two-drink minimum to come see me be heckled off the stage. I'd been so humiliated, I swore I'd never do that again. The woman insisted this place wasn't like that. She told me how much fun she was having and how she was performing almost every night now. I talked Adam into going with me.

I had been sitting on the top of the stairs in Surf Reality's hallway, the designated "tobacco" smoking area, having a Nat Sherman and trying to process what I had witnessed in the past hour: there was not only stand-up, which I had expected, but also a woman who painted with her menstrual blood and another who expelled first an onion and then a Butterfinger bar out of her vagina while a man stood silent next to her for her entire eight-minute "act" and painted his penis purple.

An extremely animated, extremely thin woman wearing a fur stole and white thigh-high go-go boots sat down next to me. "You know, you could be really hot if you only lost ten pounds. Do you know the photo shoot diet?" she said.

I sat there speechless, not knowing whether to laugh or smack this person explaining to me in day-by-day detail exactly how to lose five to seven pounds in just one week. She was on day four when the door opened and someone yelled, "Trigg, you're up!"

"Come watch me," she said. "I don't know what I'm doing, but I'd like you to see it."

I followed her into the room and in the next eight minutes saw her perform four of the most brilliant original character monologues I had ever seen.

The next performer was a man who told a story about how he had failed at everything he ever tried until he became a motivational speaker. By the end you realized he was playing a character all along—or was he? This was followed by a group of men swathed in plastic wrap who did an excerpt from their rock opera, accompanied by puppets; then an Israeli woman who sang like Aretha Franklin; and last, another man who played the guitar and sang a song about high school called "Whose Life Sucks Now." I was hooked.

For the next six months I sat in the back row every Sunday night. Sometimes it was brilliant, sometimes horrifying, but it was never boring.

I watched each week without ever putting my name in the bucket. I told myself this was not real acting, and these people would never have been at any of the auditions I had been on—while I fell in love with whatever it was. I was drawn to the freedom to experiment, something unheard of in the acting circles I knew. The truth was, I was paralyzed with jealousy and fear.

Adam finally said, "You get up and do something or I'm never coming back." A week later I put my name in the bucket and did a John Patrick Shanley audition monologue. It sucked. The next week, I tried my stand-up routine, which consisted of sticking a wad of gum on the mic stand and cursing in Spanglish, while wearing a Betsey Johnson micromini leopard-print, baby-doll dress. The dress killed; I didn't.

I hadn't planned to go back to Surf Reality again, but after the accident something inside me knew it was a place where I could at least try to be creative and where it didn't matter if I wore braces or had a visible scar. I was sure I wasn't the only one there who had been scarred.

The night I went back, it was cool for September. I had just gotten my braces tightened and they stung against my still slightly raw mouth. I planned to do a Craig Lucas monologue about death and imbue it with the sense memory of both my father's death and the death of my acting career.

When my name was called, my knees buckled as I walked to the stage. I wanted to bail. I also knew that bailing would make the death of my father and the death of my acting career the death of me. It would be suicide. I might as well throw myself in front of an F train.

The emcee brought me a stool. "It's okay," he said with real compassion in his eyes. "You can do this." He just thought I was scared. He had no idea what I had been through.

This night was another in a long line of accidents. I ditched the Craig Lucas and told my story of my father's death, the car crash, and the cable company call with my mouth sewn shut, and that my father would roll over in his grave if he knew I was now paying $50 a month to watch television—especially MTV—since I was thirty-seven years old, but so what, I liked it and I was keeping it. I didn't care if it, or I, was good or not. I didn't care if it was art. I just knew that I had to do it.

Afterward, people came up to me and said, "That was beautiful. . . . You made me think about my dad. . . . Hey, that 1-800-CABLE bit was funny. You want to be in my show next week?"

I had thought of Surf Reality as a place where only freaks went. Now I was one of them. Multiply that night and the other "alternative" stages I later braved by over a dozen years, and I would learn not only that my words had weight but that what came from my heart, my experiences, had much more of an impact on an audience—and to me—than reciting someone else's script ever could.

I became a writer without realizing it and would collaborate with some of the most brilliantly deranged minds I've ever had the pleasure of knowing. Sometimes our collaborations even included, gasp, acting.

My braces eventually came off, and after spending half of my (woefully inadequate) settlement on microdermabrasion treatments and peels, all that's left of the scar over my lip is a faint white line you can only see if you're waking up next to me.

One night at Surf, during a break in a show, I ran to the deli for a beer and saw a man who must've had a similar accident to mine. His lip line didn't meet. I dropped my bottle of Stella to the floor as I realized how lucky I'd been after all.

I finally found my way to being an artist. Becoming a storyteller may have been an accident, but it was me—and I loved it. Sometimes I wonder what my life would've been like if my father had lived or if the accident hadn't happened. Or maybe, there are no accidents.

45

RED SHEEP

Adam and I were with my Cousin Evie and her boyfriend, Alex, at *La Caridad*, the long-established Upper West Side Chino/Latino restaurant on Broadway and 77th Street. They had called saying they wanted to take us to lunch and they had something to ask us. I was excited to go, not only because I hadn't seen Evie in a while, but also because the food there was yummy.

I ordered from the old Chinese waiter, *"Ensalada bacalao y tostones con* extra *mojito, por favor."* He stuck his nose in the air and asked me if I was Puerto Rican because my Spanish was so bad. He was, of course, Cuban, and everyone "knows" Cubans speak the "best" Spanish along with Colombians, Argentineans, Spaniards, and Japanese (sarcasm intentional). Alex, always the peacekeeper, stepped in to facilitate the ordering.

When he finished, the waiter snorted, "And you must be Dominican."

The waiter was two for two; Alex was Dominican.

After our delicious lunch, I ordered an espresso to go at the takeout counter, *"Damé un café . . . negro."*

No response.

"Uh, damé un café . . . negro?"

The counterman glared at me. "What did you say?" he said in heavily accented English.

I was starting to get annoyed. Was he deaf? "I said, '*Damé un café—negro!* '"

I swear the man leaped over the counter holding a machete—or at least a butter knife. Okay, it was a spoon, but still, he leaped over the counter as if he wanted to chop me up into *sofrito*. Alex jumped between us and begged, "*Por favor!* Please! She doesn't know Spanish!"

"Yes I do," I said in an attempt to save face.

"No! She doesn't," Alex insisted. "Look at her!" and he dragged me out of there.

Once we were out on the sidewalk, Evie and Adam started laughing. "Why did he do that?" I asked. "Why did you say that? All I said was give me a black coffee."

"No you didn't, Michele." Alex could barely speak, he was laughing so hard. "What you said to that very large, very black man was, 'Give me a coffee—Negro!' "

"Oooops . . ." I said, and even I had to laugh.

The words were correct, but my inflection was in the wrong place (sometimes a little knowledge is the most dangerous thing).

So, yeah; maybe I didn't speak the best Spanish in New York City, but at least I tried. I had learned it from high school classes and hearing my relatives tell secrets and yell. What little I knew, I had absorbed from the air, like *humo*.

"Oh Michele, you're always so dramatic," Evie said, but she too was still laughing.

"Which reminds me of what I wanted to ask you guys," Alex added. "Evie and I are getting married next spring, and we want you both to be in our wedding party."

Evie and Alex were high school sweethearts and had been together for ten years. It was somewhat rebellious, I guess. There is "supposed" to be a long-standing "rivalry" between Puerto Ricans and Dominicans. My father used to say, jokingly (repeat: jokingly), that I could bring home anyone I wanted, except a Dominican.

"I can bring home a girl then, Daddy?" I had asked once, laughing.

"Yes," my father said, "as long as she's not Dominican."

My father died that summer, but if he had been there, he would have been happy for them. He loved Alex. We all did. Evie was lucky to have him. He was lucky to have her. They were lucky to have each other.

"Yay!" Adam said, hugging Alex and Evie at the same time. "Congratulations!" He smiled at me. I hesitated before smiling back.

The last time I was with someone for this long and a couple close to us had gotten engaged, it precipitated our breakup. I looked at Adam, who seemed genuinely thrilled for my cousin and soon-to-be-cousin, and thought maybe I didn't have to worry.

When my *abuelita* died, Adam, who was Jewish, was mystified by the Latin-style three-day open-casket wake with wailing and gnashing of teeth. But on the last night of my father's wake, I saw him kneeling in front of my father's casket and, before he knew I was there, overheard him say, "Don't worry Rudy. I'll take care of her."

Adam's family wasn't religious; they were what he called "Holiday Jews." They celebrated Chanukah, Passover, Rosh Hashanah ("Rush-a Homa" according to Adam), and if they were so inclined, Yom Kippur—although Adam always maintained he never had anything to atone for. I, who from my "Pentatholic" (Catholic vs. Pentacostal) upbringing welcomed a little suffering with my religion, liked the idea of fasting and reflecting for a day and sometimes did it for the both of us.

I came out of my reverie. Cousin Evie was standing in front of me, smiling. With her short hair, short dress, and big eyes she looked like her mother, Titi Dulce, had thirty years before, like the *Boricua* Mia Farrow.

"Wait till you see the dresses I picked out, Michele," she said.

I looked over at Adam and Alex and smiled. Evie and I walked back over to them. Maybe there wasn't anything to worry about this time after all.

46

A TALE OF TWO WEDDINGS

How can you tell a Puerto Rican bride at a wedding? She's wearing something old, something new, something borrowed, something blue, something pink, something green, something orange, something striped, something plaid, something leopard print . . .

I love my cousin Evie. I really do. But that dress! When Evie saw her six bridesmaids come out of the dressing room, she cried. When I saw my reflection in the mirror, so did I. The flounced, ruffled, ruched, sweetheart-necklined, asymmetrical-hemmed, dark purple satin, puffed-sleeve dress with two layers of crinoline reminded me of being a little girl at a birthday party in Washington Heights, eating Valencia cake and scratching at myself because the damn thing itched so badly. The fact that I'd be wearing it in a wedding party at the age of thirty-eight didn't do anything to assuage my horror.

For every modern Nuyorican family, there comes a time when they must finally accept the reality of intermarriage—as when my Cousin Evie married a Dominican. At Evie and Alex's wedding there was a champagne fountain, a twelve-piece salsa band, and the most segregated room since George Wallace ran for president: Santo Domingo was on one side; Corozal was on the other.

When the band started, though, and as long as the music played, the dance floor transformed into a tangle of hips, hair, and feet.

The second it stopped, an invisible Mason-Dixon Line reappeared, and the two groups would return to their respective sides, glaring at their dance partners from just a second ago. Evie and Alex didn't notice. They were in love.

I noticed. I was the pale-skinned, freckle-faced, red sheep of my family. I could hardly speak Spanish. I couldn't dance. I never fit in. And I was sure that by now everyone knew it.

I excused myself to go to the bathroom and found two of Alex's cousins sharing a Newport Light. One looked like twenty pounds of *salchica*, sausage, stuffed into a six-pound bag, the other like Dominican Gothic, in black lipstick and white tube socks. The second they saw me go into the bathroom stall, out came the Spanish.

"Oyé, quien es esa blanquita colorada?" (Hey, who's that white redheaded girl?)

"The redhead? She ain't white, she's Evie's cousin."

"Oh-oh-oh, y quien es el hombre que no puede bailar . . . tampoco?" (Who is the guy who can't dance either?)

"Him? I think he's the boyfriend. I heard he's a Jew."

"Un Judeo? Aqui? No creo!" (A Jew? Here? I don't believe it!)

"Ay pobrecita, that must be all she could get."

So yeah, my boyfriend was a Jew. A long-haired, six feet three and a half inch, gothic rock and roll Jew. The black sheep of an academic family—an artist and an outsider—like me.

Now there have only been a few times in my life in which I have exhibited any type of *cojones*, courage. This was one of them. The cousins laughed until I came out of that stall armed and dangerous with five years of high school Spanish—and thirty-eight years of playing *la boba*, the fool:

"Oyé, gordita! Tiene la hora?" (Hey fatty. Got the time?)

They stood there, their faces slowly crumbling like pieces of *morcilla*, blood sausage, as they realized I had understood everything. As they spluttered their apologies, I said, *"Mira, no me joda.* You are so busted. Have a nice day."

*   *   *

I got my revenge, though. I married my Jew. The wedding was on the eleventh anniversary of the day Adam and I met at CBGB's Gallery. And it was at CBGB's Gallery.

We scrubbed and decorated the place and called the event, "The Russo-Rican Extravaganza." We stood under a chuppa and I took communion. Adam broke the glass and I read an ancient Taino prayer. We ate *paella* and brisket, *empanadas* and knishes, *arroz con gandules, platanos maduros,* green beans almondine and chopped liver. Titi Dulce sang hymns in Spanish and had all the Rosens, Druckers, and Spiegelmans clapping for *Alleluja Jésus.* Kevin gave me away and even Titi Ofelia had a swell time.

A few weeks later, something strange happened. I started to worry about being officially "Jewish by injection." Could this mean I had unconsciously—or consciously—rejected my culture? Was I guilty of diluting the gene puddle? Had I finally betrayed whatever little ethnic identity I had?

A few years later, I came out of the subway into a cold December drizzle and saw a very tiny, very brown, very bewildered woman being asked by a well-meaning Yuppie couple: *"Uh, como su piragua?"* (How is your snow cone?)

I walked over and asked her in Spanish if she needed help. *"Por favor!"* She said she was lost and "these white people are crazy." She asked if I knew how to get to 8th Avenue.

On the way, I found out she was from El Salvador and was here to live with her sister, and study to be a dentist. *"Hace frio,"* she said. (It's cold.) Was it always so cold at night?

"Espere hasta que nieva," I answered. (Wait till it snows.)

We walked in silence another moment or two, and suddenly she stopped and turned to me and said, "You must be Puerto Rican."

"What?" I halted mid-stride and nearly tipped over. "Huh? What? Me, Puerto Rican? Wh-wh-why do you think? How do you know?"

A lifetime of insecurities that had long been swept behind sofas, stuffed into closets, and half buried in shallow graves, spilled out. How did she know? Was it my lousy Spanish? The red hair? The pale skin? The freckles? The complete absence of rhythm in my walk? What? What? WHAT?

The woman, who was at most, four feet ten inches, looked up at all five feet three and three-quarter inches of me and said, "No, I thought you must be Puerto Rican, because you are so tall."

To her, I was tall. And, of course, she knew I was a Latina because that's what I was, never mind language, dancing, food, family, politics, religion, the shape of my body, texture of my hair, my chosen profession, who I chose to share my life with, or anything else. I ran home to tell Adam.

"Yeah, so?" he said. "What's the big deal? Why do you still care so much? Can't you just be satisfied with who you are?"

Who I was? Who was I? Forty-three years and I still didn't know. Sadly, neither did he.

I didn't know it at the time, but we were beginning our slow drift apart. He was home all day painting, or trying to. I was working ten hour days at my new, but still-freelance job in what I called "Fashionland," staying an extra couple of hours every night to write shows because we still couldn't afford a computer at home. He was lonely. I was frustrated. He didn't understand that he needed to get a steady job. I didn't understand that even though I was finally realizing my dream of being a performer, maybe it wasn't good to be away from my husband so much.

And thus we continued. For a little while. Until we couldn't anymore.

47

WALKING IN COQUITO WONDERLAND

Christmastime, glasses clinking, 'cause it's time to start drinking
A beautiful sight, this bottle so bright, walking in Coquito Wonderland
Go away, Borden's Eggnog, champagne punch and Swedish Glog
What I have right here is Latino cheer, walking in Coquito Wonderland
In a blender you can put some vodka—only if you want a bellyache
Take a tip from Carmen you'll be smarter . . . to add as much dark rum
  as you can take . . .
Have a shot, you'll be smiling, not too much, or you'll be flying
It's 500 proof, you'll go through the
  roof, walking in Coquito Wonder-
  land,
Walking in Coquito Wonderland!!!*

I sang this song on stage wearing
a hat that was a cross between a fully
lit menorah and a Christmas tree, trail-
ing a thirty-foot extension cord behind
me and carrying a half gallon of Carmen's Triple-X Coquito as the audience
cheered.

It was December 2000. I was Carmen Mofongo, the Lower East Side's One and Only Latin Lady with Stuff on Her Head.

Adam and I had once spent our Friday nights drawing in the Metropolitan Museum of Art; we now spent them in Surf Reality as members of the Producers' Asylum, a small group of performers responsible for producing a show a month. Ours was *The Carmen Mofongo Show*.

Shortly after I started going to open mics at Surf Reality and its sister theater, Collective:Unconscious, I became obsessed with Carmen Miranda. Adam and I had seen a documentary on her life called *Bananas Is My Business*, and I was hooked.

What really intrigued me was learning she wasn't a Brazilian at all, but a Portuguese émigré whose family had moved to Brazil when she was a small child. That someone could completely embody and be a national symbol of an entire culture without actually being born in that culture boggled my mind.

Adam bought me a videotape of the documentary, and I watched it repeatedly. I thought, "What if the spirit of Carmen Miranda came back for our generation in the body of a Puerto Rican from New York City named Carmen Mofongo . . . me?"

Most cultures have their own version of "heart attack on a plate." Americans have bacon cheeseburgers. Italians have fettucine Alfredo. Jewish culture has chopped liver in schmaltz. Southern African Americans have chitlins. The closest to a national dish that we of Puerto Rican heritage have is *mofongo*: a mound of *tostones* mashed with shredded pork meat and crispy pork skin, olive oil, garlic, and seasonings, with stewed chicken, shrimp, or more pork underneath and a piquant, tomatoey, *criolla* sauce on top.

I decided to give Carmen Mofongo Grandma Mari's accent and my vocabulary. The idea of a thick Spanish accent saying words like "juxtaposition," "congruence" and "xenophobia" cracked me up. It was also a bit of a personal statement. It seemed to me that every foreign accent was considered elegant to most Americans, except a Latin one, which was generally depicted as uneducated and unlovely. In my own small way, I was going to break that antediluvian cultural stereotype. "Oooh, 'antediluvian!'" I thought. "I gotta add that word in too!" I started practicing.

"I think it's a dumb idea," Adam said. "No one's gonna get it. People are stupid."

I didn't listen to him. In 1998 Carmen Mofongo debuted at Surf Reality and a star was born. Or at least a Lower East Side icon.

For the next five years, until Surf Reality closed its doors, Adam and I were a theatrical team. I wrote the shows; he made the props, including Carmen's signature collection of hats.

The hats were reinterpretations of Carmen Miranda's various headdresses. Before long, Carmen Mofongo had a wardrobe of over twenty, and proudly wore them all. From the Dinner Hat adorned with components of a stereotypical Latin meal (including a packet of *Sazón*, a pork chop, a can of Goya beans, and a pack of Newports [for afterward]) to the pastel Art Deco recreation of a Miami Beach hotel complete with palm trees and dolphins to Adam's (who became known as the Millinery Mastermind) masterpiece, Carmen's Brain: a

Clockwise from top left: **Carmen's Brain, Miami Hat,
Xmas/Menorah Hat, Platano Hat, Dinner Hat**

rubber brain under a plastic dome. It was similar to the AB-Normal brain in *Young Frankenstein* but with Coney Island sideshow-inspired graphics and signs for each of its sections: Sex, Drugs, Rock and Roll, Boolean Mathematics, Eastern Philosophy, and Pork. Even Adam had to admit I was on to something.

The character and the shows became a popular cult figure on the Lower East Side performance scene, appearing at least once a week, in one space or another, along with our monthly show. In December, we had our biggest extravaganza yet: *Carmen Mofongo's Coquito Xmas 2000.*

For you unlucky ones who don't have a Caribbean Latino in your life, *coquito* is the quintessential Puerto Rican holiday libation, a tropical coconut twist on eggnog. It's a Caribbean vacation in a glass, more specifically, a delicious, sweet, creamy blend of rum, coconut, rum, milk, rum, eggs, rum, vanilla, rum, spices, and rum. The holiday tradition's various recipes are passed down from your ancient *tio, titi, abuelo,* or *abuela* and are family secrets guarded under lock and key.

Even though Grandma Mari was a devout Christian woman, she was also practical. When my mother won her building's first television in a church raffle, *abuelita* decided perhaps gambling was a sin, but gifts from *El Señor* were not. When a sanctimonious woman at *abuelita's* church chided her for wearing lipstick and having manicures, *abuelita* answered, "You think you glorify God by not taking care of yourself? God looks down on you and says, 'Woman, bleach that mustache, and in my Holy Name, shave those legs!' And although drunkenness was frowned on, a little holiday celebration was a blessing. So every Christmas, next to the *pernil,* she made sure there was always a liter or two of her famous, secret *coquito.* I knew that recipe. She never told me it, exactly, but I had watched her make it enough times to remember how.

I carried the holiday tradition with me into my adult life, eventually becoming my family's "official" *coquito* maker. Even Titi Ofelia couldn't argue with my skill.

I also brought a bottle to work every holiday season. For the past five years, my coworkers looked forward to their yearly shot of *coquito*. And each year, there would be the new employee who disregarded the veteran *coquito* drinkers' warnings that it should only be consumed in a shot glass, in the smallest portions.

This year it was the new, redheaded art director, Caitlin Lowe. "I'm from Scotland," she scoffed. "We are born drinking whiskey. Spanish drinks are *poof*." My office mates looked annoyed as she emptied nearly half the bottle into her water glass. I shrugged.

It wasn't long before she was giggling on the ground at the top of the agency's fancy staircase, with her miniskirt and cowboy-booted legs askew, and her glass drained.

This Scotswoman did not believe in panties *or* personal grooming. The company president exercised discretion when he caught an eyeful as he ascended the stairs; the production manager, who was directly behind him, did not. The next day, the entire office knew about, "Fire Down B-Lowe!"

A month later Caitlin took her art-directing skills to Miami.

Carmen Mofongo's Coquito Xmas 2000 was a big hit. All fifty-plus people in the audience had a great time watching her get visited by the ghosts of Coquito Past, Present, and Future and rescued by Santé Claus and El Diablo. And to top it off, at the end of the show, three audience members who could name all of Santa's reindeer, the seven dwarves, and the original seven astronauts (I was obsessed with reruns of the HBO series *From the Earth to the Moon*) won their very own personal-sized bottle of *coquito*. The rest of the audience was consoled with shots from a full-gallon bottle. If you weren't there, you missed it.

After the show, Adam and I were invited to the Christmas party of a well-known performer couple, the "JJs," short for Janet and Jennifer. They were queens of the neo-burlesque and Lower East Side performance scenes. They had matching nose rings, piercings in places I could barely spell, let alone pronounce, and had gotten engaged exactly six years, six months, and six days after their first date.

They were legendary. So were their parties. I was terrified.

Let me explain. Although I was a card-carrying member of the New York City performance underground, people wondered what my home life was like. Did I strut around my apartment in spiked panties while guzzling homemade absinthe and downloading vegan, transgendered, amputee porn? Not really.

I'd go home; take off my makeup; put on my angel-fairy jammies; and watch reruns of *Deep Space Nine*. The truth was I've always been a geek: a sci-fi/fantasy geek.

I've been to not one, but two Star Trek conventions. I've seen each *Lord of the Rings* movie at least twenty times and can quote long passages from all of them verbatim. I know the difference between a Wookie and an Ewok, a Romulan and a Cardassian, and even once fantasized about sex with the Elves. For a long time I believed I was the closeted anomaly in an underground world.

When people asked me what I was "into," I'd stammer and say, "Oh, you know, this 'n' that," The person usually responded with their sexiest wink and the variations on these knowing looks made me cringe. Because I was actually just going to go home, make a pot of Earl Grey tea, and read *The Two Towers*. Again.

But when I walked into the JJs' living room I saw front and center, among skull ashtrays, Rob Zombie dolls, and a Norwegian death metal collection, a perfect, six-foot-tall, live, balsam fir Xmas tree with Jean-Luc Picard on top where the angel should be. I reached up to touch it. As if on cue, the JJs appeared on either side of me. "You like Star Trek too?" the JJs asked. It was as if a holodeck opened up in their Fort Greene living room. I had found sanctuary.

Adam had not. He sat sulking on a couch as I flitted around the room. Energized, and with a cup of mulled wine in one hand and a plate of Smithfield ham in the other, I eventually plopped down next to him and gushed, "Isn't this party fun!"

"It sucks," Adam said. "No one wants to talk to me."

"Talk to them," I said. "Be friendly. What's wrong with you?"

Adam had been struggling to find his way as an artist, and I seemed to have found mine—as a performer. He enjoyed working with me on the shows, but wanted to be known and appreciated in his own right. Someone had recently made the mistake of asking him how it felt to be "Mr. Mofongo." His response, a look of pure death, ensured that no one ever asked him that again.

I returned to flitting about the JJs' living room, and when I looked back a few minutes later, Adam seemed happy talking with a small group of people. I smiled at him and he smiled back. Everything was wonderful. The party ended. A new year began.

We continued with Carmen Mofongo. I also wrote my second one-woman show and was ecstatic when it got booked for an early autumn six-week run at a popular East Village theater.

The first week of September, right before my show was scheduled to open, I impressed MTV producers with Carmen Mofongo at an open call for a new show requiring an unusual "talent." I went in full regalia and proceeded to roll my *r*'s for thirty seconds. I was invited to the callback audition the following Wednesday, the day before my show was to open.

I was floating! I soared all weekend. After all I had been through, it seemed my life was finally going to come together. But the next Tuesday was September 11, 2001.

There was no callback audition at MTV. My solo show was postponed until the final two weeks of its run in October. All of downtown was still under the cloud of the fallen towers. Hardly anyone came. But I told myself I was lucky; after all, neither Adam nor I had lost anyone.

We did a *Coquito Xmas 2001* show that December, but things weren't quite the same anymore. For anyone.

48

GOOD-BYE PUMPKIN

Dear Michele,

I did love you, Pumpkin. I really did. We were so good for each other for so long. Part of me still does love you—but I'm no longer in love with you. There's a difference. The boy you loved doesn't exist anymore. He's gone and I don't know who has taken his place, but I have to find out who he is or I'll go mad. I may already have gone mad. And that's why I have to leave. Now. Before I drown. Before I lose myself. Before there's nothing left of me.

I know this is going to come as a shock to you. But you are so preoccupied with your shows and with your writing and with Kimchi, you just don't see that there's nothing between us anymore. The other night after you performed, someone came up to me and asked me what I thought, and you know what I told that person? When my wife is onstage, I hear her; when she is at home, I don't hear her.

I understand the writing and the shows are your career now. I know Kimchi is dying. I understand. But you need to understand. I need to find where I belong.

I can't lead two lives anymore. I can't. I didn't want it to be this way. It just has to be this way.

Good-bye,
Adam
The Hangman

49

JUST IN TIME

If only we could have talked about all that before we broke up.

It was mid-August 2004, a week after Adam's thirty-sixth birthday. I went to his art studio despite his protests that he needed to finish a painting. I walked in to find him online—on a laptop I had never seen before. We still couldn't afford Internet service for our dinosaur iMac at home. His laptop didn't register to me at the time. There was something I had to know.

"What are you going to do now?" Adam asked.

When Adam told me he no longer wanted to be married, I had thrown up, collapsing onto the bathroom floor. He didn't help me up. Or walk me out. Or say good-bye to me as I left his studio. He wasn't my husband anymore. And hadn't been for some time.

Two mutual friends had asked separately if I'd seen Adam's MySpace page. They both turned away when I said he didn't have one. It took a couple of weeks to get the courage, but on that afternoon, right before trekking to his studio, I finally looked up his page.

He'd been leading a double life from his studio for over a year. He went to clubs and parties I wasn't invited to, with people I didn't know. Some of his friends were women, whose comments made clear they weren't just drinking buddies.

My legs and brain somehow worked together to get me from Adam's studio to the A train to the F train and to our apartment.

I couldn't remember the commute home, and when I eventually came to, I was sitting on the couch, staring. I couldn't believe what had happened.

Nearly fourteen years of friendship, love, and collaboration had been obliterated in one fifteen-minute conversation where Adam confirmed he had been leading another life. It was worse than shock, worse than pain, worse than being numb. I felt as if our entire relationship had been canceled out. As if it never existed.

I cried all night. At 9 A.M. I stopped. I took a shower and went to work, thinking if I hadn't gone to the studio that night, when was he going to tell me?

I later found out that Adam had had that MySpace page for over six months, and all our friends knew about it but were afraid to tell me. I don't know what hurt more, the breakup or the thought that everyone knew it was coming but me. How could I have been such an idiot? How could I not have seen that for the last year we had been living mostly separate lives? Although we spoke on the phone almost every night, if there wasn't a show I was doing or a family function for us to attend, Adam and I were together only once or twice a week. He told me he was working on a new group of paintings for a show and needed his space. The times I did question his absence, he responded, "I don't bother you with your work. Why can't you let me do mine?"

For the last nine months my life, my work had been on hold. Kimchi, one of the two kittens I got when I moved to Brooklyn sixteen years before, was ill. She had been with me since she fit into the palm of my hand, when all I owned was a futon on the floor, a box of 1980s mix tapes, and had eggplants disappearing in my backyard. She was with me through unemployment, career changes, car accidents, and my first gray hairs. She was part of the life I had before Adam and before my *abuelita* and father died. I wanted to do everything I could to help her get better—and then, when that was no longer possible, to help her stay comfortable.

Adam was going through an emotional ordeal too. His beloved Aunt Millie, the only one in his family who had truly stuck up for him when he told his family he wanted to be an artist, was also slowly dying. He started staying at his studio more and more. I hardly noticed. I had to give Kimchi medicine three times a day and would go straight home from work to take care of her.

Cats and people were dying—and we were broke. Almost our entire savings went to vet bills. I resented that Adam wasn't working and that after working all day, I went home alone. I resented having no energy on the days we did see each other.

I thought this was just a phase and it would pass. We had been through rough patches before and had always come out fine. Except now we were fighting almost all the time.

Adam was angry that "whatever little money we had, had gone up a cat's ass." My answer was to drink a half a bottle of wine every night so I could keep functioning. I was lonely. I was exhausted. I was miserable. I thought this was what I had to do.

Adam did come when Kimchi was put to sleep and his tears were real. He had known both Boris and Kimchi almost all their lives. Kimchi had always been "my" cat, but Boris used to follow Adam around the apartment like a puppy. He sat in Adam's lap while he ate or watched TV and slept on his feet while he painted in our front room.

But in the past year, Adam's studio had moved from the front room of our apartment, to the building of a couple who had become his new best friends and mentors. He got the space and a laptop in return for doing handyman work and being the woman's photo assistant. He spent almost all his time with this couple, and the times I did join them, I didn't feel welcome. Earlier that year, I saw a photograph hanging in Adam's studio of the three of them at a backyard barbecue. It was taken on my mother's birthday, a day Adam said he couldn't come with me up to The Bronx because he was busy.

At any other time, the warning bells would have rung off the hook, but as Adam said, I was preoccupied. Besides taking care of Kimchi, I had discovered storytelling.

In January 2004, on a bet with my then writing teacher, I'd gone to a competition called a StorySLAM, sponsored by an organization called "The Moth." It was kind of like a poetry slam except you told a five-minute story that was judged. This teacher, like Dr. Weber at New York City Community College, twenty-five years before, knew exactly how to motivate me as the bet was that I didn't have enough nerve to do it.

She told me I should watch it before trying it, but the first night I went, I put my name in the hat anyway. I was picked last, told a story about Titi Dulce, and won.

Later that spring I performed in the GrandSLAM, where the winning storytellers over the last twelve months competed against each other. I think I came in third, but the night was a blur to me. The day before, Kimchi was put to sleep, and that night Adam told a woman in the audience, "When my wife is on stage I hear her, when she is at home I don't."

A few weeks later, I finally came out of my preoccupied daze. I realized Adam and I had been in an unhealthy place and wanted to make things right between us. I realized that maybe Adam had felt shut out just the way I had, and if there were things I resented about him, there were probably things he resented about me too. But we never got that far.

Adam's Aunt Millie had also died, and after the funeral he said he needed to be alone and paint through it. I believed him. I was his wife. Soon after that I found out about his double life. And then I wasn't his wife anymore.

I continued to work. I continued to perform in my latest incarnation, reinventing my Carmen Mofongo character as a burlesque host. I also kept writing and telling stories.

Three years passed and Boris, who was about to turn eighteen, had a stroke. He had kept me alive those first horrible weeks after the breakup when all I did was cry and chain-smoke and drink and cry and chain-smoke and drink some more. He slept with me every night, purring until I fell asleep and stayed next to me until I got up in the morning.

Adam had wanted to take Boris with him, but I said no. Boris was the last link left to my old life, to my youth, to the twentieth century. I couldn't let him go. I realized however, that soon I would have to. And I called Adam to give him the option to see Boris and to be there, if he wanted, when it was time to put him down.

We had barely spoken since the breakup. Mostly because my initial shock and hurt turned to anger, and instead of "How could this be," my thoughts were, "After all we had been through, I can't believe this motherfucker dumped me."

A couple of months after our breakup, Adam came to get his winter clothes. As he was leaving I said, "You should have given me the chance to fix what was wrong."

He shook his head. I ran and pulled a red, heart-shaped clock that had once been on top of our bedroom dresser from the dresser's bottom drawer. On the back of the clock Adam had written, "Valentine's Day 1997. See, Pumpkin, I love you all the time." I blocked the front door to the apartment and shook it at him crying, "What happened to this person?"

"He doesn't exist anymore," Adam said.

I finally took off my rings and threw them at him.

Now, three years later, with Boris dying, I was still angry and hurt. I knew, though, that telling Adam about Boris was the right thing to do. After all, Boris had been Adam's cat too.

Boris, a Russian Blue, was no longer "strong like moose" with thick silver-gray fur like a pelt. He was now thin and frail, his coat sparse and dull. I left the apartment to give Adam time alone with him. When I came back, it looked like Adam had been crying.

For the next couple of months, Adam and I began a new relationship: he would come over once a week to see Boris, I'd make us some tea, and we'd make small talk for an hour or two. I remember thinking that in some small way this must be what it was like to be a divorced parent when the only safe thing you can talk about is the child, or, in our case, the cat.

The day we put Boris to sleep, the vet came to the apartment. I picked up Boris and he turned his small gray head to me and struggled to get away. I sensed he didn't want to leave me. He didn't want to go. I whispered, "It's okay Boris, you can go now, Adam's here."

After it was over and the vet took the body away, Adam and I sat at the kitchen table and had the conversation we should have had three years earlier. The new life Adam had envisioned didn't quite work out the way he had planned. In the first year after the breakup, he lost his art studio and the friends he thought were going to be his mentors and saviors. He said that he had been angry and that he felt as if he deserved something he wasn't getting but he didn't feel that way anymore. He had struggled to find work, a gallery, a studio, relationships, but things were starting to fall into place.

"I wish you had been kinder," I interrupted. "I know I was wrong too, but I was your wife. You owed me the truth. I deserved better."

"You did," Adam said. "I just couldn't. I didn't mean for things to turn out the way they did. They just did. I'm sorry, Michele. It's . . . just like that sometimes, you know . . ."

We sat in the kitchen and cried. For what was and for what could never again be.

You can spend a lifetime with someone and never know what goes on in the back corners of that person's mind: what secret fear fuels their secret needs. You can never wholly compensate for or fully understand what monster another person harbors, the beast that, if let out of its box, destroys everything in its path. We all have one. We all have to face it one day. Sometimes, the monster wins.

In those three years I thought I needed to replace Adam with another man and had a new round of fling, transition, and mistake. It was even less satisfying now that I was in my mid-forties, instead of my late twenties.

The day Boris was put to sleep and Adam and I sat together at my kitchen table, though, I knew that I didn't need to replace Adam. I needed to learn how to be alone. I realized people have to go through their own lives in their own way on their own timetable, and that for some couples, the timing doesn't match.

This will sound cornier than Corn Flakes and cheesier than the sappiest Frank Capra movie, but it's the truth: when Kimchi died, I lost my husband; when Boris died, I got a piece of him back. Adam and I are friends now and always will be. Some people are amazed at our rapport, and when they find out what happened between us, they say they don't think they could've gone forward. I can't speak for Adam, but I can say I didn't do it for him. I did it for me.

Adam and I were lucky. We got a second chance. Some people never get even one.

50

BROOKLYN IS NOT AMERICA

It often happens that when one native New Yorker meets another, they ask, "What are you?" which means, "Where are you from?" As in where are your ancestors from? The other person answers, maybe, "Italian and Irish," or "Polish and Greek," or "Jamaican and Eskimo." Well, not so much the last one, and not just because it's considered politically incorrect and therefore *not allowed* to say "Eskimo"anymore.

I'd been asked this question so many times in my life that declaring my ethnicity upon request was as natural to me as explaining to a disbeliever that yes, I was Puerto Rican.

"You're Puerto Rican?"

"Yep."

"No you're not."

"Yes, I am."

"I don't believe it."

"That's okay, most of my family doesn't either."

When I called Nadya, an old friend of Adam's and mine who lived in Paris, and told her about the breakup, she said, "You must come to *Paree*. It will *feex* you."

I booked a flight that day.

My family warned, "You better watch out. They don't like Americans there; why don't you go to Hawaii? At least they speak English."

I explained that if I had a friend in Hawaii, I would go to Hawaii, but my friend lived in Paris. "If no one believes I'm Puerto Rican here in New York," I said, "why would they think I'm an American in Paris?"

I got my passport. The cover had a gold eagle with the inscription "The United States of America." I flipped through the unstamped pages to find a pastel pattern of more eagles and "The United States of America" on each one.

Now, of course, I knew I was American. But I'd also lived around so many people who defined themselves otherwise, that I never really felt like one. It didn't fully register with me that I was a citizen of the United States of America—not Puerto Rico and not just New York City—until I was preparing to leave the country.

A couple of Mondays later, Nadya met me at de Gaulle airport and handed me a Metro map and the keys to her apartment. "*Au revoir*, Mee-shell," she said. "I see *vous* in *ze* Friday!" She was running to catch her own commuter plane as her job had suddenly called her to a conference in Dijon, for nearly the entire week I was there. It seemed Paris would be "*feexing*" me solo.

I'd practiced speaking French before I left New York but upon exiting the plane realized that the fifty words I had struggled to memorize meant nothing when spoken with an accent so horrendous it sounded like a cross between Carmen Miranda and Chewbacca—a squawk so unintelligible, the words were stripped of all meaning. So I decided to once and for all to clamp down on my natural vociferousness and speak as little as possible. Why not? I didn't know anybody. And I wasn't in Paris to make friends. I was here to be "*feexed*."

The city was absolutely, amazingly, and arrestingly breathtaking. Beauty was everywhere. The leaves falling to the pavement were wistful swatches of the most perfect fall colors I had ever seen. The stray *le mongrel*, licking its parts in a refuse-strewn doorway, exhibited a style and grace that belied both the location and the act. And I witnessed two *messieurs* (what back in New York I would have called bums) lounging at a Metro station holding *une discussion* . . . over a bottle of Bordeaux.

On the first evening of my trip, I went to the rooftop cafe of La

Samaritaine department store as Nadya had recommended. Pont Neuf was on one side and the Ile St. Louis on the other. In front of me, a small *plat de charcuterie,* an ice-cold glass of *Sancerre;* and the beginnings of my first Parisian twilight. Department stores with bars on the roof; . . . I could like it here.

I sat at the chic little bistro table guzzling the view instead of the wine (as uncharacteristic for me as keeping silent), when I overheard two words I wasn't expecting: "Bud Light."

I turned around and saw a group of what could only be—and I apologize for saying this, please don't hold it against me, but they had to be—Midwesterners. You know, middle-aged women with bleached-blond hair and teenage girls with still-blond hair, all sporting brand-new acid-washed jean outfits, and new white Reebok high-top sneakers.

I hadn't seen acid-washed denim since the 1990s or a pair of double Velcro-strap Reeboks since the 1980s—and didn't think I would ever see either again. But there they were. The world's last surviving pairs of De La Soul *Three Feet High and Rising* denim jeans and *Flashdance* "Maniac" sneakers.

I watched with silent *amusée* at the women's surprised expressions when they couldn't get either cheeseburgers or Budweiser and made their displeasure quite clear—in English. One of the girls said, "Mom, why don't you use your phrase book?"

To which Mom answered, "Oh, they all speak English; they just don't want to."

I tried not to look at them.

The girls wanted to go downstairs and shop for makeup, but the moms said no, the store is closing. I turned and said, *"Pardon, s'il vous plaît, le* store is open tonight until the nine."

The girls whooped and hollered and ran off while their mothers gave me dirty looks, which got even dirtier after the waiter told them, *"Mesdames,* the bar is closing, you must to leave."

"What about our children?" they asked.

"That is not my concern. You must to go . . . now," the waiter replied.

The moms left as loudly as they had arrived and I was disappointed. Not to see them leave, but because I wanted to see the sunset. I asked the waiter, *"Vous êtes fermeture?"* (Are you closing?) rhyming *"fermeture"* with "temperature," and cringed as I waited for him to throw me out as well.

Miraculously he just said, "Oh, no *mademoiselle* I wanted *les Américaines* to go. Would you care for another glass?" He answered me in English. It seemed "the mom" and my family were at least partially correct about the French not liking Americans. No matter. *"Oui,"* I triumphantly answered. *"S'il vous plaît, merci!"*

Puerto Ricans in Paris: 1. Bleached-blonde tourists: Nothing.

Five days later I was leaning against a pillar, smoking and waiting for the Metro. I was on my way to meet Nadya for our first dinner together. In the days since my first *aperitif* at La Samaritaine, I had walked through the Catacombs; seen the Mona Lisa and more art than my brain could even begin to process; climbed every last step to the tops of the Eiffel Tower, Notre-Dame de Paris, and Sacré-Coeur; sampled *crêpes marron* in Le Marais; ate *pommes frites* in Les Halles; and experienced more than one "Turkish" toilet. I was beginning to relax for the first time all year.

I was dressed all in black, except for a sparkly green scarf and Nadya's *très chic* cheetah-print umbrella. My hair was slicked back into a tight ponytail and my face was naked except for freckles, winged black eyeliner, and red lipstick. I caught my reflection in a window and thought I looked good, especially practicing my *très insouciant* French inhale.

There was something else I did, or that happened to me, that week. I spoke Spanish—unselfconsciously—for the first time in my life. My intention was to speak as little as possible, but there were certain things you had to ask for, and other than saying the *"bonjours," "bonsoirs," "mercis,"* and *"s'il vous plaîts,"* I just could not get my tongue around that damned French.

To my surprise, many Parisians I encountered spoke a little Spanish—at least as much as I did. And to my astonishment, no one pounced on me for using a wrong word or judged my accent. Without the pressure of a hypercritical *titi* hovering around, I found I was speaking Spanish better than I ever had. I was so emboldened that when I couldn't think of a word in Spanish, I just threw in a couple of French words. I called it Spench.

I met Nadya at a restaurant in the Latin Quarter. It was one of the oldest traditional bistros in Paris, she said. As we caught up with each other and looked at our menus, a group of women walked in whose resemblance to the moms from La Samaritaine was uncanny. It took a few minutes for me to realize they weren't the same moms from the rooftop bar.

They sat close by Nadya and me; close enough so that we could hear them order. And just like the group from La Samaritaine, they complained that there was nowhere in Paris to get a cheeseburger and a beer. When the waiter said, quite truthfully, if they wanted a burger, why didn't they go to *le McDonald's*, one of them said, "We didn't fly three thousand miles to go to McDonald's."

I watched as the waiter walked back to the bar, whispered to another waiter, gestured at the group, and mimed spitting in his hand. Now you don't need to be fluent in any language to know what miming a hock of spit into the palm of your hand means. I kind of understood the waiter's attitude at first. My initial reaction was to toss my glittery scarf and roll my winged eyes at them. But then a thought came to me, unbidden. Instead of seeing a group of rude, clueless tourists, I saw myself. It was kind of like an acid flashback, only instead of seeing trails, I recalled the taunts and slurs I had endured in my life. Suddenly, I felt the need to defend—all of us. It was a matter of honor, of principle.

"I don't care how *stupide* they are, you skinny French . . . fuck!" I muttered.

Nadya looked up from her menu and said, "Mee-shell, have you gone *fou*?"

Before she could stop me, I was walking toward the waiter.

"The bathrooms are on the right," he said.

"*Vous hablo* English?" I asked. I was caught completely off guard as this restaurant was not *una touriste* trap.

"Oh yes, quite well. . . . We all speak the *Engleesh*. We just don't want to."

I looked at the bleached blondes. Where had I heard that before? I was totally confused now. But I was determined to complete my mission and continued in English.

"Yeah, well, those people over there. . . . I heard what you said and I saw what you did and . . . you cannot spit in their food!"

"Why do you care?" he sneered.

"Because . . ." I grasped for words and spluttered, "Because . . . I'm American too."

"You? You are no *Américaine*. What are you? Where are you from?"

All my life I'd suffered this question. But this time it was different. It wasn't as if we could sit at a table over a bottle of Lillet or Fundador, and I could tell him about the island of Puerto Rico and about how it was a cultural stew where everyone was a mix of the conquered and the conquerors. There wasn't time to explain about Nueva York, *la pirata*, and *pecas*, the five different words for your behind, the politics of panties, *papas de sofas* or . . .

"Where are you from?" he asked again, louder.

I didn't know what to answer. Then the part of me that remembered how surprised I was to see the United States of America on my passport kicked in, and I didn't even think; it just came out.

"I'm from Brooklyn!"

"Brooklyn?" The waiter took a full breath and snorted, "Bah! Brooklyn is not America!" and turned on his heels. But not before I swore I saw a glint of *amusée* in his eyes.

I don't know what the bleached blondes ate, but I went back to Nadya and our *lapin en moutarde* and *onglet avec pomme frites*. I would later learn *lapin* was rabbit and *onglet* was *cheval*—horse steak with potatoes fried in horse fat—the *spécialité de maison*. It was the best steak, bunny, and French fries I've ever had.

Brooklyn Avenger: 1,000,000. Snooty waiter: Nothing.

I left Paris full of excellent food and a freeing feeling, both of which I had just tasted for the first time. From that day forward, I would never be self-conscious about my Spanish, or lack of, ever again, and when I was asked where I was from, the answer was now and forever, "Brooklyn."

I've been to a few more places in Europe since then. I've even been to Puerto Rico and walked down the same streets Grandpa Ezekiel and Grandma Izzy walked. But it was in Paris where I learned that being from Brooklyn could save me from, as I would say in Spench, *"uno escupo in votre coffee."*

I can't say that Paree *"feexed,"* me. But something in me was shifting.

51

BROTHER FROM ANOTHER MOTHER

Dear Michele,

You are not a bad sister. You don't have to be ashamed or upset that you did not do enough for me, but sometimes I think you could be nicer to Mommy.

I know you are mad at her for something. Try not to be. She couldn't help being in the hospital. She couldn't help going away. What happened to her was no one's fault. I had to live in Grandma's house too, you know. Sometimes, things are just the way they are.

You have given me a lot you probably don't even remember, but I do. Every time you went to a concert, you brought me back a T-shirt, and all the kids thought I was cool, even though I had no idea who half those bands were. You got us tickets for the Mayor's Trophy Game and all those other Met games. I remember acting out Jesus Christ Superstar with you when you were practicing for that play. And I remember when I was in eighth grade, you came to my school and told Mr. Nenner there was an emergency and we had to leave immediately. I started crying because I thought something had happened to Mommy, but when we got on the train, you told me to shut up—and we went to the opening day of Star Wars. I remember all of that.

But the best gift you could give me now is to help me with Mommy. I know you are married. I know you have your own life.

But I am alone with her now, and it is hard for me sometimes. I guess I just wish you would at least come see her more.

But you are not a bad sister. No way. No matter what, you do something else for me. You make me laugh. Always.

Love,
Kevin, your Anglo-Saxon Republi-Rican brother
who looks like Quentin Tarantino.

52

DEATH AND THE PUERTO RICAN

I promised God that if my mother lived, I would never call my brother a fucking douche bag ever again.

There are a few things you should know about my brother, Kevin, and me, born three years and nineteen days apart: One of my first memories is of the two of us clunking each other over the head with a Nestlé's Quik can while watching *The Three Stooges*. I was four; he was just over a year old. A few years later, I ended up in the emergency room after he bit me because I wouldn't share my Halloween candy with him. A while after that, he hid my Barbies and wouldn't tell me where they were. I took the driver from the Fisher-Price school bus and threw it at him. It knocked out his just-growing-in permanent bottom tooth; he still has the gap. Another year, he jabbed a pencil into my knee; you can still see a spot of lead. I got him back though. I stabbed him in the palm of his hand with a fork.

Then there was an interlude that I like to call the "Watchful Peace," which ended right after I turned fourteen. Kevin and his friends took my OB tampons to the roof, unwrapped them all, threw them over the edge, and started calling me Bloody Mary behind my back. When I found out, I was so furious I spit on Kevin. Twice. He punched me in the stomach so hard I threw up—on him.

After my mother intervened and cleaned us up, I told her, "I wish you had had a miscarriage." She answered, "You two are my blessings. I don't understand why you can't be each other's."

Fast-forward twenty-five years.

Almost everyone in my family who is deceased has died from complications of diabetes. Not the kind you get in childhood, but Type II—the kind you get after the age of forty when you've gained a few or thirty pounds. Maybe you've finally quit smoking. Maybe you've been pregnant too many times. Or maybe you just like traditional Latin food: a hunk of fried meat accompanied by *tostones* and a double portion of *dulce de coco*. It doesn't matter. In my family, if you are over forty and overweight, you get diabetes. And in my family, diabetes equals death. All my grandparents had it. Titi Carmen had it. And now my father had it.

My father had smoked nonfiltered Camels from the age of fifteen until forty-five when a doctor told him, "Quit smoking today or drop dead tomorrow." He quit that same day, but over the next ten years his weight went from 190 pounds to 230 pounds. The diabetes that immediately accompanied his weight gain spiraled until he became insulin-dependent.

He became worse as I was preparing to move away from home for good. This was at the same time Pasha and I broke up, and I was moving to Brooklyn, as far away from The Bronx as I could get and still be in the same city.

Now according to traditional Latin culture, children (especially girl children) are supposed to either live at home until they're married or live only a block or two away at the most—the better to facilitate unannounced Saturday morning visits and mandatory Sunday dinners of *carne mechada, arroz con salchichas,* and *queso blanco con guava*. I had already flouted that unspoken rule by semi–living with Pasha. But now I was going off on my own.

I didn't want a traditional Latin life. And furthermore, I was determined that I would never have diabetes. I trained myself not to like sweets. I ate broccoli, brown rice, and cantaloupe. I exercised: Yoga, Pilates, rollerblading, ice skating or at the very least, walking as fast as I could. I was so obsessive-compulsive about it that if I knew I was going to be drinking alcohol that night, I wouldn't have any bread all day. I wasn't going to get diabetes. Ever.

One morning, shortly before I moved to Brooklyn, my dad collapsed onto the kitchen floor after his usual Saturday breakfast of two fried eggs with sausage, two Twin Donuts, and three cups of sweet *café con leche*. My mother was in the bedroom. My brother and I were in the kitchen with him.

Kevin was finishing the same breakfast as my father, minus the coffee. I was having oatmeal and tea. Kevin ran to the telephone to call 911. I went to the fridge, took out the insulin, loaded the needle, and shot my father in the hip right through his pants, just like he had shown me on an orange.

My mother came into the room and stood there, frozen. After the paramedics had come and gone, saying my father was lucky I was there, my father said, "Little girl, if you leave who is going to take care of me?"

I said, "I don't know. Can't Mom or Kevin do the needles?"

"Kevin gets nervous about it, and I don't trust your mother." He gave a little laugh. "She wouldn't do it anyway."

The meaning behind what he said escaped me at the time. "Well then, Daddy, you have to take care of yourself. You can't keep eating donuts and sausages and fried junk. You have to start eating brown rice and broccoli and cantaloupe or you're going to die."

My father looked at me and said, "Little girl, if I eat that, I will die."

My parents wouldn't visit me in Brooklyn for over a year after I moved there, and when they finally did, I spent the entire visit trying to convince them to move to my neighborhood. It was closer to my father's job in downtown Manhattan. I could get them on the list for a senior citizen's building; I figured that by the time their name got to the top, they would be old enough. Plus, Prospect Park was undergoing a total renovation, and they could take walks or sit on a bench at the lake and feed the ducks.

But my mother said, "Parks are dangerous. You go in there alone?"

"Mom, this isn't The Bronx. It's Brooklyn!"

"Your brother lives only two blocks away from us. Why can't you move back home?" she asked.

What could I say? Kevin had become a very respectable, teetotaling Wall Streeter who lived two blocks away from my parents and liked it when my mother went over and cooked for him. I wondered why I spent so much time trying to convince my parents to move closer to me when I had intentionally moved so far away from them. Maybe it was because I could see my father's diabetes was slowly getting worse. But eventually, I stopped asking.

The years passed. I met Adam. I traded an artist's life for an actor's life. I spoke to my parents on the phone almost every week, but only went up to The Bronx for birthdays and holidays. I was okay with that. I was grown up now, I didn't need my mother—or even my father anymore. They had their life. I had mine.

One autumn Saturday I took my father to the Greenmarket in Brooklyn's Grand Army Plaza and cooked him organic butternut squash soup, kale with three kinds of mushrooms, and fresh salmon steak, a meal he politely pushed around his plate.

"Daddy, you have to take care of yourself."

"I know, little girl. I know. Would you make me a *café con leche?* Three sugars."

"No, Daddy, you have to use Equal! Who will take care of you if you have an attack?"

He didn't answer.

The next summer, he was dead. The doctors did an autopsy, which showed that not only had he suffered a massive heart attack, but there had been at least four or five others over the past five years. He had never said a word about feeling ill. Ever. The cause of death was listed as arteriosclerosis, as a complication of diabetes. Ironically, even though he had smoked two packs of nonfilter Camels a day for thirty years, his lungs were as clear as a nonsmoker's.

Soon after my father's death, my five-feet-tall, perfectly coiffed, groomed, and accessorized mother, who'd weighed 108 pounds on her wedding day and after forty-two years of marriage still tipped the scales at just 118 pounds, stopped cooking at home and turned to Mickey D's and Sara Lee for comfort. I tried to convince her once again to move to Brooklyn, but after the fifth turndown, I stopped asking. Kevin moved back home to live with her. Since he'd always lived near our parents, I figured it wasn't such a big deal for him.

I was glad my mother wasn't alone anymore and glad it wasn't me who had to be there. Now that my father was gone, it was uncomfortable for me to be in the house alone with my mother—and not much better when Kevin was there too.

Kevin and I had almost nothing in common anymore, not even the Mets. He had defected and was rooting for the Yankees now. When we were younger, I used to joke about his being a Republi-Rican, but he was now so conservative, the only thing we could talk about without arguing anymore was *Star Trek*, and sometimes not even that.

The first Christmas after my father died was spent in my mother's living room looking at photographs of my parents when they were young. The apartment felt empty without my father, and I couldn't wait to go home. As Adam and I were leaving, Kevin put on his coat and walked us to the train, something he rarely did. I could feel something was up. I was right.

"You really should come visit more," Kevin said.

"Why? There's nothing to do," I answered. "I hate it here. Why don't you guys come to Brooklyn instead?"

"Ummm, I'm going ahead to get the tokens," Adam said, running up the block as fast as he could.

"Because you're the one that has the life?" Kevin retorted. "What do you think I have?"

"Then leave. You can still live up the block or something." I paused and then said, "I would."

"I can't," Kevin said softly.

"Why not?"

"That, Michele, is the difference between you and me."

We had at last reached the corner. "You know what?" I bit back. "You're a doormat. And a dork!" Then I ran upstairs to the train.

Then came April 1999. My mother, Kevin, Adam, and I were walking down 57th Street in Manhattan after our Easter get-together when all of a sudden my mother stopped. With a panicked look on her face she said, "I have to stop. You're walking too fast."

I don't know how I hadn't noticed before, but she must've now weighed 150 pounds. My once impeccably groomed mother had vanished. A puffy-faced impostor with a carelessly tied scarf over her head and an indifferent smear of color across her lips had taken her place. She stared at me wide eyed.

"Mom," I said, "something's wrong. It's not normal to get out of breath from walking two blocks."

Her eyes narrowed. "I'm fine. You walk too fast; I'm old now."

"Mom, you're not old, you're just . . . fat. Maybe you need to go to the doctor. Maybe you have diabetes like Daddy."

"I don't have diabetes. I feel fine!"

Three weeks later, two days before her sixty-sixth birthday, Kevin called me at work and said our mother had a heart attack that morning and was in the hospital. I immediately left work and went as fast as the Pelham Express could take me up to The Bronx and Albert Einstein Hospital where I found her in intensive care, hooked up to what seemed like the hospital's entire inventory of machines.

"Mom . . . Mom . . . what happened?"

She could barely talk. The doctors came in. She was going to have a double bypass operation at seven the next morning. Her arteries were almost completely clogged; plus, her blood sugar was over five hundred. My mother absolutely had diabetes and she also had at least one or two smaller heart attacks before this one. And just like my father, she never said a word.

My mother's third artery collapsed during the operation, but they were able to save it and her. Back in the Cardiac ICU that afternoon, Kevin and I were only allowed to go into her room for fifteen minutes at a time, every hour. The two nurses who were there for the first twenty-four hours after surgery monitored the digital bells and whistles that were keeping her alive.

"Your mother is strong," one of them said. "They have to stop your heart to operate on it you know."

After what seemed like a year, but was really only an hour or two, my mother started coming out of the anesthesia. The nurses had told us not to be afraid if she seemed disoriented at first as it was normal after such a major operation.

As she stirred and moaned, my brother and I had faced off on either side of her bed. We had passed the time all day comparing the *Star Trek* series spin-off *Deep Space Nine* (which I liked) vs. the original (which he preferred). I remember we were in an intense debate over whether Captain Kirk would have been able to handle the Jem'Hadar. Then without any warning, we blew up at each other. Maybe it was fear. Maybe it was lack of sleep. Or maybe it was a combination of his resentment for being the one who moved back home and my guilt for not doing so.

"It's your fault," Kevin said. "You shouldn't have moved so far away."

"I wanted her to come to Brooklyn," I retorted. "You could have made her eat better. You shouldn't be eating all that junk either. Look at your gut. You're going to be the next one on a slab if you don't watch it."

Kevin glared, "You think you're so slick because you're skinny. I know why. It's because you smoke cigarettes and you and Adam probably still smoke pot too. I'm going to tell Mommy."

"Go ahead! Tell Mommy! I'm almost thirty-nine—I can smoke all I want—and I don't even smoke weed anymore. Maybe you should start. You need something to chill you out, you . . . fucking douche bag!"

At this point one of the nurses (who yes, sadly, witnessed it all) said she was, um, going into the bathroom (which was in the room) for just a second, would we be okay?

"Yeah, sure," we barked at her.

The other nurse said she was going to check on my mom's meds.

"Go ahead," we snarled. We didn't notice my mother was now almost completely awake and had heard the entire argument.

A rasping, gurgling sound came from her breathing tube as her long-ingrained façade and sense of propriety tried to override her condition. I knew this because I could see it in her eyes. I knew what she would have said if she could, "Why are you doing this? Why are you embarrassing me?"

And then it happened. She tried to move one of her arms and a tube in her side popped loose.

Blood oozed from the hole, and Kevin and I both freaked. Kevin ran to the door, yelling, "Nurse, Nurse!"

One nurse ran out of the bathroom, the other back into the room, and when they saw I had jammed my finger into the hole in my mother's side in a misguided attempt to try to halt the bleeding, they yelled at me to stop. I could have given her an infection, they said. Then they shooed us both out of the room.

People say there is no worse pain than that of a parent losing a child. I may not have had children, but I can tell you that for me nothing was worse than having my mother's blood on my hands. As I went to find a bathroom to wash it off, my brother hissed at me, "You killed Mommy."

I couldn't argue. I was the one who left home. Maybe that did kill her. Maybe I had killed Daddy too. I found a bathroom and washed my hands, then leaned against the sink and made my pact with the Almighty.

As it turned out, I didn't kill Mommy. That tube wasn't critical to her survival at all; it was just for drainage. And what seemed like a river of blood was just blood-tinged I.V. fluid.

My mother left the hospital a week later, and over the next year made a complete recovery. I have almost bit through my tongue on more than one occasion, but have kept my promise: the words "fucking douche bag" have not been shouted, spoken, or whispered to my brother in over ten years. Kevin is a good man and a good son, even though he is still a bit of a sci-fi dork. But then again, so am I.

My mother's diabetes remains under control. Once again she puts on a full outfit, age-appropriate makeup, and tastefully coordinated accessories whenever she leaves the apartment. And Kevin has done what I couldn't: he helped her to change her diet. She now eats both broccoli and cantaloupe, but she just won't eat brown rice. Of course not, no matter what, she's still Latin—eating brown rice would kill her.

53

SPANISH ON SUNDAY (part 6)

Another Sunday. Another supper. Only this one wasn't in anyone's home.

It was Titi Ofelia's sixty-fifth birthday, and we were all in a party room in a restaurant in Washington Heights. It was the kind of dark wood and upholstered place where off-shift doctors from nearby Columbia-Presbyterian hospital, off-duty cops from the nearby Manhattan North 33rd Precinct, and local families taking a night off from cooking, all felt comfortable.

The food was American, for a change: roast beef, chicken, and shrimp; different pastas; and salads. And it was very good. Best of all, for once, everyone was getting along fine. My family, or what was left of it, didn't get together too often anymore. I hadn't been in a room with all of them together at once since the previous Christmas, and it was now November again.

At my table was also Ofelia, her new husband Ignacio (who I jokingly called "Uncle Iggy"), my mother, Kevin, Dulce, Evie, Alex, and Cousin Ray-Ray, who would turn forty the following week.

"Hurry up and join the club, Evie," Kevin joked, "before Michele leaves it." I stuck my tongue out at him, and we all laughed but it was true. We were all getting older.

Over the years I had finally come to accept my "separate but equal" status in the family. I no longer took either offhand comments or outright criticism personally. In return they didn't laugh when I danced with my shoulders instead of my hips or complain when I proudly spoke Spanish like the American that I was.

After dinner, I even asked the DJ to play a set of New Wave in between the *salsa* and *merengue* and was amused to see how many people couldn't dance to New Order or Tom Tom Club. I gave them credit for trying. A round of salsa started up, and I went back to the table while my mother got up to dance with her sisters. I hadn't seen my mother dance since Evie's wedding or mine, and both of those were back in another century.

My mother looked beautiful. She was wearing black patent leather pumps, albeit with only one-inch heels, and a bracelet-sleeved gunmetal silk dress with a black and silver lace-and-brocade overlay and a short matching jacket she left on her chair. The dress had a trumpet skirt that flared when she twirled. Once Jackie O, always Jackie O. She looked like she was having a great time. I was happy for her. When the song finished, my mother and Dulce came back to the table, and Ofelia went off to talk to the guests.

It had been eight years since my mother's operation, and while she might not have weighed 108 pounds anymore, at this point in her life, 120 pounds was perfect. She was then seventy-four and had at least ten years on most of the other guests but looked younger than almost all of them.

Ofelia's friends couldn't believe I was in my forties either— "*Coño*, way in!" as one of them put it. They all thought Evie (who is and will always be ten years younger than I am) and I were the same age. I've never looked my age, going back to when I was a teenager. I was occasionally still proofed at bars until just recently. When I'd complained about my first gray hairs a couple of years before, my friends all said, "Good, it's about time you got something. We were thinking you had a JPEG in your closet aging for you. What do you use, anyway, Oil of Delay?"

My mother and Dulce were talking about something I can't remember as the dessert was being served. Ofelia came back to the table with a half-finished piña colada in her hand. She started talking about how she couldn't believe she was sixty-five and about how things were "back in the day" when she and Dulce were young and about how she missed *abuelita*, Carmen, and Papa Julio.

At the mention of his name, I saw my mother stiffen like she used to, but no alarms went off inside me yet. I looked for Kevin, but he'd gone off somewhere. I'd just finished the last of my "family party" limit of two Dark and Stormys and was feeling good. I didn't want anything to ruin this party. For once, being with my family had been nothing but fun.

Uncle Iggy came over. Ironically, he's the only one out of all of Ofelia's husbands I've ever called Uncle. It's a joke because he's ten years younger than she is and therefore only eight years older than I am and it's kind of ridiculous, but it works. He's a kind man who has even more energy than Ofelia and keeps both their minds occupied— something no husband or boyfriend had been able to do before. I'm glad she seems to be happy.

Ofelia didn't notice or acknowledge Uncle Iggy and went on about Papa Julio. Dulce tried to change the subject to the baby Evie and Alex were planning to adopt. But that just got Ofelia started on how she wished her "almost twenty years disappeared" son, Benny, were here. Her eyes welled up. She blew her nose. She looked straight at my mother and said, "Who would think you, the *prieta*, would still be here."

I sat stunned, but said nothing. After everything I had heard Ofelia say to or about my mother over the years, I was always mystified when she flung that racial term at her. Uncle Iggy gave my mother a pained look of apology, grabbed Ofelia by the arm, and steered her out of there. Ofelia was slightly tamed, by either Iggy, age, or alcohol, and went with him without protest. But the damage had been done.

My mother started to cry, silently. Dulce, Evie, Alex, and Ray-Ray immediately tried to comfort her, but she rebuffed them. At first I thought she was overreacting. Couldn't she see Ofelia was just being drunk and stupid?

I was just about to lean over and attempt to calm her as well when Kevin came back from the bathroom. He had missed the whole exchange and just saw my mother crying.

"What did you do?" he asked.

"Nothing," I said.

"You always do nothing," he said.

Now I was the one who was insulted. I got up and went to the bar for another Dark and Stormy. When I got back to the table, my mother said she wanted to go home, and she insisted I come with them. But I didn't want to go all the way up to The Bronx; it was almost nine-thirty. Why should I when I had to go all the way back to Brooklyn alone? I could see she was upset, but couldn't Kevin take care of her? What could I do? He always knew what to say to soothe her.

The truth was that although I always enjoyed having my mother and Kevin visit me in Brooklyn, ever since my father died, I hated going to my mother's apartment. There were too many memories in those rooms, in that neighborhood. There were too many memories of name-calling and insecurity; too many sleepless nights from speeching or anxiety; and too many ghosts of things and people I had long left behind.

I told my mother I'd a writing class assignment due that Tuesday that I hadn't yet begun. I told her I didn't have a change of clothes. I told her to come over the following Saturday and I'd make her favorite roasted asparagus, arugula, and artichoke salad. But something in her face scared me. I felt like I had the day ten years before when I had to choose between working a big face-painting picnic and spending what turned out to be my last Father's Day with my father. I might not get another chance.

I downed the drink and got into the taxi with Kevin and my mother. But I didn't go gently. "What am I supposed to wear to work tomorrow?" I grumbled.

Kevin and my mother didn't say a word the entire ride. We had barely arrived at the apartment when my mother broke her silence.

"I have to tell you something about . . . my father. . . ." she began.

My mother had never really talked about her real father before.

She stopped, and I could tell even now she was deciding whether to continue. She did.

"You heard what Ofelia called me. So what if my father was . . . half *tregieño*, half black. . . . Her father was dark too. Who is she to remind me . . ."

There was more. She told the story of Grandma Mari and the musician Beltran with the fine tightly curled jet-black hair and how she and her mother had been abandoned and why they had come to New York.

I struggled to process what I had just heard. Our real grandfather was part black? That was it? That was the reason behind the snide remarks and disdain from Papa Julio and the others all these years? How could they? What did it matter? But then again, it was a different time with different beliefs and values and people were ignorant of many things, for many reasons.

As I tried to rationalize it all, I looked at Kevin. He had obviously heard none of this before either and was as shocked as I was. He tried to touch my mother's arm, but she pushed his hand away.

There was more. She told us what her childhood was like and what Papa Julio had done. I had kind of always sensed that, but was afraid to ask. I could never ask my mother about anything like that when I was young. It would have caused a month of sleepless nights. So I had always remained silent about what I, too, had endured.

I was exhausted. I was also feeling a little woozy from the bumpy taxi ride and from downing that third drink; it had been a double. But there was still more.

She revealed what it had been like for her in the hospital: the isolation and the endless pills she pretended to take. She told us how she had missed us so much, how she blamed her mother and Papa Julio for putting her there, how she blamed my father for not rescuing her, and how she never really forgave him for that.

"I needed patience," she said. "I needed love. I needed understanding. I didn't need to be put away . . ."

Her words trailed off. She hung her head for a moment, then picked it back up and began to scream. I hadn't heard her yell like that in twenty-five years. It was as if she had launched a lightning bolt of rage and grief around us. I thought the once endless fury inside her had, if not subsided, at least been subdued by age and time, but it erupted all over again.

She was seventy-four. She'd had triple-bypass heart surgery; there was a zipper on her chest. What might this rush of emotion do to her now?

I looked at my mother's face, and the sight of her pain was overwhelming. It was not my pain, but it was pain nonetheless and that was something I understood. But no matter what I had gone through, she had it far worse. At the very, very least, I had a father.

I thought about my father and about how there was always something strange and distant between my mother and him. And now I knew why. I remembered when I was nineteen and breaking up with Brendan, I'd asked my father why he didn't run when my mother was in the hospital. His answer was, "A man doesn't run from his mistakes."

Maybe he stayed with us because he did love my mother, and maybe it was because he loved Kevin and me. Or maybe it was because he felt guilty that he hadn't done more for her, that he allowed the hospitalization, that horrible year to happen.

The realization made my stomach drop. He should have known better. They all should have known better. But they didn't. And dammit, that family of hers could've been nicer to her.

Suddenly, the rum left my system and disconnected thoughts came—unwanted, but undeniable. Grandma Mari wasn't there when my mother needed her. My mother hadn't been there when Grandma Mari needed her. And my mother wasn't there when I needed her. I'd always been angry, so, so angry about that. I was angry that no one knew what was happening in *abuelita*'s house; angry that my mother was so preoccupied, angry I could never talk to her the way my girlfriends did with their mothers; and angry that I had to be careful whom I invited to the apartment, just in case something triggered my mother.

And I was angry that she hadn't fought back. She'd just accepted all that sorrow and pain and never confronted the fuckers who hurt her. And then . . . the connection. I hadn't been there for my mother, just like she hadn't been for hers, but I was in the room with her now. All my life I had convinced myself I didn't need my mother. Maybe that was true, but tonight, she needed me. The pattern could be broken. Tonight. Here.

I reached for my mother, and she came into my arms. I held her as if she were the child, and it made me uncomfortable. This was Kevin's domain; I was always the one who made things right with my father. As she sobbed, I realized I couldn't remember the last time my mother and I held each other.

I could feel her fragility, her fatigue, and her age. I could also feel something else inside her: a core of strength that by force of will had kept her alive, if not entirely whole all these years. She could have chosen differently. But she did not. At that moment I knew I had that force too. "It's okay, Mom," I said. "It's okay. I love you. Let it go."

She said that she had been holding those secrets all these years, and she was sorry. I didn't know what she was apologizing for. Or maybe I did. I kissed her hair and told her Papa Julio was dead. Grandma Mari was dead. My father was dead. They were gone, but Kevin and I were here.

But instead of winding down, her sobbing escalated, and I became afraid of what might happen if it went on for much longer. Maybe it would never be all right for her. Maybe there are some things, some people for whom it will just never be all right, but she couldn't continue like this. I didn't know what to do, but I had to try something. So I did what has always come naturally to me. I opened my big mouth.

"Wow, really? I knew it! Well, that explains everything!"

My mother slowly looked at me with a mixture of shock and horror.

"I always wondered why we've always looked so good for our age," I continued. "Black don't crack and Puerto Rican's no creakin'! That makes Kevin and me what, octoroons? So what? Who cares? We be lookin' good and they all be jealous of us!"

My mother's sobs abruptly stopped. She broke our embrace. I wondered if this time I had finally gone too far and said the unforgivable. I looked at Kevin, my Republi-Rican, Quentin Tarantino–looking brother who was standing right next to us. He was staring at me with his mouth open. He looked as if he was about to say something, but not before I had one last chance to shove both my feet into my mouth even deeper, all the way down to my *fundillo*.

I raised my hand for a high five. "Yo, brotha! Dyn-o-mite! Yo, Sanford! Yo, Sam-bo! What up?"

Kevin shot me a look that can only be described as deep disgust crossed with incredulous, begrudging appreciation, and I could tell he was torn between telling me off—for good—and bursting out laughing. The laughter won; he cracked up and high-fived back.

Kevin said, "Sho' 'nuff, sis. We should all go to Ofelia's next birthday wearing whiteface. We can sing 'Mammy' to her . . . in Spanish! You can paint us."

I answered, "Okay but you best start practicing *su Español* now, we only gots a year."

"*Si, bueno, si*," Kevin said. "How's that?"

My mother had moved to stand in between us, and I saw her face change from shock and horror to anger and disbelief . . . to the face of a mother with two incorrigibly mischievous children. She swatted at the two of us and told us we were both terrible and had better repent.

"But Momma," I said, "I tries to be good, but . . ."

Then, unexpectedly and amazingly, my mother started laughing. Laughing and crying and crying some more, but these tears were different. She hugged Kevin and me, tightly. "My children," she said. "My children."

I thought about when Kevin and I were growing up and were in the living room trying to do our homework. The TV would be on, our father would be on the sofa snoring, a train would rattle past every five minutes, and our mother would be speeching in another room out the window. But when Kevin or I would occasionally ask her something, she'd stop and calmly answer whatever it was, then go back to her venting. We'd go back to our long division or book reports. She'd always been our mother, even when she couldn't be herself.

I went to work the next day in my party dress. I'm sure my coworkers thought I was doing the "walk of shame," but I didn't care. On the way back to Brooklyn that evening, I thought about how nothing I tried my entire life had satisfied me for very long: drawing, graffiti, friends, drugs, art school, work, marriage, performing—nothing was ever enough. I had tried so hard not to be like my mother, yet in a way, I was exactly like her. Something had never been right for me either.

I took that thought back to my apartment, and when I got there, I sat down at my computer and started to write. My new cat, Jubilee, jumped up on the table and tried to lie across the keyboard. She hadn't eaten for two days. She wanted her dinner. Still, she purred.

I was home. Exactly where I was supposed to be.

54

WHEN THE MIRACLE DOESN'T COME

Dear Michele,

I was angry for a long time. I'm still angry sometimes even now. I wasn't crazy when they locked me away, but I'm sure I was when I came out. You don't know what that is, to cry for help and have no one listen, to feel like you can't count on anyone or anything, to feel totally abandoned and betrayed. Or maybe you do.

You think I didn't give you anything? You had two things I never had. One was your father. The second was freedom. The freedom to make your own choices. The freedom to be yourself. I think you realize that now. There was never ever a time when I didn't love Kevin and you. You are my blessings. My children.

Love, always and forever,
Mom

1 Corinthians 13:6–8: Love does not delight in evil but rejoices with the truth. It always protects, always trusts, always hopes, always perseveres. Love never fails.

Ephesians 4:31: Let all bitterness, and wrath, and anger, and clamour, and evil speaking, be put away from you, with all malice.

Hebrews 11:1: Now faith is the substance of things hoped for, the evidence of things not yet seen.

P.S. I think your Titi Ofelia needs a facelift, don't you?

P.S.S. You should think about getting another cat. I think Jubilee is lonely.

55

THE RETURN OF THE QUEEN

I did get Jubilee another cat, but not until the following March. This day was Christmas Day, 2007.

"Who's the white wizard again?"

"That's Gandalf, Mom. He's like God. Well, not really God, but like one of the angels."

"And who is the Red Eye?"

"That's Sauron. He's the Devil. Well, not really the Devil, but his emissary. You know, sent by the Devil to take over the Earth. Uh, Middle-earth."

"And the one with the Ring. The little one. Is he gay?"

"In real life? I think Gandalf and Pippin are, but I'm not sure about Frodo."

"Such a big deal about a little ring."

"Yeah, I know. But it's a good story isn't it?"

Ten years since my father died. Three years since my marriage broke up. Six months after my eighteen-year-old Boris, the little gray kitten whose big poop had once saved me from starvation, and whose last days had sparked another miracle, had also died. I was sitting in my living room with my mother and Kevin after Christmas dinner trying to watch *The Return of the King*.

It was like an episode of *Mystery Science Theater 3000*, only Latin style. I don't know about you, but I was a teenager before I realized people actually watched TV in silence. Every TV viewing I had ever experienced that included any member of my family contained an ongoing parallel dialogue that didn't end until either the dial/remote had been finally switched off or one by one they began to snore and drool in their respective places, exhausted, no doubt, by the exertion of running nonstop color commentary that only took a break *during* the commercials.

"*Mira a ese Cher,* how can she show her belly button like that? *Que sinvergüenza!*"

"I know who shot JR. It was his momma!"

"That sweater Mr. Huxtable's wearing—I saw the exact same one at Korvettes—on sale!"

"Mr. Neelix? I think he's gay. They let gay aliens be on the *Enterprise* now, right?"

"MOM!" Kevin yelled, as he rewound the DVD back for the fifth time in an attempt to watch The Battle of the Pelennor Fields scene once, just once, without interruption. "Mom, they're Hobbits!"

"Ho-bits?" she asks.

"Hobbits!" he answers. "Little people."

"Like dwarves?"

I try to help, "No, Mom, Gimli's the dwarf."

"Which one is he?"

"The elf Legolas's friend," I say.

"Are they gay?"

Now my mother is not and has never been dumb. When I was young, she considered Carl Jung and José Ortega y Gassett light reading. And she is not homophobic. She has met Kevin's and my gay friends and loved them all, even though she couldn't resist trying to convert them.

She has, however, been obsessed by gay movie and TV characters and actors ever since Rock Hudson, one of her favorite actors of all time, had to leave one of her favorite TV shows of all time, *Dynasty.* I remembered that night . . .

"They say Rock Hudson is not coming back to the show."

"No he's not, Mom. He has AIDS."

"He can't have AIDS. Only gay people get AIDS."

"That's not true. But he does have AIDS."

"He doesn't have AIDS. He just has a cold. He kissed Linda Evans last season."

"Mom, he's gay."

"He is NOT. He kissed Doris Day too and almost married her."

"Mom, that was in 1950. It's 1985. He married Jim Nabors. He's gay!"

"Jim Nabors? You mean Gomer Pyle?"

"Yes, Mom. Rock Hudson married Gomer Pyle. They're both GAY."

"Well, maybe that Jim Naples is, but not Rock Hudson. He's too handsome. You believe everything you read."

My mother doesn't believe anything she reads. Or hears. Or sees. If it contradicts what she believes is the Orderly State of the Universe, it doesn't exist. My mother's universe left off in 1955, when she left accounts receivable at Gimbels to marry my father.

We settled down to watch the Battle of the Pelennor Fields scene. Again.

"Those big elephants, Michele, are they mastodons?"

"Well, kind of, Mom, but not really. They're imaginary creatures."

"And those people on them with all the makeup, are they supposed to be from the Middle East?"

"Well, kind of, but not really. They're allegorical."

"Allah? So they're Osama Bin Laden?" She turned and blurted at the TV, "Get them Gandalf! Get them! Slay them with your white light!"

I looked at my mother. She is who she is, as I am who I am, and there are some things that just won't change. Ever.

My mother watched the rest of the movie, giving her opinion on every costume, line of dialogue, and plot point.

By the end, Kevin was exhausted. He went into my bedroom to pet Jubilee. She tried to bite him—just like Kimchi always did.

"That was a great movie," my mother said. "Now I know why you read those books so much when you were younger."

"I still read them. I think Tolkien is one of the greatest fantasy writers of all time. Did you know he was also friends with the poet and novelist C. S. Lewis, and they were both Catholic? They put a lot of their beliefs into their writing and . . ."

"Were they gay?"

Kevin yelled from the bedroom, "Mom! . . . Ow!"

I laughed. It is going to be okay. Finally. It wasn't too late. For her—or for us.

56

FISH OUT OF AGUA

I did see my great-grandmother one last time.

She was walking toward me, walking across the field in front of the hospital where she had died. Only she looked the way she had in the old photograph abuelita had shown me when I was a child. She was tall and strong, with jet-black waist-length hair, skin the color of a cinnamon stick, and cheekbones too sharp to endure. A princess. A priestess.

With every step she took, grass sprouted from the ruined earth. Withered trees blossomed, the once scabrous pigeons grew new feathers and sang, and many-colored butterflies appeared out of nowhere, sacrificing their lives to adorn her like living jewels. She came nearer, arms outstretched, speaking first softly, then imploringly. And when she finally got close enough for me to hear . . .

I woke up choking back a scream, with sweat pouring down my face and my heart pounding as it never had before. She had been speaking to me in Spanish. And I couldn't understand her. I didn't understand.

As I lay back down and tried to calm myself, I drifted between the waking world and the other world, and at last I knew what my great-grandmother had been trying to tell me all along. I understood what she had meant every time she spoke to me without talking, looked at me without seeing, grasped me without those iron hands. It was my *abuelita*'s job to be the caretaker and my mother's job to be the criticizer—and the criticized. My job was to be the recorder. And now that I finally understood this, great-grandma's job was finally done. Mine was about to begin.

GLOSSARY

It is my sincere wish that those who read this book come away knowing at least as much Spanish as I do. So with *lengua* firmly in cheek, the following is provided for the enhancement/enjoyment of *Fish Out of Agua*.

Note 1: Generally, the **ita** suffix serves as a diminutive, or term of endearment; **on** or **oso** suffix adds emphasis to the verb, that is, *gordo* = fat, but *gord***on** = very fat.

Note 2: Some of the terms contained herein are fabrications (*papa de sofa*), expletive or vulgar slang (*coño, bicho*), or extremely politically incorrect insults *(cocolo)*, which, if used, may cause immediate retribution and/or bodily harm to the user. The author and publishers of *Fish Out of Agua* accept no responsibility for use/misuse of any terms contained herein, and we suggest extreme discretion/caution be used in their application. That said, enjoy!

FOOD

Alcapurrias: *empanada*-like pastries with spiced meat filling.

Arroz con gandules: rice and pigeon peas.

Arroz con salchichas: rice and (Vienna) sausages.

Arroz dulce: rice pudding.

Arroz y habichuelas: rice and beans.

Bacaláitos: fried codfish cakes.

Bizcocho: cookie.

Café con leche: café au lait; espresso with steamed or heated milk.

Café negro: black/espresso coffee.

Carne mechada: pot roast.

Cerveza: beer.

Coquito: traditional holiday drink: eggnog made with spiced coconut cream, milk, eggs, and rum.

Criolla: Creole style.

Dulce de coco: coconut candy.

Dulce de leche: caramel.

Empanadas: pastries filled with meat, vegetables, or both.

Ensalada bacalao: codfish salad.

Galletas: crackers.

Maduros: single-fried sweet yellow plantains.

Mojito: a condiment of fresh chopped garlic, lemon or lime juice, and olive oil; also the summertime cocktail of light rum, sugar, crushed mint, and lime juice.

Pasteles: traditional holiday/special-occasion food: boiled patties made with grated plantains, root vegetables, meat, and *sofrito*.

Perñil: traditional holiday/special-occasion meat: roast shoulder of pork.

Piccadillo: ground or shredded beef simmered in a rich *sofrito*, sometimes with peas and French fries added.

Platano: Plantain; cooking banana used ripe or unripe.

Pollo guisado: chicken stew.

Queso blanco: traditional Latin white cheese, often eaten with guava jelly and *galletas*.

Recao: an aromatic herb used to flavor *sofrito*.

Refresco: soda, Kool-aid, Hawaiian Punch, etc.

Sabor: flavor.

Salujos: fried cornmeal fingers stuffed with *queso blanco*.

Sazón: commercial Latin spice blend used to flavor meats and *sofrito*.

Sofrito: a highly seasoned cooking sauce made with any combination of the following: onions, garlic, mild or hot peppers, tomatoes, olive oil, capers, olives, recao, cilantro, and Sazón.

Sopa de pollo: chicken soup.

Tostones: double-fried unripe green plantains.

PEOPLE

Abuela/abuelita: grandmother.

Abuelo: grandfather.

Blanquito/a: (European/American) white person.

Bobo/a: fool; dunce.

Boricua(s): Puerto Rican people; from "Boriquen," the original name of the island of Puerto Rico.

Chinos: specifically Chinese; also used as an all-encompassing slang term to describe any person of Asian descent (can be offensive). Oddly "china" also means orange, as in *jugo de china*: orange juice.

Chiquito/a: tiny.

Cocolo [no exact English translation] roughly: coconut head (very offensive slang).

Esposo: husband.

Flaco/a: skinny.

Gordiflona/gordita: overweight female; fatty.

Gordo(a): fat.

Gran mamichula: hottest among hot women.

Gran vieja: really old woman; i.e., your grandmother's oldest sister.

Hombre: a man.

Ingladesas: Irish.

Italianos: Italians.

Judeos: Jews.

Jibaros: country people (the equivalent of "hillbillies").

Jamona: old maid; spinster.

Jamona virgeña: virgin old maid.

Mami: mother.

Mija: dearie; honey; sweetie (endearment).

Moreno: brown one (can be either offensive or an endearment depending on context and tone).

Mujer: woman.

Muñeca: doll.

Negrito: black one (can be either offensive or an endearment depending on context and tone).

Niñita: little girl.

Novia: girlfriend.

Novio: boyfriend.

Nuyorican: first/second generation born to island-born parents.

Padre: father (also priest).

Papi: also father.

Pelo rojo/colorado/a: redhead.

Prieto [no exact English translation; offensive].

Princesa: princess.

Tregieño [no exact English translation; can be offensive].

Viejo/a: old man/old woman.

PHRASES

Adulto: adult.

Ahora: now.

Ay bendito, que paso? Oh dear (blessed be), what happened?

Bago: sluggish, wishy-washy.

Cállate: Shut up.

Chistes: jokes.

Complicado: complicated.

Coño: expletive [no real English equivalent]; the closest literal translation depending on context would be "shit," "damn," and "hell" combined.

Damé un café . . . negro! Give me a coffee . . . black one!

Damé un poco de algo: give me a little something.

Dejala: Leave her (alone).

Delicioso: yummy.

Desacuerdo: disagreement.

Desilusión: disillusion/deluded.

Dime que me quieres: Tell me you want me.

Dios mio! Oh my God!

Decepcionado: disappointment.

Espere hasta que nieva: Wait till it snows.

Esposo verdad: true (real) husband.

Explica: explain.

Hace frio: It's cold.

Humo: smoke.

Lento: slow.

Mal de estomago: tummyache.

Mala: bad.

Malissima: the worst.

Me lo dijo cállate o te voy pow-pow! I said, be quiet or I'll smack you one.

Mi amor: my love.

Mija: dear, sweetie, honey.

Mira: look.

Mira a ese: look at that.

Mira, no me joda: Hey, don't (fucking) bother/annoy me.

No puedes fumar aqui: You can't smoke here.

No puedo escribir mas: I can't write anymore.

No te preocupes: Don't worry.

Nuestra familia: our family.

Nunca: never.

Papa de sofa: literally, couch potato [I made this up].

Perezoso: lazy.

Pero no tocar: but don't touch.

Pobrecito/a: poor thing.

Poco minuto: Just a minute.

Por favor: Please.

Por que: Why?

Porque: because.

Quien es? Who is it?

Semilla malo: bad seed.

Siempre: always.

Siempre vaya a bailar primero: Always go dancing first.

Sinvergüenza: shameless.

Sola: alone.

Sus chuletas siempre son sabroso, abuelita: Your pork chops are always tasty, Grandma.

Tenga cuidado! Watch out!

Tocarme bicho: Touch my dick.

Vamos a comer: Let's eat.

Vamos a resar por ti: We'll pray for you.

Ven acá: Come here.

Vergüenza: shame.

Yo te promeso: I promise.

PLACES

Cabo Rojo: small city on the southwest coast of Puerto Rico.

Calle Ocho: Eighth Street; famous Cuban neighborhood in Miami, Florida.

Corozal: small town near the center of the island.

El Barrio: Spanish Harlem: a neighborhood in Manhattan roughly bordered by 96th Street to the south and 125th Street to the north, from the East River to Fifth Avenue.

El Buyé: beach near Cabo Rojo.

Nueva York: New York.

RELIGIOUS TERMS

Catolico: Catholic.

¡Gloria Allelujahs! Glory Hallelujahs!

¡Gloria al Señor! Praise the Lord.

¡Gloria Jesus! Praise Jesus!

Guardeños el Señor: Keep us, Lord.

Luterano: Lutheran.

Milagro: miracle.

Pentecostal: Pentecostal Christian congregation with varying degrees of fervor, strictness, and doctrine.

Salmos: psalms.

The Way of the Saints: an all-encompassing term for nontraditional pantheistic forms of worship such as Paganism, Santeria, and Voodoo.

THINGS

Bicho: dick (vulgar slang).

Cabeza: head.

Caldero: low, wide cast-iron or steel cookpot, similar to a Dutch oven, used for cooking rice and stews.

Chancla/chancleta: slipper.

Cheechos: the flesh around your hips (slang).

Cocotazos: traditional Latin punishment: a rap on the side of the head or in the fleshy part of the upper arm or thigh by two upraised knuckles.

Colador: old-fashioned device of a circular socklike sieve on a stick, used for making Spanish coffee.

Cuerpo: body.

Cuerpo cortao: literally, "cut body": nonexistent exhaustive disorder of mysterious origin.

Culo: ass.

Dolor: pain.

Escuela: school.

Fantasia: fantasy.

Finca: farm.

Fogón: outdoor cooking hearth.

Fundillo: behind; butt.

Guagua: bus.

Iglesia: church.

Lengua: tongue.

Luz: light.

Merengue: traditional Caribbean Latin dance.

Monga: mysterious flu-like ailment.

Musica: music.

Nadie: no one.

Nalgas: butt cheeks.

Novela: Spanish-language soap opera.

Pecas: freckles.

Pipi: child's unisex word for genitalia.

Plancha: iron: the device used for smoothing wrinkles from *sus ropas* (as opposed to the mineral).

Puerco: pig.

Salsa: traditional Caribbean Latin dance.

Sus ropas: your clothes.

Toto: vagina (slang).

Virgen: Virgin.